Star Actors in the Hollywood Renaissance

Star Actors in the Hollywood Renaissance

Representing Rough Rebels

Daniel Smith-Rowsey
Sacramento State University, California, USA

First published 2013 by
PALGRAVE MACMILLAN

Palgrave Macmillan in the UK is an imprint of Macmillan Publishers Limited,
registered in England, company number 785998, of Houndmills, Basingstoke,
Hampshire RG21 6XS.

Palgrave Macmillan in the US is a division of St Martin's Press LLC,
175 Fifth Avenue, New York, NY 10010.

Palgrave Macmillan is the global academic imprint of the above companies
and has companies and representatives throughout the world.

Palgrave® and Macmillan® are registered trademarks in the United States,
the United Kingdom, Europe and other countries.

ISBN 978–1–137–31038–5

This book is printed on paper suitable for recycling and made from fully
managed and sustained forest sources. Logging, pulping and manufacturing
processes are expected to conform to the environmental regulations of the
country of origin.

A catalogue record for this book is available from the British Library.

A catalog record for this book is available from the Library of Congress.

*To my wonderful, patient wife, Irena,
and our beloved sons, Darwin and Rainier*

Contents

List of Illustrations

Acknowledgments

I would like to thank my doctoral supervisors, Roberta Pearson and Gianluca Sergi, for their seemingly inexhaustible patience and flexibility when it came to my topic, my writing, and my personal needs. None of this would be possible without the generosity and support of Sharon Monteith, Ann McQueen, and the entire department at the University of Nottingham, including the amazing assistance from the faculty, staff, and my fellow student colleagues. I also want to thank Peter Krämer for help with early drafts. Any errors are my own.

1
How to Represent a Rough Rebel

> There is a book to be written on the importance of
> ugly men in cinema.
>
> Anthony Lane, 2007[1]

Introduction

For its first 46 years, *Time*, America's newsweekly of record, invariably
featured illustrations of important people or events on its cover. The
very first *Time* cover photograph, dated February 7, 1969, featured not
a world leader, astronaut, or international conflict, but Dustin Hoffman
and Mia Farrow, appearing in suggestive close-up and adorned by a
headline that read "The Young Actors: Stars and Anti-Stars." The article, written by Stefan Kanfer, Jay Cocks, and Carey Winfrey, positioned
Hoffman and Farrow as nothing less than Hollywood's best response to
the counterculture. It read:

> *The Graduate* and *Rosemary's Baby* spin a new myth of lost innocence,
> of the individual against the wicked system. The new young actors
> themselves represent the death of many movie myths—among them,
> the one of the movie star. The big press buildup, the house in Beverly
> Hills baroque, the ostentation and the seven-picture commitment
> are giving way to a stubborn kind of performer who is as suspi-
> cious of the Hollywood system as a student rebel is of the university
> trustees.

The article quoted Hoffman: "Art has never been for the masses, but
now people seem to see what's good. The least I can do is try to make

1

what I do as artistic as possible." The article eventually associated even this kind of "anti-star" with artifice:

> The anti-star attitude itself threatens to become a new pose or convention in which the Hollywood swimming pool is replaced by the interesting East Side pad, the Valley ranch by a Martha's Vineyard retreat, the antic table-hopping by frantic political activism.

This was a partial reference to Hoffman's campaigning for Eugene McCarthy; when more leftist candidates were available, Hoffman had taken Mr. McCarthy's daughter to the Oscars as his date (for his nomination for *The Graduate* (1967)), and had stumped for Mr. McCarthy on college campuses, urging students to "Get Clean For Gene." *Time* was particularly interested in Hoffman as a representative of a new sort of male movie star both offscreen and on:

> As comedy grew steadily blacker and as audiences grew steadily younger, hipper and more draftable, the old concepts began to erode. The invulnerables like Peck and Holden and Wayne seemed lost in a country full of people whose destinies were not in their own hands. The nation of cities needed new images, and suddenly Hoffman became an archetype.[2]

If *Time* was right that we needed new "images," who or what were the others? What exactly did Hoffman's "archetype" represent? And what effect did his type have on cinema and American culture more generally?

In this book, I argue that male "anti-stars" of the late 1960s and early 1970s exerted deterministic power over the most transformative cinema of the time. They were more than just actors in films; on magazine covers and in popular discourse, they were positioned, promoted, and received as Hollywood's best possible response to the young educated adults who ostensibly "did not trust anyone over thirty." (The fact that these men were at least thirty years old is only the first of their interesting contradictions.) By close textual analysis of nine representative films made and released in a crucible period, I show how the performative styles of the most popular star-actors signified an absurdist, ironic alienation as well as the exclusion of women. By sampling the critical reception of the time, I show how these star-actors' discursive constructs were understood and contextualized. Overall, I show that the star-actors functioned as privileged symbols for navigating the contradictory modes of resistance and traditionalism inherent in the films and the wider discourse.

Many books about cinema, and many non-fiction books that mention films, refer to motion pictures by their name, year, and director—for example, "*The French Connection* (William Friedkin, 1971)." This is only the initial way that directors are privileged as singular, determinative artists of films. My book aims to show star-actors' precise influence on films, partly as a corrective supplement to director-centered auteur theory, and partly to better understand the crucial nature of the actors' contribution. How can we really understand cinema without more careful consideration of the power and effects of its star-actors?

For each time the press quotes a film's director, then and now, the film's star-actor is perhaps quoted ten times as often. But the "anti-star" quotes of the late 1960s were different from their predecessors: in the 1950s, Marlon Brando almost never mentioned Elia Kazan, James Stewart was not on record about Alfred Hitchcock, and so on. In contrast, the Rough Rebels often extolled their directors. They confirmed the power of the director and of themselves for having the agency and taste to choose the right directors. When Dustin Hoffman was asked why he chose to star in *Little Big Man* (1970), he said, "You go for a director, of course."[3] This particular "of course" was almost unheard of in the classical era. It is also true that the "anti-stars" moved quickly into independent producer alliances, and that Jack Nicholson even directed a film in this period (*Drive, He Said* (1971)). But far more often, these new stars presented themselves as stars and equal partners with the director on a film, as when *Look* wrote "Hoffman and [director Arthur] Penn turn Hollywood upside-down"[4] or when Nicholson described the working process on the Mike Nichols-directed *Carnal Knowledge* as "Let's run it by Nick and Nick."[5]

Steve Neale points out that the first wave of so-called American auteurs is generally understood not to be late-1960s innovators like Arthur Penn and Sam Peckinpah, but instead the young men that became famous directors in the 1970s, such as Francis Ford Coppola, Peter Bogdanovich, Martin Scorsese, Steven Spielberg, and George Lucas.[6] If this is true, it seems more than a coincidence that thirty-year-old(ish) everyman "anti-stars," promoted as counterculture heroes, narrowly preceded these thirty-year-old(ish) everyman directors in the public discourse. It is more likely that the young actors' creative and discursive triumphs gave rhetorical license to those of the young directors.

Paul McDonald identifies "the greatest gaps in research" regarding "what happened to the Hollywood star system after the breakdown of the vertically integrated studios." The problem he identifies is, "In the absence of such research, it is not clear, for example, what differences may have existed in the organisation of the star system between the 1960s and 1970s, and how those periods compare to Hollywood stardom in the 1990s."[7] Responding to McDonald, this book addresses a relatively unexplored region in film studies, one that examines star-actors' roles (in both senses) in representing the style and themes of a relatively contained cinematic period.

In 1972, Marsha Kinder wrote that films of what she called "the new American humanistic realism"—she named only *The Graduate*, *Midnight Cowboy*, *Easy Rider*, and *Five Easy Pieces*—"render suspect their own 'revolutionary' perspectives by easing back into the values they appear to be questioning" partly because "the value of several of them depends largely upon performances, such as Dustin Hoffman's in *Midnight Cowboy*, Jack Nicholson's … in *Easy Rider*, and, to some extent, Nicholson's in *Five Easy Pieces*."[8] For Kinder, this was sufficient as a one-off observation to set up her analysis of what she saw as more challenging films. However, I suggest that categorical statements like hers warrant a great deal more unpacking.

To this end, I closely examine films featuring three star-actors—Dustin Hoffman, Jack Nicholson, and Elliott Gould—who moved from Academy Award-nominated supporting roles to newsweekly magazine covers and leading roles during this period. By all measures, they were central to film culture and even American culture at this time. I have chosen their representative films based on box-office success and Oscar nominations. I have seen no history of the "New Hollywood"—I prefer the more distinctive term "Hollywood Renaissance"—that does not include at least one (and usually many more) of the films and directors examined here. If part of my work is to complicate received history, these projects are a good place to start. All of these films were promoted as expanding the general possibilities of cinema, including but not limited to being the "first" to break some kind of taboo, usually regarding sex, violence, and/or profanity.

The following films are closely analyzed herein:

Midnight Cowboy (1969), directed by John Schlesinger—featuring Dustin Hoffman
Little Big Man (1970), directed by Arthur Penn—starring Dustin Hoffman
Straw Dogs (1971), directed by Sam Peckinpah—starring Dustin Hoffman
Easy Rider (1969), directed by Dennis Hopper—featuring Jack Nicholson

Five Easy Pieces (1970), directed by Bob Rafelson—starring Jack Nicholson

Carnal Knowledge (1971), directed by Mike Nichols—starring Jack Nicholson

Bob & Carol & Ted & Alice (1969), directed by Paul Mazursky—featuring Elliott Gould

M*A*S*H (1970), directed by Robert Altman—starring Elliott Gould

Beröringen (The Touch) (1971), directed by Ingmar Bergman—starring Elliott Gould

Why only 1969 to 1971? Why nine films, three in each year, three by each actor? What does this schematic approach demonstrate that other approaches might not have? First, the period beginning in 1968 (when these films went into production) and ending in 1971 was a crucible time for both Hollywood and American culture more generally—the words "seismic shift" would not be hyperbole. From 1968 to 1971, social unrest, protests against the Vietnam War, and the counterculture surged (or perhaps raged) and peaked. In response, the mainstream press interviewed—and as often as not, anointed—every "symbol" of young discontented adults it could find. Almost coincidentally, the studios were in their worst-ever financial straits, the rating system had just been overhauled, and Kodak had recently perfected the dull tones of much color (minimizing the previous "brightening" effect of color that had made it seem garish for serious dramas). As often noted by film historians, the general spirit of experimentation led to the validation of entire new genres, such as blaxploitation, mainstream pornography, road movies, and disaster movies.

The first Nixon administration was thus a period of unique fluctuation and maximal opportunity for filmmakers, establishing standards for succeeding decades. (The only other four-year period of comparable change in America and its film industry would probably be 1928–31, and in fact there are interesting parallels between the very polarized public perceptions of early-1930s gangsters and late-1960s countercultural rebels.) However, historians, in their rush to celebrate the young auteur directors of the period, rarely mention the change in onscreen personnel. Dennis Bingham provides a welcome corrective to this when he writes:

> A massive generational turnover, the likes of which had not been seen since the coming of sound, took place in only a few years—roughly 1967–71. It gave these "New Hollywood" actors opportunities for

lasting power as producers, directors, or actors as auteurs. They displaced a generational cohort that, in the youth wave and the collapse of the mass-audience blockbuster, lost the bankability many of them had owned for two decades or more. Among these were Bob Hope, Bing Crosby, Frank Sinatra, Doris Day, Audrey Hepburn, Rock Hudson, Burt Lancaster, Kirk Douglas, John Wayne, Charlton Heston, Henry Fonda, Gregory Peck, Elizabeth Taylor, Jerry Lewis, Dean Martin, William Holden, Jack Lemmon, Marlon Brando, and James Stewart.[9]

Bingham suggests that new dramas were hardly going to star Bob Hope and Doris Day; new faces were needed to assure young audiences that someone was speaking for and to them.

Why three films for each of three actors? I suggest not merely that Dustin Hoffman had a determinative influence on a crucial transition period of American cinema; actors like him did. This focus is justified through the neglect of close analysis in most histories of the period and the need to limit my sample. Too many more films and star-actors would have been belaboring the point; fewer star-actors would have been a more narrow, subjective argument. Robert Sklar writes in *City Boys* about a type that was apparent "in a number of movie performers of the 1930s and 1940s" but he chose to focus on James Cagney, Humphrey Bogart, and John Garfield "because of their diversity and because of their similarity (and, to be sure, personal preference)."[10] Echoing Sklar, I can say that I also might have chosen other subjects, like Gene Hackman, Robert Duvall, Gene Wilder, Richard Benjamin, Bruce Dern, Donald Sutherland, or Alan Arkin. Any of the men on that list, along with my subjects, could be considered Rough Rebels. (As a side note, Warren Beatty, Robert Redford, and Steve McQueen were Rebels, but were not quite as rough. It speaks to the Rough Rebels' ascendance that in 1970—a year after the smash hit *Butch Cassidy and the Sundance Kid*—Robert Redford starred in zero films and Elliott Gould starred in four. Warren Beatty went through a similar [brief] eclipse, only to reappear in full beard in 1971 in *McCabe and Mrs. Miller*. In other words, at their peak, Rough Rebels were actually preferred over more traditionally handsome leading men. This didn't last.)

Defining Rough Rebels

Webster's Dictionary defines "rebel" as one who rebels, which means "to oppose or disobey one in authority or control" and "to act in or show opposition or disobedience: to feel or exhibit anger or revulsion." Webster's defines "rough" as "marked by inequalities, ridges, or projections on the surface: coarse," and "characterized by harshness, violence, or force," and "presenting a challenge: difficult," and "coarse or rugged in character or appearance," and "crude in style or expression: indelicate."[11] While some of these descriptions might apply to the "gangster" actors of the 1930s and some to the famous 1950s Method rebels, they are united in the Rough Rebel figures. Because the Rough Rebels "did not look like stars" and carefully disclaimed some aspects of Hollywood, they were often called anti-stars, anti-heroes; they were actors first and stars second, according to their publicists and an often complicit media. As star-actors, they aligned with Horatio Alger myths, which often meant that their publicity emphasized their humble origins and the fact that they were not "Hollywood royalty" (meaning they were not born into fame, unlike, say, Candice Bergen or Michael Douglas). They performed their contradictory rise to stardom in a time that questioned stars, articulating themselves as uniquely qualified to represent the problem and the solution.

Hoffman, Nicholson, and Gould differ strongly in their performance styles, though the press often positioned them as signifying the same sort of rebel figure. By contrasting their performative differences to the films' commonalities, the actors' choices are made clearer while suggesting some degree of commutation test—how casting other actors would have altered the films. And indeed their films had many commonalities. For example, they featured many of the same supporting actresses. They were made in a sort of gritty (filmmakers then called it "gutsy"), unforgiving color, usually featuring long lenses. Their films could be said never to have left the present, although this is debatable: *Little Big Man* is a western but narrated from the 1960s; *Carnal Knowledge* goes back to the 1950s but extends as far as the near future; *M*A*S*H* takes place during the Korean War but audiences only understand this because of a last-minute title insert. The point is that these Rough Rebels were mostly seen as contemporary figures, not to be shoehorned into costume pieces of the past. Throughout the 1970s, their films did not veer from comedy, drama, war, and western—no science fiction, no horror, no musicals (Nicholson made *On a Clear Day You Can See Forever* (1970) before he could choose his scripts), no documentaries, no short films, and no avant-garde on the level of Bruce Conner, Kenneth Anger, or Andy Warhol. This fact alone—along with similar genre preferences from their peers Warren Beatty, Robert Redford, and Steve McQueen, and their successors Al Pacino and Robert DeNiro—worked to privilege "realistic" genres over other genres for a decade, and to privilege main-stream drama over other sorts of experiments. Hoffman may have gone back to the stage (briefly) but Nicholson did not return to the sort of films he'd made throughout the 1960s with Roger Corman. Gould, established as a song-and-dance man on Broadway before his break-through in *Bob & Carol & Ted & Alice*, might have been wise to return to musical theater, but he did not.

All of the 1969 films analyzed here, for which these Rough Rebels received Oscar nominations, directly engage the counterculture. For example, they all have at least one scene of characters "making the scene" by going to a gathering where young people are dancing while showing off their paisleys and beads and other bright plumage. All of the 1970 films analyzed here are picaresque and specifically "anti" something—*Little Big Man* is anti-western, *M*A*S*H* is anti-war, and *Five Easy Pieces* is in many ways anti-genre. In 1970, "anti-stars" were mobilized for oppositional virtues. Even today these films remain some of the most prestigious examples of their "anti" type. All of the 1971 films analyzed here use a Rough Rebel as a leading villain, and they were all made outside the United States. Not coincidentally, during 1971, all these star-actors were criticized for their reach exceeding their grasp. Not unlike America, then, by the end of 1971 the Rough Rebels' radical potential had been both realized and somewhat curtailed.

Robin Wood summarizes the prevailing themes of the period when he writes about a "collapse in confidence of patriarchal authority," religion as "marginal to the point of irrelevancy," "sexual games, erupt-ing into games of violence, which escalate in turn into real violence ending in total and irreparable breakdown," learning as "hypocrisy," a "descent into disillusionment," "debased existential absurdism," and "the disintegration of American society and the ideology that supports it is presented as total and final, beyond hope of reconstruction."[12] However, Wood omits the fact that *stars* were the most visible signifiers of these themes of alienation, which led to a certain distanciation, irony, farce, and good humor about the whole enterprise, on and offscreen. The Rough Rebels could be frustrated with society, but they "got it" as surely as any of the leading comedians of the day, as they demonstrated in their extended interviews to *Playboy*. Cued by the Rough Rebels, the films tended in this same ideological direction, and away from any real challenge to the "patriarchal authority" Wood mentions.

Did the heroes of the period have to be men? Although women's voices were not unknown, most of the movement's representative fig-ures, particularly star-actors and directors, were men. As Peter Krämer points out, this was in stark contrast to the female-centered films that had dominated American cinema only a few years before.[13] It is this mainstream exclusion that many scholars cite as crucial precedent to the wave of feminist film studies that arrived in the 1970s. Looking back on this period's fluctuations of societal standards and industrial control makes the lack of female agency all the more poignant. Toward this understanding, Eve Kosofsky Sedgwick's groundbreaking work *Between Men: English Literature and Male Homosocial Desire* (1985) can be usefully applied to the work of the Rough Rebels. Sedgwick herself warns that "any attempt" to treat her "book's formulations" should be regarded with the greatest care, because her analysis is clearly bounded by geography and history. Her admonition has barely slowed some scholars, particularly those who briefly cite Sedgwick as they tag as "homosocial" any unusual bond between two heterosexual male characters. Sedgwick's schema is more nuanced than simple male bonding, and more helpful for reading the Rebels' represented masculinity of the period. In her introduction, Sedgwick describes the goals of her book:

> first, to make it easier for readers to focus intelligently on male homosocial bonds throughout the heterosexual European erotic ethos; but secondly, to use the subject of sexuality to show the usefulness of certain Marxist-feminist historical categories for literary criticism.[14]

I hope I employ Sedgwick's insights in the manner she finds "dialectically usable," stretching the "heterosexual European" to include Hoffman, Nicholson, and Gould, whose represented "rebellion" in this period necessarily excluded women even as it frequently included other men.

In this, they differed from the famous movie rebels of fifteen years before. Offscreen, Marlon Brando, Montgomery Clift, and James Dean admitted to some sort of homosexuality even at the time; Hoffman, Nicholson, and Gould have never come close. On screen, compared with the rebels of the 1950s, Rough Rebels' films rarely featured a fully characterized "good girl" that they were meant to reform for; at the same time, the Rough Rebels' roles were not as feminized as some of the 1950s rebels' roles. The Rough Rebel had some affinity with the British Angry Young Man, a type defined as demonstrating "conflict with parents, conflict with the law, heterosexuality, occasional moments of ranting."[15] After the Freudian difficulties (and "good girl") of *The Graduate*, the Rough Rebels' characters rarely dealt with their parents or their children. Instead, the men they played defined themselves against their peers, with special hostility toward women.

For Sedgwick, men verify their masculinity not always through simple conquest of women, but by taking women for granted, by constructing a masculinity that assumes female compliance. Sedgwick applies this to centuries' worth of fictional characters in literature narrative, but I suggest that her observations can also be applied to stars, whose discursive constructs also represent narrative. Sedgwick's schema is useful for understanding any male star doing press, because the "male–male love ... is set firmly within a structure of institutionalized social relations."[16] Because star press is not presumed to be exclusively for heterosexual female readers, the tone of the articles assumes and even negotiates that male heterosexuals (fans) can love a male (star). Reasons are given for this love (e.g. talent, appearance, being a man of his moment); these reasons only prove the viability of the male star as a model for behavior. However, what many feminists have missed about the dominant male type of the time is that much like, say, the National Organization for Women, the press surrounding 1970s Rough Rebel star-actors tended to borrow the language of victimhood and "unheard voices" from the civil rights movement, making their "authenticity" more difficult to counter. They weren't new stars the way that, say, Tony Curtis was once a new star; they were ethnic everymen.

Hollywood had more at stake with Hoffman, Nicholson, and Gould in 1970 than it ever did with the City Boys, the famous 1950s rebels, or any other set of "everymen" at any other time. With the industry in unprecedented financial turmoil, it depended on college audiences, who were asked to verify the Rough Rebels' authenticity. Contemporary sources on the Rough Rebels reveal a "lady doth protest too much" tendency. Whatever Hamlet's mother may have meant when she said it to Hamlet, the phrase is generally used today to mean that one who belabors a point begins to lose credibility or at least raise suspicions of one's hidden motivations. Indeed, the Rough Rebels were so widely and consistently praised as challenges to the system that one must question their nature. I argue herein that in "protesting too much," Hollywood negotiated its own social relevance by incorporating its supposed upstarts.

The rise of the Rough Rebel figures was directly enabled by at least two broad socio-historical trends and one industry in crisis. The 1960s saw the lionization of both ethnic (or "-American") figures and young adults, particularly young adults who felt alienated from the previous generation. At the same time, Hollywood's business model fell into a disarray unlike any other point in the industry's history. Without any one of these factors, the Rough Rebel figure might not have dominated American dramatic films of the 1970s.

Ethnicity

Dustin Hoffman describes the theater scene when he arrived in New York in the early 1960s:

> If you got Back Stage, the casting notices said Leading Men, and then Juveniles, and Leading Ladies, and then Ingenues. And then, next to that, it said Character Leading Men, Character Juveniles. And that word—"character"—meant that you were not attractive: You were the funny-looking person next to the good-looking person in high school. And everybody knew it.[17]

The over-simplified version of the subsequent transformation is represented by Molly Haskell:

> We no longer demanded 'role models' and instead went to see real actors—or even 'real people'—saying inaudible things in unpleasant films that would make us think. This was the sixties. Pop went the American Dream as it had been floated by Hollywood, and out of its rubble emerged the American art film. ... No more stoical heroes with a tough-guy swagger, but slouching, sensitive boy-men.[18]

Actually, there were still plenty of "stoical heroes with a tough-guy swagger," and even some emergent ones like Clint Eastwood and Charles Bronson. But Haskell's comments are indicative of an over-reading that I stress in order to correct it.

Though previous stars—say Humphrey Bogart, Edward G. Robinson, and Spencer Tracy—arguably articulated the "everyman," their press barely mentioned it; the media surrounding the Rough Rebels insisted on their "everyman" stature. This can be fairly read as code for something else. The Rough Rebels both performed and complicated dominant notions of whiteness. Regarding my three paradigmatic figures, Hoffman and Gould were reported to be Jewish, while Nicholson was often received in the press as Irish,[19] and thus it is fair to say that all three men were white, but "ethnic." This gave them ineluctable liminal positioning between the mainstream and the deviant, at a serendipitous historical moment.

Many events of the 1960s might be named as fostering more ethnic awareness and pluralism, from the beginning of forced school busing to the Second Vatican Council's advocacy of pluralism to Sandy Koufax's refusal to pitch a World Series game on Yom Kippur to the Supreme Court's 1967 decision striking down "miscegenation" statutes in *Loving v. Virginia.* Philip Gleason identifies two events from 1965 that precipitated new degrees of ethnic identification: the Civil Rights Act and the immigration law that eliminated national origins from selection criteria. Gleason finds that the "white ethnic" movement was a reaction to these two changes as well as a reaction to the Black Power movement. In 1968, *after* the black "legitimization of ethnicity,"[20] whites began to encourage use of "something-American" labels. Gleason names as determinative the two Consultations on Ethnic America in June 1968 and the 1970 National Project on Ethnic America, all of which were principally sponsored by the American Jewish Committee, and promoted (to secure funding) as efforts to reduce racial tensions—they were named Depolarization Projects. Many sociologists agree that the 1968–71 period was a uniquely privileged time to assert ethnic identity, and for other Americans to affirm that assertion.

For Ronald Segal, "The Irish and the Jews, indeed, go far toward explaining the persistence of popular faith in the American creed." Regarding the former, Segal cites the prodigious success of the Kennedys, the immigrants becoming "virtually synonymous with the police," and the Irish Catholic Church's evolution from British persecute to wealthiest and largest church in America. Regarding the latter, Segal cites the influence over all New York City institutions, including "art, entertainment, fashion, advertising, the communication of news and ideas."[21] For Segal, the generalized success of Irish-Americans and Jewish-Americans is proof that the promise inscribed at the base of the Statue of Liberty can be made reality. One might add that Jewish-Americans, as prominent leaders of the counterculture, as victims of the Holocaust, as winners (by association, anyway) of the Six-Day War, also had a rare and unique claim on the American imaginary by 1968. Irish- and Jewish-Americans had recently and famously been killed in the service of American values (the Kennedys and the freedom riders), giving their representations the authority of blood. From this perspective, the Irishness of Nicholson and the Jewishness of Hoffman and Gould serve to rescue the American Dream at its most embattled, or perhaps, in their disillusionment, to demonstrate the depths to which that dream has become corrupted. Certain ethnicities may actually seem *more* American than the apparent White Anglo-Saxon Protestant ideal, because their appearance represents the Horatio Alger myth of hardscrabble success more than a WASP's appearance can.[22] As an over-simplification, the Rough Rebels connoted America's immigrant story, suggesting often-successful assimilation even—especially—as they represented the ostensible death of the American Dream at the end of the 1960s.

Certainly in Hollywood history, ethnic groups were often asked to perform in similar ways, as James Naremore writes: "As a general rule, Hollywood has required that supporting players, ethnic minorities, and women be more animated or broadly expressive than white male leads."[23] The Rough Rebels worked in distinctive styles to break down this truism, much as Sidney Poitier had just before them. Mark Harris makes clear that Sidney Poitier's career was partly enabled by a campaign by the National Association for the Advancement of Colored People for greater inclusiveness. *Variety* wrote about a common joke in the mid-1960s: "It has become much too ironic to [rewrite] the part for a white actor if Sidney Poitier is not available or not interested."[24] This was directly related to sexuality, as Calvin Hernton made clear in 1966: "Why can't Sidney Poitier … make love in the movies? … By desexing the Negro, America is denying him his manhood."[25] A year later, Poitier agreed as he discussed white producers and studio heads: "So they have to make him—the Negro—kind of a neuter. … You put him in a shirt and tie … you make him very bright and very intelligent and very capable … then you can eliminate the core of the man: His sexuality."[26] The "ethnic everymen," the Rough Rebels, can be seen as a reaction to Poitier's career, to its discursive potential and its limits. While Poitier might have been "denied his manhood," Hoffman, Nicholson, and Gould would all insist on theirs, playing shirtless love scenes in beds in their first films with Hollywood budgets (respectively, *The Graduate*, *Five Easy Pieces*, and *Bob & Carol & Ted & Alice*). Because these generally exceeded narrative demands (meaning the scenes could have been done with shirts on without changing the story) it was almost as though the Rough Rebels were verifying their whiteness, or off-whiteness, as sufficient for a new sort of "manhood." The Rough Rebels represented an engagement with the times without being too much of a break, as casting, say, Bruce Lee might have been.

There is a danger regarding essentializing white "ethnicity" per se. Different groups have different roles in the American consciousness. For example, with the exception of *A Streetcar Named Desire* (1951), Polish-Americans have never seen much overt representation by Hollywood, perhaps partly because Chicago is not in Los Angeles. In large numbers, Jews are firmly in favor of laws against housing discrimination, while Irishmen are firmly against such laws.[27] Some sociologists have suggested that pluralism and inclusiveness may not be seen by everyone as a zero-sum game. Movies about the problems of white ethnic men may, instead of invoking solidarity with blacks, in fact do just the opposite by proving that white problems are just as valid. Andrew Greeley implied as much when he wrote that white ethnics (he named, first, Jews, Irish, Italians, and Polish people) were substantially alienated by the progressive movements of the 1960s.[28] It may make the most sense to see Hoffman, Nicholson, and Gould—and successors like Al Pacino and Robert DeNiro—as liminal figures, ethnic palimpsests upon which several historically charged meanings can be mapped.

Film reviewers and entertainment writers rarely used the word "ethnic," preferring labels like "anti-star," "everyman," "ordinary-looking," and "non-matinee-idol." But ethnicity was an indispensable if unspoken aspect. As a caveat, this book is not meant to perpetuate what some scholars have called "lookism."[29] It is not my personal belief that Dustin Hoffman, Jack Nicholson, and Elliott Gould are less attractive than Warren Beatty, Robert Redford, and Steve McQueen. In terms of looks, I rely upon legions of studies which demonstrate that specific appearances have proved advantageous in everything from salary increases to making a baby smile.[30] If we are not to dismiss every press account of the period, then the three studied star-actors "did not look like" leading men. If anything, this work is meant to complicate received notions and constructions regarding appearance. Informally, one wonders if the very unconventionality of the new leading men was something that gave them more authority. After all, authority figures in most walks of life had hardly been matinee idols. By the end of the 1960s, most Americans were accustomed to authority exuding from anchormen, NASA officials, Pentagon spokesmen, activists, marchers, and other "everymen" (with the notable and "ethnic" exception of the Kennedys). Perhaps Hoffman/Nicholson/Gould's resemblances to a politician, scientist, doctor, or beloved father actually imbued them with gravitas that, say, Robert Redford could never have commanded. Perhaps ugliness aids intelligence and authority in ways that cannot be faked; Andy Martin suggests as much in his work on "the phenomenology of ugly."[31] Or perhaps "uglier" men are more inherently masculine, because some have suggested that "pretty boys" carry an inherently androgynous connotation.

Youth and alienation

The Rough Rebels' most frequently assigned connotation was a sort of youthful rebelliousness, something that the star-actors abetted by their nature and proclivities. The baby boomers, roughly defined as the disproportionate surge of Americans born between 1943 and 1962, brought a new focus and privileging to the young. In 1959, the United Nations made its "Declaration of the Rights of the Child," which the US Senate ratified; in 1960, the birth control pill was made widely available. As the 1960s began, a President known for his youth directly solicited the younger generation's involvement, not only by saying, "Ask not what your country can do for you, ask what you can do for your country," but also by founding the Peace Corps. President Kennedy suggested that even without going to war, young men and women could represent American values as well as anyone. Youth was understood not as those attending elementary school (as in today's media), but as young adults, particularly college students. At the end of 1966, *Time* put "25 and Under" as its "Man of the Year." With every passing year of the 1960s, young adults demonstrated steadily more fealty to attitudes and morals that can generally be characterized as both liberal and libidinous, as sympathetic to raciness, radicals, and racial-integration movements. If the studios were not to ignore every press source, they had reason to believe that young adults would prefer style and content that was more thematically challenging than 1950s' fare.

While young adults were not the only evidence of change in the 1960s, they spearheaded the new and unprecedented. For cinema, they were both the crucial audience and the real-world version of what was being represented. In perhaps too neat a comparison, young people were to the 1960s what the era's nascent star-actors were to films: not necessarily the ones pulling the strings, not always, but certainly the ones that bore the burden of representation, of identity, of legitimizing the latest thing. This is another reason why the examination of star-actor behavior is important to understanding films that have until now been mostly characterized as director-driven visions.

By the end of 1964, young adults were reported to be interested in both Berkeley's Free Speech Movement and the civil rights movement, particularly after a couple of white (Jewish) college students were slain while trying to register voters in Alabama. Then, mere months after President Lyndon Johnson had won one of the most convincing landslides in electoral history, he was loudly and publicly excoriated by his former youthful supporters for the post-Gulf of Tonkin buildup. Two years after the March on Washington, one year after the landmark passage of the Civil Rights Act, and six months after the murder of Malcolm X, the explosive Watts uprising may have represented a tipping point for the civil rights movement. No longer could it depend upon the sympathies of the average white American; bitterness began to increase on both sides.[32] By the end of 1965, the so-called conflict in Vietnam had reached the point of no return. Todd Gitlin wrote that "those young radicals moving leftward were already prone to a deep and passionate alienation from the whole ensemble of American normality, its racism and suburbs, its sexual hypocrisy and cultural fatuousness alike." Alienation, for Gitlin, had become part of the young American identity.[33]

Among the books that this generation named as favorites were *The Catcher in the Rye* (1951), *One Flew Over the Cuckoo's Nest* (1962), *Catch-22* (1961), *Stranger in a Strange Land* (1961), and especially Jack Kerouac's *On the Road* (1957). Kerouac presented a potent vision of detachment and disillusionment, yet he still kept his humor as he scoured America looking for hope. Famously, in both book and film, *The Grapes of Wrath*'s Tom Joad ended his odyssey by saying "I'll be there": he'd be wherever social justice was being abridged. In contrast, Kerouac's characters would be anywhere, fatalistically hoping for something better, and never finding it, laughing about the futility.[34] The ironic fatalism was a crucial distinction between World War II veterans and the "don't trust anyone over 30" generation.

It almost goes without saying that young adults were also interested in music. The single most popular and influential American musician of the 1960s was Bob Dylan. In 1963, *The New York Times* treated Bob Dylan as a curious but isolated phenomenon; in 1965, the same newspaper reported that "every new songwriter is trying to imitate him."[35] In a recent collection of essays, scholars concur that Bob Dylan articulated ironic alienation. Dylan may have expressed hope in the early 1960s, but by 1968, he expressed mostly futility and reflexive suspicion of protest.

Dylan, like other folk singers (e.g. Woody Guthrie and Pete Seeger), and Jack Kerouac, like other original Beats (e.g. Allen Ginsburg and William S. Burroughs), sympathized with the poor and downtrodden, but came from a place of white (and ethnic, New York-based) male privilege. Dylan's lyrics were rarely about true penury or deprivation; his scathing criticisms of American institutions came from relative affluence. Likewise, *On the Road* vouchsafed the disillusionment of a middle-class man with enough money to afford a soul-searching road trip. Furthermore, both artists were known for satirical jokes that kept their work from being understood simply as assaults against any establishment. Not to put too fine a point on it, Dylan and Kerouac (and Andy Warhol, in the new "pop art") permitted the humor-loving middle class to be part of an emergent absurdism. This shouldn't be confused with the more Dionysian aspects of the counterculture. If current students wonder why famous fiction films of 1969 to 1971 show very little of the actual counterculture (as represented by the Summer of Love, Woodstock, and Haight-Ashbury psychedelia), one answer is that younger filmmakers and star-actors were looking less to hippies and more to men like Dylan and Kerouac. By 1969, Bob Dylan had disavowed the counterculture too many times to name. Right up to his untimely death in 1969, Kerouac went on talk shows (like William F. Buckley's *Firing Line*) to rail against the hippies for getting his ideas wrong.

From today's perspective, it is easy to over-estimate late-1960s Americans' sympathy with the New Left. In 1972, Frank Armbruster published *The Forgotten Americans*, a study that included more than fifty tables of morality/values questions, charting Americans' attitudes (or what they told pollsters) from the 1940s to the then-present. Over-reductively, majorities of Americans supported government solutions even as they opposed some of the 1960s more radical ideas (forced busing, tax-supported birth control information).[36] Gitlin's history of the New Left claims that majorities of Americans, as late as 1967, did not favor American withdrawal from Vietnam.[37] Were young people looking for change? Yes. Were they necessarily looking to the counterculture or the New Left? No. The films of the Rough Rebels, cannily marketed to young people as hip *and* disillusioned, eventually served as evidence that the studios understood and perhaps influenced the distinction.

Ten years after the first publication of *On the Road*, in the beginning of 1967, the Dylan–Kerouac brand of restless, hip, wry alienation had not really been seen on film screens. That would soon change. And when it did, many of Dylan and Kerouac's pro-male, anti-female biases would also come to the fore. As early as 1973, in *Popcorn Venus*, Marjorie Rosen noted that films like *Easy Rider* and *Midnight Cowboy* actually extended patriarchy, even more than films had done before, partly through more explicit representation and partly by not favoring the domestic.[38] Dennis Bingham writes, "An irony of the male left, as reflected in postwar art especially, is that rebellion against the dominant order is too often blindsided by a misogyny and phallocentrism that ensure the order's continuation."[39] Indeed, this was one more aspect that the Rough Rebels would borrow from the Beats and folk-rock music. However, just before the Beats came to Hollywood, Hollywood found itself in a uniquely hospitable situation for them.

Studio malaise

A key discursive element of the Rough Rebels is that they were asserting agency in a supposedly "post-studio" world where actors could make up the rules. Despite the rhetoric in the press, actors as determinants were hardly new. The biggest stars had consistently been understood as decision-makers regarding their films—especially after they created their own production companies—from Charles Chaplin to Douglas Fairbanks to James Cagney to Burt Lancaster. However, more Hollywood actors developed more agency as studio system power eroded. One under-appreciated reason for this was World War II, because the US government, raising funds for the war, began taxing salaried studio (and non-studio) employees in higher-income brackets by as much as 80 percent.[40] Non-salaried talent, the kind that required a new contract for every project, was taxed at the much lower capital gains rate. These tax code changes were an important reason why the 1940s saw an exponential increase in independent production companies, some managed by actors. Prior to the war, agents for actors and directors perhaps met with studio executives once a year. In 1950, James Stewart became the first star-actor to negotiate for "back-end points." With every successful deal, agents and actors accrued more and more power, until Lew Wasserman, the city's most powerful agent and manager of MCA, actually took over Universal Pictures in 1962. By the time of the Rough Rebels, star-actor power was less a new force and more a discursive approach to appeal to young adults.

Wasserman's takeover of Universal was only one of many battles the studios lost after their business model peaked during the 1940s. In the 1950s, the studios, fighting for their lives with television, came to make more and more "epic scale" productions to distinguish their product from the small screen. Hollywood's swords-and-sandals cycle seemed to represent, even profilmically, the bloat and excess of the major studios. After the death and retirement of the last few remaining classical-era moguls, perhaps some change was inevitable. In the mid-1960s, Warner Bros. merged with Seven Arts and was integrated into Kinney National Services, TransAmerica acquired United Artists, Gulf and Western purchased Paramount Pictures: studios were clearly vulnerable to corporate takeover. They were more open to new ideas—even ideas from actors—than they might have been ten years before.

After the 1948 Supreme Court decree against vertical integration in *United States v. Paramount Pictures*, exhibitors' relationship with distributors became more and more strained. Without sufficient product to fill the screens, exhibitors increasingly had to rely on movies made outside the Hollywood studio system. This gap in supply was handily addressed by B-film companies like American International Pictures, by foreign films, and by producers of pornography. By the mid-1960s, as Dennis

Hopper would later remark, there were 600 art-houses, without one Hollywood film to fill them.[41] In the mid-1960s, industry regulation was upended as never before or since. Since its rigorous enforcement began in 1934, the Hays Code had endured increasingly predictable challenges: a film pushed the limits enough to get publicity, then sued over its First Amendment rights, then marketed itself as the "film they don't want you to see." Each time, the Code frayed a bit. By the end of 1965, because of films like *The Pawnbroker* (1965), breasts were coming out, and the Hays Code was rendered all but obsolete. The new ratings system arrived only after the studios witnessed how foreign and home-grown "titillating" films had parlayed their notoriety into major profits. New rules would bring new faces.

In 1968, the new President of the Motion Pictures of America Association, Jack Valenti, unveiled a new rating system for Hollywood films: G for General Audiences, M for Mature Audiences (later changed to GP, then PG), R for Restricted Audiences, and X for minors to be excluded. By then, however, most of Hollywood's talent had had the opportunity to work on at least one picture during the seemingly unreg-ulated years of 1966–8, and many filmmakers had taken advantage of the relaxed rules in some manner. Increasing amounts of blood, nudity, and profanity, then, were naturally tied to new notions of what it meant to be realistic. The exhibitors, for their part, did not complain about being able to show what had never been shown. In the same year, an MPAA-sponsored study found that 48 percent of box-office admissions the previous year were from persons aged 16–24, and concluded "being young and single is the overriding demographic pre-condition for being a frequent and enthusiastic moviegoer." In 1967, Bob Evans, then 37, said, "The strongest period in Hollywood history was in the 30s, when most of the creative people were young. The trouble is that most of them are still around making movies." Evans even boasted that 28 of 48 then-current directors at Paramount had no directorial experience prior to 1963.[42] It's hard to imagine a studio executive even wanting to make such a claim in any prior year, and executives have hardly been bragging about that since the 1970s.

At the end of 1966, to apologize that his year-end top ten list would only include two American films, *The New York Times'* canon-maker Bosley Crowther wrote, "Experience has long prepared us to accept the uncomfortable fact that the best work in motion pictures—the most intelligent, progressive, astute and alert to what is happening to people—is being done abroad."[43] It is certainly possible to over-state the influence of European films over American filmmaking; nevertheless, certain tendencies seem to have been appropriated. The fabled "neo-realist" films of Italy were celebrated for revealing an aesthetic where everything captured inside a frame would have a natural, unrehearsed quality and an affinity with the common man. Critics praised this cinema that made fiction films appear, at a glance, similar in many ways to documentaries. Siegfried Kracauer wrote that this sort of realism demanded a new sort of actor: the "non-actor," who could seem like an ordinary, unfilmed person. If a man looked ordinary enough, he seemed more "realistic": this was "playing oneself."[44] Star-actors like Hoffman, Nicholson, and Gould, simply by appearing as themselves without makeup on, had a privileged claim on realism before they even opened their mouths. Like the Italian professionals Anna Magnani and Aldo Fabrizi, their star images benefitted from the sense that they just showed up out of nowhere.

At the end of the 1950s, the French *nouvelle vague* films infused the neo-realist aesthetic with style, irony, and hipness. The narrative rules seemed broken by disjunctive editing, fourth-wall-breaking, and flash-forwards. *Nouvelle vague* films like *A bout de souffle* (1960) and *Jules et Jim* (1961) asserted, as Raymond Williams would later call it, as a compliment, "the critical and self-critical wing of the bourgeoisie."[45] The middle class was *right* to feel bad about itself even as it joked and did nothing to change the system. For all their despair, these European filmmaking auteurs that came to prominence in the 1960s had never known what it meant to go days without eating or to sleep in the street. Unlike films like *Ladri di biciclette* (1948), the *nouvelle vague* films paired disillusionment with a certain arch irony. In this, they were well aligned not only with their American counterparts, but with the men running the corporations that were taking over the Hollywood studios. New Wave films were popular with young adult audiences, and that meant that when American filmmakers looked across the Atlantic for inspiration, they saw both disenfranchisement and playfulness. (Asked about *Easy Rider*, Dennis Hopper said, "I wanted to make the first American art film."[46]) Less noted by historians is the fact that most of the hit *nouvelle vague* films were also about young people, rarely over the age of 35. To the degree that Hollywood echoed these films, the studios weren't exactly going to cast people like Cary Grant and Elizabeth Taylor.

Technology improvements meant that handheld cameras now produced images that studios considered suitable for the big screen. Improved Kodak stock meant that people could look human without need for heavy makeup. In general, the trend of the color palette of films, as opposed to that of its movie stars on the red carpet, ran toward the less garish and more muted. Color's new ubiquity, arguably, had the effect of liberating it from its former "brightening" effect (as when Dorothy lands in Oz). If color was everywhere, negative shades could have colors as well. And if color could pick up "dirty" details without seeming dirty itself, this in many ways could enable the Rough Rebel. There were also changes in sound quality; improved recording equipment could pick up mumbled lines. The vaunted realism of the coming movement, then, was partly a matter of timing.

Bonnie and Clyde and *The Graduate*

Among the many, many films that influenced the Rough Rebels, two deserve special mention here. 1967's *Bonnie and Clyde* and *The Graduate* spent 1968 earning record fortunes and were singularly influential regarding the films and actors that succeeded them. Even when it was in theaters, the *Hollywood Reporter* said of *Bonnie and Clyde*, "Not in a generation has a single Hollywood movie had such a sudden decisive and worldwide impact."[47] Its influence and power has been noted by many historians of the period (including many not focused on cinema), often in terms of "anarchic individualism" and righteous violence in the face of capricious authority. For this film, alienation meant trying to steal the American dream (including that of attaining celebrity) and getting killed for it; the film's realism was of the open-road, stylized variety. Before 1967 was over, *Bonnie and Clyde* had emerged as a watershed, not just formally and thematically, but also as "a small victory for the independent judgment of audiences against the guiding advice of mass journalism."[48] After his denunciation of *Bonnie and Clyde*, Bosley Crowther was asked to leave *The New York Times* after more than twenty years as the paper of record's critic of record. As much as any person, Crowther had served as the Bourdieuan arbiter of the line between art and kitsch; his departure signaled that standards were changing. Crowther was replaced at the *Times* by Renata Adler, who was more sympathetic to less traditional films. *Time* underwent an even more stunning and notorious reversal. Six months after it ran a pan of *Bonnie and Clyde*, a *Time* cover story of December 1967 called the film a hallmark of a New Hollywood and officially announced a "renaissance" of American cinema; *Time* identified complex narratives, hybrid plots, stylistic flourishes, and taboo subject matter as its hallmarks.[49] Its young stars were also celebrated as part of its appeal.

Bonnie and Clyde is pointedly more about image than substance. Its screenwriter David Newman said,

> In our view, what kills Bonnie and Clyde is not that they broke the law, because nobody liked the fucking banks—but that they put a tattoo on C.W. Moss. His father says, "I can't believe you let these people put pictures on your skin." This is what the 1960s turned out to be about.[50]

To some extent, this is what the films of the Rough Rebels turned out to be about. Film by its very nature privileges image over substance, but Newman was discussing the diegetic level, implying that the look of the actors mattered at least as much as what they were saying and doing. Most films featuring the Rough Rebels can seem leftist, but in fact the major characters tend to distrust all totalizing solutions, whether offered by hippies or Nixon voters. And like *Bonnie and Clyde* and *The Graduate*, they would laugh instead of cry, representing irony and disillusionment at the same time.

What *Bonnie and Clyde* did to validate mainstream violence, *The Graduate* did to validate mainstream lasciviousness. While the book and script seemed to call for a lead like Robert Redford, the film's centrality of the Dustin Hoffman persona appeared to vouchsafe its hipness and daring. Many in the press positioned *The Graduate* and Dustin Hoffman as a force of the counterculture. Hoffman had told Nichols: "Clearly, the character, the graduate, 'Ben Braddock,' isn't Jewish." Nichols replied: "No, but he's Jewish inside."[51] *Life* wrote: "Nichols gambled that Dusty's talents would triumph over his appearance. He has won his gamble. ... Dusty is one of the few new leading men in Hollywood who look like people rather than profiles in celluloid."[52] *Life* began the positioning of Hoffman as a subversive yet authentic anti-hero, and the mainstream press followed suit. *Life*'s headline read "a swarthy Pinocchio makes a wooden role real," and others would follow with similar off-color comments. The many critics that praised *The Graduate* did not name Hoffman as Jewish; they hardly needed to. Instead, they went out of their way to praise the everyman persona. In twenty-plus researched sources, no review of Hoffman's performance bothered with the word "innovative," "revolutionary," or even "Method." His significance was distilled to his subversive persona matched with his unlikely looks. America had seen this sort of thing before, but the press made it sound as though it were learning it all over again.

Of course *The Graduate* was hardly as subversive as, say, *The Battle of Algiers* (1966), and many critics rightly took it to task at the time. But marketing as in the *Life* article encouraged people to "get it," to position the joke, the film, and the off-beatness of Hoffman as a way to freak the squares. Adopting Hoffman as a cultural symbol became a way for America's largest generation to prove they knew better than their parents. When it came to Hoffmans of the late 1960s, baby boomers' tastes leaned closer to Dustin than Abbie. Witty alienation resounded louder than liberal activism. And the Hoffman archetype signaled a change for Hollywood casting. Mel Gussow noted in September of 1968 that "He's given hope to hordes of homely men." He predicted that

> rejected producers will start asking for *a* Dustin Hoffman ... "But there'll come a day," predicts the original Dustin Hoffman, "when a face like mine will not be able to get work. Ten years from now, they'll say, 'I'll give half my kingdom for a walking surfboard.'" But for the next ten years—watch out.[53]

This was, as it happened, quite prescient.

Sam Peckinpah spoke about *The Wild Bunch* (1969) as an effort to "out-Bonnie and Clyde Bonnie and Clyde,"[54] and he was hardly alone. Using the *Time* cover headline "Violence ... Sex ... Art" as a starting point, one way of understanding the nine studied films is how they pushed boundaries of violence and sex further than *Bonnie and Clyde* and *The Graduate*. *Easy Rider*, *Little Big Man*, *M*A*S*H*, and *Straw Dogs*, for different reasons, represent a deepening of the violence seen in *Bonnie and Clyde*, and *Midnight Cowboy*, *Bob & Carol & Ted & Alice*, *Five Easy Pieces*, *Carnal Knowledge*, and *The Touch* try to expand the representations of sexual freedom of *The Graduate*. Perhaps a previous generation of stars with a more "traditional" appearance and performance style (say, Gregory Peck) could have "pushed the envelope" on representation, but that isn't what *Bonnie and Clyde* or *The Graduate* signified.

Another way that the Rough Rebels' films echoed *Bonnie and Clyde* and *The Graduate* was the use of a single star surrounded by previously unknown actors. While Arthur Penn and Mike Nichols's *previous* films had followed typical (though never absolute) Hollywood convention in featuring at least a couple of established personalities, *Bonnie and Clyde* featured Warren Beatty and a group of non-stars while *The Graduate* featured Anne Bancroft and a group of non-stars. This point is occluded by historians that celebrate supposed non-star casts in this period; the truth is there were just as many films of the period that featured emergent stars alongside more established talent, and these were the ones that earned a lot of money and awards. It is no coincidence that when Linda Ruth Williams and Michael Hammond name truly leftist films from the period—*Greetings* (1968), *Medium Cool* (1969), *Hi Mom!* (1969), *Zabriskie Point* (1970), *The Strawberry Statement* (1970), and *Getting Straight* (1970)—they name only films without stars, with the exception of the last one, and we will see that Hollywood turned away from its star.[55]

With the idiosyncratic exceptions of *Billy Jack* (1971) and *American Graffiti* (1973), Hollywood dramas without stars released during the Nixon administration faded quickly from theaters. *Easy Rider* featured Peter Fonda; *Bob & Carol & Ted & Alice* featured Natalie Wood; the other films studied here featured at least the stars under discussion. (*M*A*S*H* is a liminal case; Gould was not really a star, though he was Barbra Streisand's husband and Fox had just signed him to a three-picture deal on the strength of a clip from *Bob & Carol*.) The point is that the Rough Rebels were deployed not to show the lunatics running the asylum but instead something closer to the Horatio Alger myth. Anyone could succeed in Hollywood; anyone could be in bed with Natalie Wood or Ann-Margret. This distinction matters because it speaks to how the most successful Rough Rebel films were less than a systemic overhaul and more of a continuation of Hollywood norms. This "one star rule" was neither codified nor strict, but it certainly exerted determinative influence over the films. One only has to imagine *Midnight Cowboy* with Elvis Presley as Joe Buck or *M*A*S*H* with Jack Lemmon and Walter Matthau as Hawkeye and Duke, which were ideas that some executives supported in pre-production. Supervising producers like Richard Zanuck and Robert Evans lionized "fresh faces" (especially everyman faces) but were generally careful to have at least one known quantity in the cast. It's easy to see how, after the Rough Rebels proved its ongoing viability, this template went on to enable the biggest hit films of the 1970s: *The Godfather* (1972), *The Exorcist* (1973), *Jaws* (1975), and *Star Wars* (1977). These apparent everyman blockbusters, particularly the latter two, led some scholars to conclude that stars weren't important during the 1970s, but this is based partly on ignorance of the "one star rule."

"Post-studio" stars

Thus far, I have said that prestige films from Europe, a popular mood of disillusionment, and studio tumescence (including a breakdown of censorship) were key antecedents to the Rough Rebels. Yet if these trends somehow gave rise to the Rough Rebels, one might have expected a very similar movement to have arisen in the early 1930s, when these conditions also existed. In fact, in many ways, it did, according to Robert Sklar. Two of his three City Boys, James Cagney and Humphrey Bogart, honed their acting abilities in 1920s Broadway plays that then exemplified what was being called the "new realism." Sklar reviews the very real crisis that the studios faced in 1930 to ask why any Broadway actor would risk a move to Hollywood at the time, and explains:

> Hollywood had the welcome mat out for Broadway veterans. They had already shown that they could act and talk at the same time, a feat not every silent screen performer had mastered; perhaps more important, they were willing to work for salaries well below the prime Hollywood pay rates of the free-spending 1920s.[56]

The Broadway stage has always provided discounted talent for Hollywood, but the 1960s proved a particularly acute case. People like Carl Reiner, Mel Brooks, Mike Nichols, and Barbra Streisand helped casting director Marion Dougherty convince some producers that opportunities for talent and "everyman" publicity lay with Rough Rebels from Broadway like Hoffman, Gould, Gene Hackman, and Robert Duvall. Dougherty probably deserves her own chapter in this book, or even her own book; she championed the Rough Rebels against what she called "the Tabs and the Troys."

There lies a contradiction for star-actors of the period that began in the 1960s: for the first time, new stars emerged without signing extensive studio contracts, theoretically empowering stars, yet somehow stardom itself seemed diminished. In response, Joshua Gamson defines what he calls "post-studio" stars: "Their success, in either case, is a merited one: either because their natural charisma is recognized or because they fulfill the American dream, becoming stars through their own blood, sweat, and tears."[57] This is crucial, because we might say that the first ideological significance of a star is not only being, as at least three scholars separately put it, "ordinary and extraordinary" (as, say, filet mignon might be described), but also "naturally" charismatic and/or connected to Horatio Alger myths that celebrate success for the deserving few. Such myths should have only become stronger in an era when star-actors supposedly controlled their own images.

Celebrities are caricatured by scholars like Gamson and Barry King as "human pseudo-events," meaning things that are only important because they have claimed themselves to be. Gamson writes that in the 1950s, "Terms began to change: the celebrity was becoming 'merchandise,' 'inventory,' 'property,' a 'product,' a 'commodity,' while the fans were becoming 'markets.'"[58] King sees the same trend toward commodity status and writes that "stars begin to show a distance from their own image, which becomes an object for manipulation in relation to character." If Gamson and King are right, then at some point during the 1960s, stars became complicit in making stardom itself more ordinary, more human, less glamorous, and perhaps less powerful. In another essay, King says that because stars are now proprietors of their own image, star images "take on a reflexive, i.e. accountable, relationship to the actorly and communication aspects of his or her work."[59] My book indeed goes some distance toward substantiating his point.

Where Gamson and King differ is their description of the predominant tendency that follows this "disenchantment" of stardom. For Gamson, "post-studio" stars now relentlessly perform irony and knowingness:

> Through irony, these celebrity texts reposition their readers, enlightened about the falseness of celebrity, to 'see the joke' of the performed self or become it. Cynicism, irony, and invitations behind the scenes engage. ... The irony is more than defensive; it is proud. These texts offer telling new resolutions to the underlying cultural tensions. The anxiety about public selves, for example, is no longer met only with the continual promise of personal revelation. The private self is no longer the ultimate truth. Instead, what is most true, most real, most trustworthy, is precisely the relentlessly performing public self.[60]

By this reckoning, film stars in interviews are almost always telling some sort of joke, referring to themselves in an offhand, ironically amused way where the presumed audience is either "getting it" or not. Gamson's analysis works well for some stars, but less well for any star that consistently conveys sincerity in their roles or appearances.

King, on the other hand, says that the ostensible breakup of the studio system led to "a corresponding emergent emphasis on character." Because every film now has to "stand on its own merits," now "a successful characterization must 'stand' on its own terms." Because "character" is now "an integral variable in its own right, no longer simply collapsible into star image," King offers the "apparent resolution" of developing an "'actorly' image, i.e. to claim technical excellence as the basis for reputation." This is closer to what the Rough Rebels often convey. King admits that "professional and commercial success" are unlikely to be consistently joined, and suggests "the alternative of developing a star image that indicates the 'social issues' indicated [sic] by carefully selected narratives since these issues transcend particular films."[61] King, unlike Gamson, seems to leave no room for 1970s stars with relatively consistent images (e.g. Burt Reynolds, Ryan O'Neal) who do not seem to engage "social issues." The stars with the "actorly image" are the ones whose films seem (somewhat) more politically conscious. This book means to join Gamson's and King's critiques together—stars as both seriously alienated and ironically playful. It is with this two-pronged consideration that the social and ideological implications of their image construction become more fully apparent.

All three of my Rough Rebel subjects were offscreen leftists, but as nascent stars Hoffman and Nicholson were quite institutional (like Paul Newman or Paul McCartney), distancing themselves from radical movements, while Gould embraced radicals (closer to Marlon Brando or John Lennon) and said that mainstream audiences did not "know what was good for them."[62] If their characters were sometimes too fatalist, the star-actors generally rushed to make it clear that this was only in the name of virtuoso performance, and that in fact they were as hip as anyone (unlike some of their more stone-faced Method actor successors). This complexly ironic approach to alienation played a crucial role in subverting revolutionary logic to star logic.

Performance

Ultimately, a responsible book on film actors must try to understand exactly what actors are doing onscreen. One problem with previous attempts at such understandings is an over-emphasis on generalized explanations of techniques; these techniques include the Delsartian code, the Stanislavski-derived Method, and the neo-realist style of "playing oneself." A crucial problem for scholars is that no one can say exactly which technique an actor uses in a given scene. Even the actors are not always certain. Nonetheless, scholars often connect techniques to film performances as though a favored acting teacher, such as Lee Strasberg, had been directing the films. Techniques provide guidelines for analysis and occasional signposts for behavior, but to suggest that a given formula leads directly to a specific onscreen gesture or expression is usually misleading.

Enumerating the signs used by actors—the gestures used to communicate different feelings—is one more way of understanding the work of the actor. Such work dovetails with analysis, because most scholars are predisposed to seeing the actor as something of a sign him/herself. The first sign that an actor manipulates is his own appearance, and many scholars have pointed out that no actor can go far beyond his looks. Barry King, often quoted in this regard, says,

> The actor's product—a given performance—is inseparable from his or her physical attributes. ... If we now ask what acting in general is we can define it as the process of subsuming the self—a personal identity, operative behind all roles and settings—into a character in a limited, e.g. written, social setting ... for some social theorists the distinction between self and role is typical of all forms of social activity. In this sense we are all actors.[63]

Vsevolod Pudovkin articulated a similar perspective:

> The image the actor builds as his work develops, on the one hand is constructed out of himself as a person with given individual characteristics, and on the other is conditioned by the interaction of this personal element and the intention in general of the play.[64]

Thus, judging acting is measuring the difference between self and role, or measuring the extent to which actors are going beyond the restrictions of their appearance—their initial "sign."

Scholarship that interprets actors as performing signs (in more than one sense) suffers from at least two recurrent problems: lack of historical specificity and lack of explication of ideological functions. Scholars have addressed a perceived lack of historical awareness by returning to the "applied aesthetics" of François Delsarte (1811–71), less as a direct influence on contemporary performers than as a helpful taxonomy of gestural significances. However, there exists an English-language manual older than Delsarte's, which serves to better underscore scholars' implicit point that the more things have changed, the more they have remained the same. M. Engel's *Practical Illustrations of Rhetorical Gesture and Action, Adapted to the English Drama* was translated from the German into English by Henry Siddons in 1807, and it includes illustrations of what it calls "passions" (we would now call them emotions or feelings) such as Love, Jealous Rage, Servility, Loftiness, Tranquil Joy, Quietude, Anger, Despondency, Indifference, Expectation, and about fifty more. Several would be familiar coding for any modern viewer, and several would not.[65]

Some scholarly books on actors use *Practical Illustrations* to call attention to the highly schematic, formalized set of gestures that influenced

American theater at the turn of the previous century. However, reading the two-centuries-old text reveals a great deal of awareness of nuance. Siddons, having read over Engel's work, wrote,

> [T]he same expression or modification of a passion is delineated by various ways in various persons, without a necessity of any *one* of those modes being superior to the *other*; and that we must likewise consider the personages in their characters, national and private, the age and sex, and the thousand complex &cs. belonging to them, before we can safely say what is the *best* expression or modification of a peculiar passion.

> (emphasis his)

In other words, even in 1807, the author(s) promoted a temporizing and equivocal prescription for good acting of "passions." Siddons did not believe that simple slavish onstage reproductions of the illustrations would be sufficient for effective performance:

> There are but two counsels to give the actor on this head: first, that he ought to seize all occasions of observing nature, even in those effects which are unfrequent in their occurrence; and, in the second place, that he should never lose sight of the main end and grand design of his art, by shocking the spectator with too coarse or too servile an imitation.[66]

This was never a code of crude pantomime, but instead a supplement to desired naturalism.

One reason that I linger on *Practical Illustrations* is that, at several points, Engel offers his German's version of what he calls Italian gestures. So we already see that to enounce is to mimic the more ethnic, the more marginalized. Siddons also uses a distinctly ethnic example as a guard against those who would over-essentialize the work:

> Shylock, in the *Merchant of Venice*, affords a fine example to illustrate transitions of passions and affections. Shylock experiences the most bitter anguish, whilst recalling to his mind the precious jewels he has lost by the flight of his daughter: he evinces the most lively joy, whilst learning the catastrophe of Anthonio ... these two opposite sentiments alternately succeed in the soul of the Jew: grief seems to take the place of joy, and joy to assume that of grief, without any intermediate sentiment.[67]

Even two hundred (and four hundred) years ago, representations of ethnic men were not restricted to one-dimensional stereotype, and in fact
were even deployed to assure polyvalence and richness of character.

Moving forward to the era of cinema, perhaps the most comprehen-
sive set of actor sign interpretations is provided by Cynthia Baron and
Sharon Marie Carnicke, who convincingly demonstrate that varying
historical taxonomies can be productively applied to contemporary
films.[68] They do not advocate that one particular analytical structure is
superior to another, and thus I think they would approve of my picking
and choosing among their methodologies to scrutinize my subjects; I
make particular (but not single-minded) use of their rubric for what has
become known as Laban Movement Analysis.

Rudolf Laban (1879–1958) was an actor, dancer, and teacher who
was born in Bratislava and eventually immigrated to England. Laban
noticed that actors generally focused on their lines and their "character," and tended not to control their own body movements with the
rigor of dancers. He eventually pioneered a system he called "notation,"
an exhaustive accounting of the significance of gestures and movements. Laban was well aware that any particular movement might be
interpreted in more than one way (much as spoken homonyms are),
yet he maintained throughout his life that actors could benefit from
more attention to an audience's general understanding of their body
language. Laban worked with dance and theater programs for more
than forty years before synthesizing his observations into *The Mastery
of Movement on the Stage* (1950), where he described gestures as "expressive *releases* rather than practiced achievements."[69] Laban offered many
caveats against over-simplification; nonetheless, he eventually provided
a simplified system, or taxonomy, so that actors would have some sort
of baseline to work from. Laban suggested that the "releases" in performances could be usefully understood through the four following
metrics:

Spatial aspects
Place, direction, shape of movement
Direct versus flexible (indirect) movement
Temporal aspects
Speed and rhythm of movement
Sudden versus sustained movement
Weight/strength
Degree of resistance to gravity
Strong versus light movement

Energy flow
Degree of control of movement
Bound versus free-flowing movement

But this taxonomy was not specific enough to describe routine acting choices. Eventually, Laban and his collaborators settled on eight basic efforts, charted as follows:

	Sustained	Sudden
Strong, direct	Press (crush, cut, squeeze)	Thrust (shove, punch, poke)
Strong, indirect	Wring (pull, pluck, stretch)	Slash (beat, throw, whip)
Light, direct	Glide (smooth, smear, smudge)	Dab (pat, tap, shake)
Light, indirect	Float (strew, stir, stroke)	Flick (flip, flap, jerk)

I find these to be a good starting point for *what an actor is doing* onscreen, particularly because certain efforts imply more strength and directness than others. As a *very* broad generalization, strength and directness connote a sort of moral force, a certainty, while lightness and indirectness often suggest flexibility and even looser morals. This is not always the case, and indeed many actors intentionally nuance their characters to complicate easy understandings of their motivations. However, beginning with these terms helps to show how actors make characters live by certain moral leanings, often varying over the course of the narrative, and this serves as a start of an examination of ideological representation. One reason scholars have generally avoided such examination might be summarized as: an onscreen cough doesn't directly challenge dominant ideology any more than an onscreen smile directly reinforces it. However, many scholars have been letting the actors off too easily; there is still political and social significance in gestures and expressions.

Summary

To summarize this opening chapter: if Hollywood both changed and stayed the same in the late 1960s and early 1970s, star-actors' complicity and responsibility in that evolution is neglected. The films and their stars, whom I call Rough Rebels, were positioned as simultaneously upstarts and moderate alternatives. Events of the decade gave good reason for Hollywood to valorize the "ethnic," ordinary, young, alienated everyman. By 1968, studios in crisis sought young audiences, and the unexpected success of *Bonnie and Clyde* and *The Graduate* suggested new, or revised, styles of casting and filmmaking. Ostensibly "post-studio" stars are described by Barry King as developing an "actorly" and "technically excellent" reputation that engages "social issues," and described by Joshua Gamson as ironic and bringing in their audience on the joke. I join King's and Gamson's rubrics together to better explicate the Rough Rebel figure. There are many ways to read performance, but I prefer Laban Movement Analysis as a starting point for what an actor is doing onscreen and what sort of ideology the actions signify. In the following case studies, I show how the star-actor Rough Rebels functioned as privileged symbols for the simultaneously alienated, ironic, and male-privileging natures of their seminal films, with considerable implications for major stars and major films that came afterward.

2
Dustin Hoffman: The Artistic Star

This chapter situates Dustin Hoffman's incipient star career as a negotiation of tension between appealing to young educated adults and maintaining Hollywood traditions. To an unexamined extent, Hoffman's performance style and contemporary interviews to the press exerted a considerable influence over what became known as the "Hollywood Renaissance." Hoffman's stature as an ethnic everyman, anti-hero, and unlikely star was a determinative signifier in his films, his ancillary discourse, and the movement more generally. As much as any actor, Hoffman established the Rough Rebel star image: not conventionally handsome, white-ethnic, committed to and excelling at performance, careerist, liberal but not radical, and privileging male–male relationships over male–female relationships.

As I noted, Robin Wood characterizes the major themes of the new dramatic films as "collapse in confidence of patriarchal authority," "uncertainty about the values of any possible American future," "collapse of confidence in ... traditional sexual relationships," religion as "marginal to the point of irrelevancy," learning as "hypocrisy," a "descent into disillusionment," and "the disintegration of American society and the ideology that supports it is presented as total and final, beyond hope of reconstruction."[1] These themes were presumed to be attractive to college-age and art-house audiences; thus, new, hip films needed actors that could perform them. Hoffman's expressive, highly attenuated performance as Ratso Rizzo in *Midnight Cowboy* does indeed exemplify these themes. As David Sumner in *Straw Dogs* Hoffman updated the more ironical Benjamin Braddock persona he had developed in *The Graduate*, and as Jack Crabb in *Little Big Man* Hoffman performed farcical absurdism. Hoffman's performative distanciation from Wood's themes of alienation, combined with his developing star construct as a nice, easygoing fellow (in contrast to how he and other ostensibly strictly Method actors were later perceived), served to compromise the themes Wood names, and to reify the good-humored attitude that Hollywood's biggest stars had usually implied.

As explained, according to Barry King, after the societal and industrial changes of the 1960s, stars found incentive to develop an "actorly image," which would engage with "the 'social issues' indicated by carefully selected narratives since these issues transcend particular films."[2] The star-actor would demonstrate acting ability and "character" through differing, though often sincerely empathetic, sorts of performances onscreen while showing a consistent sincerity about social issues offscreen. For Joshua Gamson, however, in this same period, "Cynicism, irony, and invitations behind the scenes engage. ... The irony is more than defensive; it is proud."[3] The star-actor demonstrates a sort of "winking" falseness onscreen and a cynical perspicacity in interviews. These two models are at odds: King does not reckon with stars that flaunt their ironic approach to the world, and Gamson does not recognize stars that attempt sincere engagement with social problems. Herein I argue that Hoffman, as a Rough Rebel star-actor, tries to reconcile these distinctions, attempting a somewhat genuine disenfranchisement with society while also making clear his hip, ironic distanciation. Whether alienated or ironic, Hoffman consistently favors male–male relationships over male–female ones, and this is well in line with what Eve Sedgwick calls her "formulations" on homosocial coding. As I wrote, I will mostly rely upon Laban's taxonomy, because I believe it provides the most useful correlation between gesture/movement and rough ideological signification.

As an entry point, sincere alienation and ironic distanciation are both central to how Hoffman's films revised the codes of the western genre at this time. The opening moment of *Midnight Cowboy* features the sound of cowboys and Indians in a battle; the camera zooms out from the all-white image to reveal a blank screen of a deserted drive-in theater. The implication is that the western is dead even if some vestige remains. Throughout the film, Joe Buck calls into question the viability of the modern cowboy type on the streets of late-1960s New York, its repugnance represented by Ratso Rizzo. *Little Big Man* brazenly renegotiates many western generic codes, positioning Custer's soldiers as the antagonists and the Indians as the righteous victims, with Jack Crabb wavering until finally damning Custer to his deadly fate. To twenty-first-century audiences, *Straw Dogs* may not seem to have much to do with repositioning the western, but for contemporary reviewers the film was contextualized exactly as Sam Peckinpah's new sort of anti-moral western brought to the modern age, with David as the man whose pacifism enables a dispiriting violent denouement. In all these cases, women are marginalized if not excoriated.

Of all genres, the western has always had a privileged place in American cinema. Westerns are where American men learn to uphold American, Christian, and masculinist values in a harsh frontier wilderness. Westerns were often more nuanced and complicated than reviewers of the 1970s implied, but taken together, *Midnight Cowboy*, *Little Big Man*, and *Straw Dogs* considerably deconstructed the genre, infusing it with both existential malaise and a certain distanciation from that malaise. It would be far too much to claim that Hoffman "killed" the western, but through his portrayals of Ratso Rizzo, Jack Crabb, and David Sumner, western myths were challenged and later filmmakers arguably found it more difficult to present those myths straightforwardly. This was one legacy of the Rough Rebel figure.

Midnight Cowboy: Textual analysis

Through Dustin Hoffman's characterization of Ratso Rizzo, *Midnight Cowboy* illustrates Voltaire's principle of futility in ambivalence, a genuine and non-ironic disillusionment that eschews solutions. Playing a homeless, hopeless man, Hoffman takes this conception further than the book or script dictates, with an apparently "sincere engagement with social issues" as Barry King describes. Hoffman's limp, a shammy redolent of a stammering vaudeville performer, succeeds in making Joe Buck's loping, heavy-booted gait look normal by comparison. According to several sources, the moment in the film where Ratso crosses a Manhattan street with Joe, and nearly gets hit by a taxi, was an improvisation.[4] The production did not have the resources to actually close New York streets. During this improvisation, when Rizzo and Buck cross the street, a taxi truly almost hits Hoffman; famously, the actor spits out his half-smoked cigarette, bangs on the hood of the car and yells, "I'm walking here! I'm walking here!" Hoffman continues to yell at the driver even as he honks and drives past the two of them. Hoffman flips up one arm and hits its elbow with his other hand, the "f you" gesture. He grabs Buck's arm, never losing his imperative as Buck's shepherd, and likewise never losing the limp. Rizzo says, "Don't worry about that, actually, that ain't a bad way to pick up insurance." This can be read as a sort of meta-line: Hoffman's ostensibly Method, fully immersed performance "ain't a bad way" to perform (and insure) the central theme of useless desperation.

Illustration 2.1 Joe Buck (Jon Voight) and Ratso Rizzo (Hoffman) cross the street

In Laban terms Hoffman is strong but indirect, with poorly allocated moral authority. Hoffman as Rizzo asserts his rights to the taxi driver, yet it's obvious that such an assertion is absurd. Rizzo had hardly looked both ways before crossing, and gave off the air of a man who would run a red light anyway. This sort of character work is barely suggested by the novel or the script, suggesting it is truly Hoffman who provides Rizzo in microcosm here: petulant, righteous, confrontational against even benign parts of the world, but also, crucially, not really hot-headed as much as resigned to a pathetic fate. To a considerable degree, this describes the tone of the film, a clear example of how an actor's performance defines a film's themes. It is moments like this that substantiate Wood's claims about despair, as well as King's claims about social engagement.

If the film as signified by Hoffman is markedly alienated, that doesn't make it radically leftist. For a film made in the summer of 1968, *Midnight Cowboy* demonstrates a trenchant skepticism about leftist sentiment. One key to this is that as Hoffman plays Rizzo, he doesn't seem to come from the middle class. The despair of Rizzo and Buck in *Midnight Cowboy* doesn't come from having everything and not knowing what to do with it. Yet their futility is just as self-defeating, as when, less than a minute after the near-collision with the taxi, Ratso Rizzo walks through a group of protestors and tells them to get a job, in perhaps Hoffman's deepest tonal register of the film. His voice "hardens," much as his face hardens at another point, when he talks about how his condemned front door keeps out "punks and creeps." This strong indirectness (in Laban terms) suggests forcefulness without achieving concrete purpose. Hoffman goes beyond the script's concept of Rizzo to show that Rizzo is so individualistic that he rejects his most natural allies. The music complements this theme even as it furthers Hoffman's star image. *The Graduate* had broken ground by using a pop-folk song, Simon and Garfunkel's "The Sounds of Silence," as the internal monologue of Benjamin Braddock (played by Hoffman), beginning with the line "Hello, darkness, my old friend"; *Midnight Cowboy*'s pop-folk song, by Nilsson, begins, "Everybody's talkin' at me, I can't hear a word they're saying, only the echoes of my mind." In both cases, a retreat into self makes more sense than social solutions. Unlike some other contemporary films about alienation (e.g. *Medium Cool* (1969), or *Getting Straight* (1970)), *Midnight Cowboy*, keyed by Hoffman's performance *and* star image, distances itself from revolution.

In Laban's language, Hoffman plays Rizzo as rigidly as a doll, and his every movement is an unrolling of energy all the way to his hands and feet, which seem almost to shake in reaction. Given this struggle, Rizzo is remarkably driven and direct; when the cab almost hits him, Rizzo seems as upset about losing his gait as anything. A few film minutes later, a shot begins with a close-up of a "society" woman's shapely legs getting into a horse-drawn cab, her legs in the top of the frame as Rizzo in wide shot (with Buck trailing behind) walks forcefully forward across the street without looking around. This is how the film updates the most famous tableau from *The Graduate*, Mrs. Robinson's leg framing (or trapping) Benjamin. If Benjamin was paralyzed by Mrs. Robinson, Rizzo instead goes forward heedlessly, against better judgment. As Hoffman plays Rizzo, in Laban terms, Rizzo is an odd combination of bound and free-flowing; like a shark that must keep moving or die, he flows but he doesn't seem free. When Rizzo finally gets Buck inside his apartment, Rizzo for the first time moves somewhere besides forward; he actually spins (locking the door) in 360 degrees and then walks *sideways* to a bathroom. In this way, beyond the script directions, Hoffman performs restlessness finding only futility. Hoffman does not play Rizzo with the subtlety of many prior representations of the indigent, the sort of "plainness" of most neo-realist actors. If he had, the futility might be mistaken for nobility.

Hoffman's performance style continuously abets the film's themes. After Rizzo invites Buck to his apartment, they ascend stairs to get there, the only time this ascent is ever seen (though the story provides many other opportunities). The script suggests that Rizzo leans on a handrail as he walks up; it does not mention which way Rizzo should look. In the film, Hoffman, probably from his own initiative, eschews handrails despite his "bum leg," and looks back at Buck again and again. On the street, in contrast, Rizzo never looks back at Buck when they walk together. Rizzo's journey up the stairs, in Laban's taxonomy, is distinguished by Hoffman keeping his body surprisingly light and free. One way to interpret this is that Rizzo's dreams are coming true in getting the young handsome Joe Buck up to his flat. But if stair ascent can be aligned with rising action, the constant looks back also suggest a fear of falling back into an abyss, or Hell. In this way, Hoffman foreshadows a crucial later scene of literal falling action, where Joe, accompanied by a new girlfriend, walks away from Ratso, and Ratso slips, falling down the stairs. This is Rizzo's final fall. After this accident, he finds he can't walk, signifying the end of act two; the third act consists of Rizzo and Buck trying to get him to Florida for medical attention. But Hoffman's performance suggests that Rizzo was on his way to the ground all along. This isn't alienation that can find a solution (like, say, Terry Malloy's (Marlon Brando's) in *On the Waterfront* (1954))—this is alienation that can only end with death, well in line with Wood's themes.

However, it would not be fair to suggest that nothing is important to Rizzo. As Hoffman plays him, Hoffman-as-Rizzo's "homosocial" behavior certainly privileges a male–male relationship, and positions women as outsiders, just as with most of the characters in Sedgwick's study. In Rizzo's first full scene, Hoffman holds his glass bobbing in the bottom of the frame, like he is barely afloat. (Joe Buck, in a parallel close-up, doesn't have that bobbing effect.) A woman repeatedly comes between them—literally, in the frame—and Rizzo treats her with hostility even as he refuses to look at her. Again, the script doesn't specify: Hoffman could have probably looked wherever he liked. Ratso says, "More goddamn faggots in this town." He's calling this woman a faggot because she's coming between them. The word is a sign, but for Ratso, not the sign we might think it is; in the same way, Ratso may not be the sign we think he is. In Laban terms, Hoffman as Rizzo is indirect, indicating insecurity, as he keeps his shoulders scrunched, and his eyes wide, as he looks only at Joe. He says, "Oh that's all right Joe, I mean, I'm used to these types that get their kicks picking on cripples, I mean the sewers are full of 'em." She interrupts him to ask, "I just got one question for you cowboy. If he's here, and you're all the way over there, how's he gonna get his hand in your pocket?" The double meaning is clearly money and sex. She rises to leave, parting by saying, "Oh but I guess he's got that figured out already." Hoffman as Rizzo continues to focus on Joe, not denying her words directly. Rizzo looks at the woman for the first time as she leaves, only as she can't see him. He shouts "faggot" twice to her, and she shouts "provolone" back, an ethnic slur. In Hoffman's first full scene as Ratso, then, he establishes his duplicity, self-hatred, and his yearning for Joe all at once, even as he makes it clear that the woman is secondary to the bond between Rizzo and Buck.

Hoffman's performance as Ratso complicates apparent revelations of homosexual desire. When Ratso dreams, he does picture Joe shirtless running down a beach. But he runs right past him and into his life as a hotel host. Hoffman could have lingered his gaze at Voight, but throughout the entire film, he never does. In Laban terms, Hoffman's general strong indirectness keeps the two at a remove. When the pair arrive at a party, Rizzo collapses onto Buck, letting his head be caressed by Buck. Hoffman smiles with relief but pointedly not amorousness; it's still not all that clear if it's more than homosocial friendship. (It's also foreshadowing; Buck's head will be caressed just outside the party.) Shirley asks them, "Don't tell me you two are a couple!" Joe laughs; neither says no. This is less suppressed tendencies than it is deliberate ambiguity. At one point, Ratso says, "What am I dragging my bum leg around town for? I mean, tomorrow some dish is liable to be scratching your back at the Plaza and where am I gonna be?" On paper, these are the words of a spurned lover, with a possible Freudian connotation for Rizzo's "bum leg." (Similarly, later, when Joe takes a broken cigarette from Rizzo and Rizzo lights it, this could also be somewhat Freudian: Rizzo as half-potent.) But Hoffman doesn't play these scenes with whiny desire. His voice is matter-of-fact, his hands are low and dispassionate. Hoffman behaves in a similar way when Rizzo gets Buck into his apartment. Rizzo says, "You want to stretch out, make yourself comfortable?" Another actor easily could have played this as a seduction, with the simplest flit of his eyelids. Hoffman walks around somewhat freely, says the line like a brother, as though Rizzo's not sure if this is even supposed to be a seduction. It's easy to imagine the scene played more confidently, or alternatively with guile, particularly Rizzo's next line, "do you want to take a nap?" in a very mock-innocent way. But Hoffman's Rizzo is less concerned about even his own desires, and more just trying to keep his head above water. Directly after, when Joe awakes from his nap, worrying about what Rizzo's after, Joe tells Rizzo, "You don't look like no fag." Hoffman does one of his most direct punctures (in Laban terms) when he replies, "What's that supposed to mean?" Indeed, what?

Hoffman's vocal and movement choices, then, keep Rizzo at a level of deliberate ambiguity regarding sexuality. It is homosocial because women are absolutely excluded while homosexual feelings are barely

Illustration 2.2   Rizzo (Hoffman) reprimanding

acknowledged. With barely a trace more "camp," Hoffman could have made the film a gay fable; instead, Hoffman keeps the film in the realm of the homosocial. *Variety* magazine had already reported in summer 1967 that it could not find one theater that refused to play Condemned films; the producers of *Midnight Cowboy* well knew how lurid they could be.[5] Arguably, the originality of the film is that it presents a sexually free world with unprecedented clarity while assuring that this clarity and freedom does not enable its two lead characters in any sense. When Joe accuses Rizzo, "I bet you never even been laid!", Hoffman doesn't narrow his eyes and barely registers the remark; he plays it as though sex is beside the point. Hoffman as Rizzo moves masculinity's emphasis away from sexual conquests of any sort and more toward survival in a harsh world. Because of Hoffman's performance, the film is less about love, even fraternal love, and more about the difficulty of surviving. Men of past films, especially the westerns of Gary Cooper and John Wayne invoked during the film, were problem-solvers. Rizzo and Buck in *Midnight Cowboy* cannot even solve or save their own lives, with sex or without it. Thanks to Hoffman's choices, Rizzo is alienated from the world and himself.

Midnight Cowboy and 1969: Critical reception

Now that Hoffman was representing a sexually ambiguous character onscreen, he rushed to declare his heterosexual *bona fides* offscreen. On February 7, 1969, after the end of principal photography but months before the release of *Midnight Cowboy*, Dustin Hoffman appeared on the cover of *Time* with his *John and Mary* (1969) co-star, Mia Farrow. The article was titled "The Moonchild and the Fifth Beatle." It was a piece of star management worthy of the classical age: *John and Mary* had barely started filming and would not be released until the end of the year; *Midnight Cowboy*, then in post-production, would come out in May; here was Hoffman on the cover of America's premier newsweekly looking like he was in bed with the young and lovely ex-Mrs. Frank Sinatra. In this way Hoffman made sure to position himself for romantic leads, whatever the reception of *Midnight Cowboy* might be, while still holding forth as a new breed of "anti-star." *Time* wrote:

> As comedy grew steadily blacker and as audiences grew steadily younger, hipper and more draftable, the old concepts began to erode. The invulnerables like Peck and Holden and Wayne seemed lost in a country full of people whose destinies were not in their own hands. The nation of cities needed new images, and suddenly Hoffman became an archetype.[6]

These words were written before Richard Nixon was inaugurated as President (and before the release of *Easy Rider*), for a cover story in America's best-selling news periodical. It is striking that this was published before most people had heard of any of Hoffman's "anti-star" character actor peers, like Jack Nicholson, Elliott Gould, Gene Wilder, Donald Sutherland, and Gene Hackman, never mind the actors that would play young mobsters in the *Godfather* films. These actors' agents, managers, and publicists could now present this *Time* cover story to producers as proof that their clients well represented the authenticity and masculinity that their films needed.[7]

The press helped construct a performer who could play "ordinary" as well as extraordinary men and was still a powerful male presence. Hoffman helped to construct his own image, particularly in these ostensibly post-studio times; an example can be seen in the interview he gave *The New York Times* that appeared on March 16, 1969. Besides echoing much of the *Time* hagiography (with terms like "virtually unprecedented"), this was the first announcement of his upcoming role in *Little Big Man*, couched in respect for Hoffman's ability and range. Here Hoffman actually anticipated his career's most prevalent criticism:

> I've begun to think that playing eccentrics all the time, is, for me, a copout. The tough thing for me is *not* to have a particular voice

or gait for a part, to have to play a guy like John, who is close to me physically and in age and so on. I have this strong fear that if I am just myself, I'm going to be dull. I don't have the leading man's charisma. I mean, I've always felt that *I* better do a helluva lot of acting.[8]

This was a telling statement. Perhaps all this new male verisimilitude was simply the pleasure of watching ugly men work harder because they *had* to. Hoffman would have to demonstrate excess just to seem more authentic, or perhaps just to get work. The confusion between the two was a sign that Hollywood would surely be able to incorporate the Rough Rebel figure.

Hoffman was complicit in structuring his image of an anti-hero ethnic everyman. In June 1968, Hoffman began to agree with his press by saying: "I am the boy next door, only the boy next door is not supposed to have pimples." With this quote, Hoffman proved willing to spearhead the new paradigm, sincere Kingian alienation leavened with Gamsonian humor. Hoffman now knew he would be representing alienation in *Midnight Cowboy*, and he decided to go along with the humor and fun of his "ordinary man" status, though he clearly knew he was hardly the first star not to resemble Clark Gable. Admitting to "anti-hero" status, he said: "Wasn't Bogart, even Tracy, off the conventional line—for their time? Isn't the anti-hero simply the alienated man?"[9] Hoffman agreed with and promoted his own role in the discourse—"everyman" looks as a way to authenticate alienation, to reach out to disaffected youth. Hoffman told interviewers that he wanted to play Malamud's Raskolnikov, Brecht's Arturo Ui, *Catch-22*'s Milo, Holden Caulfield, Malcolm X, Che Guevara, and especially Adolf Hitler. (He would never wind up playing any of these roles.) He said, "Now I can articulate the feelings of those who aren't in a position to talk."[10] This was true, as long as the marginalized could have their story represented by a mostly conventionally made Hollywood film starring a heterosexual white male who joked with the press. Hoffman was situated in the new middle, just ambitious and talented enough to be useful to studios, and just "everyman" enough to appeal to young adults and art-house audiences.

With the release of *Midnight Cowboy* in May 1969, critics celebrated Hoffman's portrayal of a truly marginalized figure. One found Hoffman "able to turn scrounging into a gallant, Robin-Hoodish activity."[11] Another said, "Hoffman gives an excellent performance; he has both the limping walk and the Brooklyn accent down pat. What is more he has in his face the ineffable sadness of the character."[12] Another review said, "Dustin Hoffman is wonderful. His portrayal of a dying, down-and-out city con is perfectly realized … yet there is nothing *depressing* about Ratso. He has a kind of tawdry panache."[13] This was also telling, of the distance between actor and character. We could watch Hoffman for two hours, as we might never watch a real Ratso Rizzo for two hours, knowing that his exaggerations were all in the name of good character work and service to a script. This was the sort of alienation and futility leavened with hip distanciation that Hollywood could and would rush to incorporate.

Hoffman was anointed the anti-John Wayne, with attendant ideological implications. In July of 1969, between cover stories about the moon landing and Woodstock, *Life*'s cover trumpeted: "Dusty and the Duke: A Choice of Heroes." Wayne was the "he-man," Hoffman the "every-man." Wayne's image was "strong, decisive, moral, and nearly always a winner." Hoffman's "characters … are conspicuously short on these traditional qualities. His people are uncertain, alienated, complex, and, by any familiar standard, losers." Wayne's old-Hollywood performance wisdom was reprinted one more time—"I don't act, I react"—near a caption that read "Every role Dustin Hoffman has played so far has been unique." Among other contrasts: Hoffman revealed that he's still seeing an analyst, said that it's not "particularly courageous for an actor to speak out politically" as he had about McCarthy, and he felt an actor shouldn't do at fifty what he did at thirty. Wayne blamed irresponsible professors for current student unrest, while Hoffman said, "The youth outburst in this country is a good thing. The kids are angry because the American leaders have made mistakes and refuse to admit it."[14] *Life* positioned John Wayne as residual and Dustin Hoffman as emergent, Wayne as a relic of conservatism and Hoffman as aligned with young idealism. *Life* positioned Hoffman close to what King means when he describes social engagement, running contrary to Gamson's claim that post-studio stars had to exhibit ironic lack of attachment.

In Hoffman's case, his talent for excess *was* masculinity, was proof that he was proficient at being a man. After the adulatory reception of *Midnight Cowboy*, Hoffman explained to one magazine that his manager had talked him into doing the upcoming *John and Mary*. The article said:

[H]is manager thinks that the fans want him back as he was in *The Graduate*—more or less. Hoffman may, in fact, have a better instinct about this. The film industry is in a state of some confusion about the box office success of movies without stars, such as *The Graduate, Goodbye, Columbus*, and *If ...* What these films have are the new faces of good young actors rather than the expensive presence of familiar stars, who come to each new role trailing clouds of old associations from previous appearances. To be durable now it may be necessary to positively avoid acquiring any of the old "star quality"—to become Promethean in aspect, in fact to take on character roles.[15]

This was written next to a photo of Hoffman inside a star-shaped frame without irony. In a time when articles began by saying that Hoffman is "small, too small certainly for hero or lover," audiences were "learning" that talent outshines looks: that was the supposedly new measure of masculinity. That they had learned this before (with the many stars that did not look like Cary Grant or Burt Lancaster) was almost never mentioned: that was the measure of successful publicity. As mentioned before, this "lady doth protest too much" sort of over-straining underlines the artifice of the construct.

Sedgwick's point about homosocial desire is less that it enables male–male affection than that it enables and even demands female marginalization. Sure enough, Hoffman's casual sexism in the press mostly went unchallenged at this time. He said in *Life's* cover story that "film acting [seems] to me to be more of a female profession. The director, who has all the creative power, really uses the actor. I don't know many actors who enjoy the work of acting."[16] Years later, talking about his competition on this film with Jon Voight, Hoffman hadn't changed his tune much: "Actors are like women. Women check each other out in a way that men don't. ... Because they're in competition with each other. Actors check each other out in a not dissimilar way."[17] In 1971, he compared working with a director to a marriage. "It's his painting and I'm just a color in it; I think it's very important to know what wavelength the director's on; a director and an actor always have a silent war going on sometime things aren't always going good, just like in a marriage."[18] In the same piece he said that film is "purely the director's medium, it doesn't really matter what you're doing, if the director's not getting it, not covering it ... it doesn't mean anything." Hoffman's sexism was of a piece with the Rough Rebels, patriarchy being one of the things they did not rebel against. Even as Hoffman validated the notion of white male "character actors" becoming leads, he did nothing to challenge other strains of stereotyping.

Hoffman told another source, "Art has never been for the masses, but now people seem to see what's good. The least I can do is try to make what I do as artistic as possible."[19] He also declared, "I will no longer accept anything unless the character is rich, the story important, and the director acceptable."[20] Some scholars ask if stars weren't merely in the right place at the right time. That may be, but Hoffman was canny about making his time and place suit his abilities and taste quite rightly. Hoffman's tastes were the press's version of antiestablishment, even when they were opposed to countercultural values. Hoffman refused to find fault with actors that do commercials, even though he hadn't:

> Get what you can! Certainly. But at the same time shrewdness, quite apart from any kind of artistic integrity thing, tells me that I will have more longevity, and more respect, the straighter I play it.[21]

However genuinely alienated Hoffman had played Rizzo, with this statement he situated himself as an artist who makes smart business decisions. This Gamsonian positioning was better appreciated than some of his peers' more radical posturing, and provides a lens with which to view his major film of the following year.

Little Big Man: Textual analysis

Largely because of Hoffman's wildly variegated performance, *Little Big Man* veers away from alienation and toward a less strident absurdism. One of Barry King's four performance codes, the vocal, is a key to Hoffman's work in *Little Big Man*. Few films have a lead actor that uses three entirely distinct voices throughout. In contemporary interviews, Hoffman did not like to discuss his acting in this film except for his work as the elder Crabb. Oddly then, the character has less than four minutes of onscreen time, restricted to the framing device of a modern interview with an old "Indian-fighter" in a rest home. The elder Crabb is heard in voice-over, however, throughout the film, foregrounding Crabb's subjectivity and by inference, Hoffman's. As the 121-year-old narrator of the life of his younger self, Hoffman considerably alters his voice, far more than, say, Orson Welles once did to play the elder Charles Foster Kane. His register is higher and frailer, in the familiar way of the elderly. It's an "old coot" kind of voice, rascally, ornery, and spirited, not attempting the gravitas of lower registers. His line readings are somewhat rushed, perhaps because of the dense narrative, but this also works to undermine the elder Crabb's authority. Hoffman's "coot" voice lends itself to jokes like "At first sight of an Indian camp, what you think is, I see their dump, where's the camp?" But this becomes a problem later, when the elder Crabb narrates, "There's no describing how I felt. An enemy had saved my life by the violent murder of one of my best friends. The world was too ridiculous even to bother to live in." This might have been a powerful statement of disillusionment, like Nicholson's "This used to be a helluva country, I don't understand what went wrong" from *Easy Rider*. Instead, because of the "coot" nature, it sounds more like farce, more like Gamsonian distanciation and less like Kingian sincere engagement.

Hoffman's old-man voice is exaggerated enough to obscure the difference between his other two voices: the folksy-yokel that he uses in the "white" world and the innocent, almost beguiling voice that he uses in scenes with Native Americans.[22] The folksy-yokel is more Appalachian than Southern, more backwoods than redneck, with a squinty sound that drops the g's at the ends of gerunds. The film does not ask viewers

Illustration 2.3   Hoffman in elaborate makeup as 121-year-old Jack Crabb

to understand Cheyenne (or read subtitles); instead, viewers are asked to realize that Cheyenne is being spoken because Hoffman has changed his accent from folksy-yokel to something more unmannered. Hoffman pioneered a connotation that was all the more radical for its subtlety: the Indians were the "normal" ones, the whites the afflicted ones. This was concurrent with the Cheyenne's practice, featured in both book and film, of calling themselves "Human Beings." But even this apparently progressive performance choice is problematic here, because of Hoffman's vocal and gestural choices as, separately, the Little Big Man and the younger Crabb.

For about ten minutes of screen time, an actor that looks like a teenage Hoffman lip-synchs Hoffman's voice while the adolescent Crabb undergoes a few youth rituals as an adopted member of the Human Beings. But even after the real Hoffman appears, and his character is anointed the Little Big Man, Hoffman uses the same voice he was using for his teenage doppelganger to lip-synch: a voice with an almost-girlish softness, a register from the back of the throat. He sounds young and naïve, as he says, lifting his hand with a Laban light-indirect flick, "Why would they kill women and children?" With a few exceptions during the 140-minute film, Hoffman keeps this tone as the (supposedly-Cheyenne-speaking) Little Big Man, implying innocence to the point of incredulity. His gestures are similarly guileless, almost a pantomime of purity. His head and shoulder movements, in Laban terms, do not seem much weighted by gravity, giving him a flexibility paired with a sort of insubstantial nature. When Old Lodge Skins tells the Little Big Man of approaching white soldiers, Hoffman listens with wide eyes and as much innocence as he can muster. He looks as though this is all new information. He shoves out his hand in a somewhat awkward use of space and says, "Grandfather, I think it is a good day to die." Hoffman gives the "die" two syllables. Hoffman as the Little Big Man conveys a surprisingly immature puerility, furthering the absurdism.

As the young adult Jack Crabb speaking English in the white world, Hoffman's folksy-yokel voice and gestures promote a measure of absurdity and a sense of farce. This characterization is introduced during a battle with whites when, for no clear reason, the Little Big Man switches sides, saying, "G-God bless George W-Washington!" The elder Crabb muses in voice-over, "Before I knowed it, them words just popped out of my mouth!" Hoffman changes accent as he yells at the soldier, "Do I have to cut your throat to get it through your head I'm a white man!"

His body changes; he goes from a feisty fighter to a recumbent man resting on one elbow, a Laban strong "gliding" gesture that suggests

Illustration 2.4   Hoffman transitions from the Little Big Man to the young Jack Crabb, with a Captain (Jack Bannon)

a man without severe agitations. The film (like the novel) never offers any kind of explanation for Crabb's sudden change of heart. In a later scene, when Custer says that Crabb looks like a mule skinner, Hoffman shifts his weight from foot to foot, stares with an open mouth, smiles with an "aw shucks" simpleton grin, and replies quickly, "Well I don't know anything about mules, sir." Hoffman's country-bumpkin intonations and gestures also suggest guile, to the point of obviating guilt. Hoffman's mobilization of backwoods stereotyping probably isn't helping either way; he's either a bumpkin that's complicit in genocide or not smart enough to see what's right in front of him. The novel and script do not dictate these acting choices; Hoffman has probably come up with them himself, and it's easy to imagine another actor doing something very different. Because of Hoffman's performance, the film implies that things just happen, and no one can explain them, which is absurdist at best, anti-progressive at worst, much closer to Gamson's "proud irony" than King's social relevance.

Following Hoffman, the film often shifts between significances, furthering an absurdist effect. On the one hand, as the elder Crabb,

Hoffman spurns an academic's re-reading of Custer: when the academic tells him that Custer's experience isn't representative of the historical genocide (he clarifies that genocide means extermination), Crabb says "shut up, now you just sit there, and you learn something." In this way, the film is anti-academic, cleverly counter-counterculture. On the other hand, what Hoffman/Crabb teaches, the idea that Indians may be the good guys, seems closer to the pro-aboriginal, dreamcatcher-adorning biases of the counterculture. Likewise, Hoffman's performance wavers even when reacting to the same sorts of events, from solemnity and contempt to cartoonish expressions. Hoffman encourages the audience to read the film either as a sort of quixotic journey or as a postmodern series of unconnected events.

Deliberate ambiguity comes to characterize the film's attitude toward Native Americans, about whom Crabb claims to have "knowed for what they was." Hoffman's three performances enable a sort of provincial racism and sexism. When Crabb meets Mrs. Pendrake, played by the white Faye Dunaway, she is wearing a white dress, and she hovers over Crabb with beatific splendor. Hoffman allows the costumes and camerawork to cue his performance: he plays it as though he is seeing an angel. In Laban terms, he is floating and flicking, nervous and rootless, easy to manipulate, childlike, a gape-jawed babe in the woods. For a few scenes, Hoffman acts like Dunaway is the most beautiful woman, or perhaps the only woman, he has ever seen. Hoffman behaves with a longing and passion for Mrs. Pendrake that we never see him display for any Indian woman. Later, Crabb "crosses three states" to find his white wife Olga, but repeatedly refuses to sleep with a group of immediately available, young, concupiscent Native American women. When Little Big Man's Indian wife asks him for support, Hoffman puts on a "henpecked husband" kind of groaning motion and voice, as though he's endlessly put upon by her demands. In Laban's language, he is strong and direct as he whines, indicating a perhaps misplaced righteousness. Without compromising the novel or the script, Hoffman could have played these scenes quite differently, with more interest in the Natives and less interest in the white women. Hoffman's performance allows Gamsonian irony or perhaps even a white-privileging interpretation in the midst of purported counter-history from the Native American side.

The nature of the story was problematic at its inception, because while Native Americans are the nominal protagonists, as with colonial myths since at least Rudyard Kipling, the natives still need a white man to save them. However, beyond the novel and script, Hoffman's wide-eyed innocence and Laban indirectness as both the young Crabb and the Little Big Man suggests that the white man is just an innocent bystander victimized by historical forces. Furthermore, by associating native dialect with the feminine and innocent, Hoffman manages to promote "noble savage" stereotypes. The problem with such Rousseauian idealization, as Steven LeBlanc and Katherine E. Register remind us in *Constant Battles: The Myth of the Peaceful, Noble Savage*, is that it diminishes the voices and rights movements of Native Americans who turn out to be less than perfectly Luddite.[23] Custer's arrogance and hubris are condemned by the film, but it is left to the folksy-yokel Crabb to foil him. Hoffman's performance privileges the theme of the little white man against a bully, instead of the theme of the Cheyenne resisting the American military. Had Hoffman played the younger Crabb closer to the way Richard Mulligan plays Custer, the film could have condemned whites more generally, but instead audiences are positioned by Hoffman's performance into a somewhat unjustified innocence. This runs counter to the film's apparent situating of whites as villains, making the film, taken as a whole, absurdist.

Hoffman's very casting makes for a measure of absurdity. At one point, the film makes clear that it has been presenting Hoffman play someone no older than 17 for at least fifteen filmic minutes, through war, displacement, and an entire new life with white people. If then-31-year-old Hoffman as a 22-year-old three years before (in *The Graduate*) was a stretch, this film asks the audience to accept the preposterous. Perhaps this is meant to further accentuate the absurdist tone. Taken as a whole, the attitude of the picaresque film toward Native Americans and women is somewhat compromised. But the attitude of the film toward Hoffman is not: in the final third, he is all that there is left to support. Hoffman's polyvalent performances of Jack Crabb ultimately serve to privilege absurdism, or perhaps star love, over progressive values.

Eve Sedgwick writes about a "heterosexuality that succeeded in eclipsing women," and indeed we see that in *Little Big Man*, Hoffman specifically performs a male-privileging behavior that sometimes goes beyond the novel and script. Hoffman makes the script's homosocial coding believable. In Laban terms, his body language is mostly light and indirect, floating instead of moving with deliberation, and this gives the impression of a casual figure without traditional morals. Hoffman's simple but not fey gestures normalize the facts that Crabb cares more for men than women and he saves all his honesty and trust for men (namely, Old Lodge Skins and the stranger historian in the rest home). The audience never sees him truly confide in his sister, in Mrs. Pendrake, or in either of his two wives, and Hoffman's behavior implies that he does not care to confide in them. Every woman in the film is attracted to Hoffman's character, including his sister. Considering all the liberties that the film takes from the book, *Little Big Man* could easily have been similar to the myth of Pocahontas, where the white man falls in love with the squaw and thus decides to defend the natives against the Yankees. But the story differs from the tale of Pocahontas in that the man as played by Hoffman is never all that in love with his squaw, and is more loyal to a man (Old Lodge Skins) than anyone else. During the Washita massacre, as in the novel, the Little Big Man saves Old Lodge Skins, but does not save his wife. The novel did not include the Cheyenne's resident homosexual, whom the Little Big Man roundly rejects when he proposes marriage. Even in a history this revised, then, Jack Crabb's masculinity is not so different from that typically portrayed by John Wayne.

Homosocial coding cannot account for all of the masculinities Hoffman performs in this film. Unlike *Midnight Cowboy*, which clearly demythologized the cowboy figure in most of its scenes, the more adventitious *Little Big Man* uses Hoffman's star image for a wide array of meanings. On the one hand, Crabb once says that "arrows versus guns never seemed like a fair fight," and he argues with a person who thinks that a white woman kidnapped by Indians is better left for dead. On the other hand, when Hoffman as Crabb is with his white wife Olga, Cheyenne whoop and cry and attack whites in a messy manner that is contrasted to the orderly nature of white battalions. Hoffman behaves in the same light indirect manner in both scenes, not telling the audience which is to be taken more seriously. Richard Dyer writes that whiteness implies straight lines, and Natives' chaotic movements in space imply savagery. If this is the case, the film seems to be playing from both sides, making it hard to take it entirely seriously, leaving viewers more questions than answers about both masculinity and the film itself. Perhaps this is intentional, part of Penn and Hoffman's abstract reading of the world.

Hoffman also mobilizes his previous star turn as Benjamin Braddock. As Mrs. Pendrake bathes Jack Crabb, he narrates "It was the greatest bath of my life," and Hoffman seems high on a sort of extended orgasm. Just as in *The Graduate*, once again he is the boy, smothered and mothered in a fantasy world by an ostensibly older woman, living a 1960s-era fantasy of the woman taking full control of a loving seduction. *Midnight Cowboy* treated this type of sexual idealization more like an unrealistic fantasy, but *Little Big Man* returns to fulfilling adolescent dreams. While Mrs. Robinson's leg overpowered Hoffman in the frame of the most

iconic moment of *The Graduate*, in *Little Big Man*, Hoffman's leg domi-
nates the frame in the bathing scene, and he lifts it just as Dunaway
seems to bathe her private area, causing her to say, "Are you thinking of
Jesus, Jack?" Hoffman moves his limbs like a child, and gapes his jaw;
this woman is just as much of a curious object as Mrs. Robinson once
was. Mrs. Pendrake says that unlike Moses, Jesus was a Gentile "like
you and me," while Mr. Pendrake sees the bathing and says that he
"looks like a pretty well-growed child if you ask me." The film reverses
Hoffman's previous representation of Braddock, a Jew playing a Gentile.
This only adds to the wide variety of representations, making the film
too scattered to make a consistent statement.

Little Big Man and 1970: Critical reception

The mobilizing of *The Graduate* is significant because *The Graduate* was
not a particularly homosocial text; Benjamin did not date Mrs. Robinson
or her daughter simply to define himself for another man. One might
think that nearly all films exhibit some homosocial tendencies, some way
of privileging a male–male relationship against one involving a female.
This may be the case, but I suggest that Hoffman's films from 1969 to
1971 exhibit a sort of overwhelming privileging of the inter-masculine
over the feminine. As in the manner that Sedgwick describes Shakespeare,
Tennyson, and Dickens, Hoffman was unlikely to be advancing a masculinist (much less homosexual) agenda, but more simply responding to
his intellectual influences. The homosocial aspect of the Rough Rebels'
personas became crucial antecedent to two very important legacies of the
era. One of them was the beginning (or maturing) of the "buddy movie"
and/or "road movie" as discussed in several essays in *The Road Movie Book*
(1997).

    The second legacy was exemplified by Robert Hughes' Emmy-winning
television documentary, "Arthur Penn 1922–: Themes and Variants,"
which aired on PBS just before the release of *Little Big Man*, and
explained the project as a collaboration between Hoffman and Penn. It
may go without saying that a star-actor who appears in and/or narrates
every single scene of a film will have some influence on the product. Yet
this was not how classical-era films were typically understood. In an era
when the studios had been discredited, promoters actually emphasized
the control exercised by Hoffman and Penn, to assuage wary audiences
that they could trust in these artists' visions. As I said in Chapter 1,
there doesn't seem to be any record of star-actors celebrating their director to the press before the 1960s like, for example, Brando on Kazan,

Stewart on Hitchcock, Wayne on Ford, or anyone else. Interviewed about *Midnight Cowboy* years later, Jon Voight said that he was looking for a relationship like Max Von Sydow had with Ingmar Bergman, and he clearly implied that no such relationship yet existed in America in 1969. Before Martin Scorsese ever met Robert DeNiro, Hoffman and Penn pioneered a working relationship like theirs as the core of a film's creative process—and, concurrently, each other's indispensability. This would have far-reaching implications. Thus, a mild corrective: the new "buddy movie" was not only pairings like Paul Newman and Robert Redford; especially with individualists (and careerists) like Hoffman and Nicholson, it was a star-actor and his director.

As an example, one headline read, "The Good Guys Wear War Paint: Dustin Hoffman and Arthur Penn turn Hollywood Upside Down." Hoffman was given equal credit with his director for a movie that was celebrated for subverting the Old Hollywood. As when an actor appears on the cover of any magazine, it was left to the actor (in this case, Hoffman) to lecture pedantically: "It's based on historical fact, although the lead character is fictitious. When the whites won a battle, it was a victory. But when the Indians won, it was called a massacre."[24] Hoffman very directly presented the film's intended ideology. Of course, films used star-actors to do press before the late 1960s, but contrary to some accounts, stars like Hoffman were *more* valuable, at least while doing publicity, in a time when Hollywood struggled to be relevant to young adults. The newly negotiated message, which the industry mobilized for decades afterward, was that viewers could continue to trust Hollywood because of star–director partnerships like Hoffman's and Penn's.

Penn even sounded somewhat homosocial as he became protective of his star. When asked why he chose Hoffman to play Jack Crabb, Penn replied, "He takes a very pure choice, going back to classic acting and reading. He asks, 'Why did this take place?' He doesn't engage in the game, 'I'm here doing this, but you and I know different.'"[25] This was disingenuous because Hoffman was indeed engaging in that "game" on camera. This marks Penn's comment as a rhetorical construction; positioning Hoffman as more immersed in his role than other actors was an apparent dismissal of a more naturalistic performative style. Penn lauded Hoffman for asking questions, suggesting that his favored acting involves a lot of digging for truth, instead of, say, appearing effortless by actually *being* effortless. Penn had done as much as anyone to promote representation by the untrained everyman when he went from the fluid, Method-trained, strikingly handsome Warren Beatty in *Bonnie and Clyde* to the stilted, untrained Arlo Guthrie in *Alice's Restaurant* (1969). But now Penn shifted gears again, and lauded technique hybridized with everyman looks, settling on Hoffman's version of the Rough Rebel.

Esquire agreed with Penn, and found Hoffman's "image" to be "unerringly chosen" by Hoffman. The magazine said,

> America is after all a nation full of men to whom girls like Katherine Ross never paid any attention in high school, and of women who long to prove that, unlike those other girls, those beautiful nasty self-centered girls, they have great stores of love to give to a deserving young man, if he be only as charming as Dustin Hoffman.[26]

This writer did not stop at including any man who ever needed a break; she made sure to hail all non-"nasty" women as Hoffman's natural allies. To resist the appeal, the volition, and indeed the very masculinity of Hoffman would surely be tantamount to approving superficiality and narcissism.

Esquire codified the new "anti-star" discourse:

> [T]he second publicist was ultimately replaced with somebody hipper, but he left his press releases behind him, a legacy of the old Hollywood for the new Hollywood to giggle over. In fact, Dustin read those releases and groaned a little, for surely that unlikely-star routine is dead by now: surely the publicists can think of something else to say. For Dustin Hoffman is, after all, an authentic star, and to call him a 'phenomenon' and look for reasons for his success is to overlook the fact that, like the Kennedys and the Beatles, he possesses star quality the way other people possess blue eyes. Three years before *The Graduate* ... whenever he came onstage the audience would squeal ... Bob Dylan didn't understand either, at first, why people wanted to touch him. Contemporary stars differ from the stars of the past in that their star quality is involuntary.[27]

There are plenty of specious claims here: did Hoffman "in fact" read and groan? How many audiences truly squealed upon their first sight of Hoffman? What does it mean to equate star quality to blue eyes? But the rhetoric was unmistakable: audience members were *dragging* Hoffman into stardom, as reluctant as any non-conformist ever was. In this way audiences were assigned complicity; people that "got it" were more responsible for his star status than they were for other stars'. "We" maintained a shared interest in keeping his (anti-) stardom alive. This "involuntary" nature was not particularly different from star publicity of the past, but in this case fans were flattered that they had the same agency as the new star-actors. At the same time, the "new Hollywood" was "giggling" at the expense of anyone who ever enjoyed films from hardly ten years before. If this was the triumph of the common man, it certainly was having uncommon elitist fun. And this sort of elitism would eventually harm the sorts of films that the anti-stars wanted to make.

As Hoffman's "political" film arrived, the press positioned him as a signifier of artistic brilliance over disenfranchisement. In December of 1970, *Little Big Man* came out and was generally received well. Reviewers praised Hoffman for spearheading an ideologically complicated western, a metaphor for American brutality in Vietnam, an epic with irony. Hoffman may have been telling Little Bighorn from the Indian perspective, but he was hardly positioned in the manner of, say, Huey Newton advocating for civil rights. Hoffman was treated as an actor performing a role, his talent assuring simultaneously the credibility and the relative safeness of the enterprise. *Newsweek* wrote, "Hoffman's performance is a marvel, alive at every moment, generous to those who play opposite him, and full of dazzling surprises from the Keatonesque seriousness of his gunslinging posturing to the sudden anger he unleashes."[28] The *Los Angeles Times* said, "Dustin Hoffman is the Little Big Man, creating a character different than any he has done before, in a performance which could have been blindingly vivid and showy (and which now and again is), but which in the crucial quiet moments has an almost self-effacing quietness which is perfect."[29] The *Hollywood Reporter* added, "In a role that's a far cry from the contemporary Benjamin, Ratso, or John, Hoffman tackles his most difficult role to date. For the most part, it is a virtuoso performance, demonstrating a refined sense of several kinds of comedy, age and seriousness. He acquits himself admirably, and it's good to see him in such a demanding enterprise."[30] This was a star-actor guaranteeing the product by doing things he had never done before, by behaving contrary to viewers' expectations. At least on the level of critical reception, this wasn't dutiful star persona maintenance as Richard Dyer describes it, but instead an emphasis on ability to diversify, meaning Barry King's "actorly" qualities, joined to his sense of social engagement.[31]

The onscreen Hoffman was widely praised for navigating ambiguity and chaotic elements, the guarantee of clarity in an unclear world. In a rave in *New York* magazine, Hoffman's range was that which legitimized the "picaresque, Tom Jones-like lilt" and power of the film:

> *Little Big Man* deals with a man of both worlds and in its concern
> for humanity approaches universal truths that transcend a particular

color of skin. Dustin Hoffman embodies this man, a good crea-
ture neither fool nor hero, who survives to put a holocaust into
perspective ... his genius and the range of his gifts become apparent
in the many facets he gives to Crabb's character, in the droll as well
as dramatic moments, in his responses to each situation. How wrong
we were to think he was limited to the over-age adolescent to which
his previous roles confined him![32]

Time likewise praised the elements of confusion: "In the title role, shut-
tling incessantly from the red to the white side, Dustin Hoffman adopts
precisely the right attitude of bewildered reality lost in myth, a photograph projected on a Fredric Remington painting."[33] Winfred Blevins
saw the same befuddlement less charitably in the *L.A. Herald-Examiner*:

For unifying these diverse elements, we are given only the non-
hero Jack Crabb. ... As far as we can see, all these people and events
never add up to anything coherent in Hoffman. They simply pass
through him. So they never congeal for us. It makes an uneven
experience—brilliant in its parts, frustrating as a whole. ... Hoffman's
performance, judged as a task of rendering character, is excellent. His
sequences as a man 121 years old are amazing technical feats. But I
wish we could like the character Hoffman plays better than we do.
His passiveness is a central problem in the film.[34]

Differing critics agreed: Hoffman, playing a so-called non-hero, validated
the reduction of narrative elements to diffusion and chaos. During its
theatrical run, the lengthiest consideration of *Little Big Man* appeared in
The New Yorker. There, Pauline Kael struck a careful balance:

The hip epic is a tricky form, because it functions without heroes, and
when the leading character in a movie doesn't have heroic dimen-
sions, when we don't really believe in him and aren't emotionally
drawn to him, we try to fill the void by fixing our hopes on someone
who will make us feel good. Hoffman, with his hopping walk and his
nasal vocal tricks, is a good character actor, but one wearies of Jack
Crabb's openmouthed bewilderment.[35]

Certainly, one may disagree with Kael's subjective interpretation of
the film, particularly her invocation of the royal "we" for audiences. But
her reading of the film aligned with those of kinder reviewers. Dustin
Hoffman was still a character actor, and his "tricks" left something to be

desired. If not always an anti- or non-hero, he was explicitly not a hero, while still the symbol of agency for a film that "sticks it to the audience," as we will see Jack Nicholson put it in the next chapter. In the end, Hoffman stood for a collapse of confidence in not just the American Dream, but in any sort of solution. Kael suggested that in the face of the Devil,[36] the best we might do is forestall an inevitable apocalypse "with his hopping walk and his nasal vocal tricks." The poster agreed with the mixed message: it showed Hoffman with a near-smile, suggesting not only that we could predict an apocalypse but laugh about it as well, a promotion of fatalism with a crucial satirical element.

During their peak years, Rough Rebels like Hoffman did not always represent violence as directly as, say, Clint Eastwood in *Dirty Harry* (1971), but their reputations validated a certain revised approach. At the time, newspapers were filled with speculation about the shocking levels of violence in society. The general feeling expressed by directors that used blood in this period, including Dennis Hopper, Sam Peckinpah, Arthur Penn, and Robert Altman, was that this blood was realistic and seen as a documentary would have shown it. For example, Altman claimed that the blood of roadside car accidents was much darker than what one usually sees on film, and that he had to fight Fox to include that sort of blood in surgery scenes in *M*A*S*H*, to show blood and violence as it really was.[37] In one interview, Penn contrasted the styles of *Bonnie and Clyde* and *Little Big Man*, calling the former more histrionic: "There won't be any high speed, low speed, jump cuts. ... It'll be dull. ... I've made my point about slow motion and violence. ... This is a GP film—anything like *Bonnie and Clyde* would have been too obvious."[38] For Penn, *Little Big Man* would seem more real for being less flashy. Star-actors like Hoffman, Nicholson, and Gould were associated with a cinema that basically said: you need to see this much blood and violence to prove our authenticity.

Jack Nicholson and Dustin Hoffman split ranks on the issue of violence. Nicholson, as shown in the following chapter, condemned Sam Peckinpah at this time. Hoffman represented a carefully specific approach to violence when he complimented *Little Big Man*'s portrayal of the Washita massacre:

> It's not romanticized. Audiences don't like to see violence as it really is. It's simple, undramatic. People want to be uplifted by violence. Like at a funeral, they want a certain amount of pomp. To the Indians though, death was a very simple thing, for life was just an appetizer.[39]

This quote is notable for at least two reasons. One is that, like Nicholson (in a different interview), Hoffman praised the virtues of giving audiences what they did *not* want to see. By implication, previous attempts at representation have been unrealistic, and audience members must be forced, almost medicinally, to accept life "as it really is." Hoffman may have been on welfare three years before, but now he positioned himself as one of the elite that knew what the masses needed more than they knew themselves. This was also part of appealing to young audiences, but a part that would eventually harm the movement's appeal.

The second point, quite opposed to Nicholson, and better understood while watching *Little Big Man*, is Hoffman's evolving perception of realistic violence. (If *Little Big Man* truly aspired to a documentary-like vision of violence, two immediate fixes would be eliminating the non-diegetic music and amplifying the gunshot sounds.) Hoffman gave the previous description of Penn's style in November 1970, knowing that he was in pre-production for the Sam Peckinpah-directed film *Straw Dogs*. Did Hoffman truly consider Penn and Peckinpah's violence "simple" and "undramatic"? (If he saw the two styles as distinct, then he risked alienating his new director, Peckinpah, in this piece.) The Rough Rebels' discursive construction was not only one of alienation and hipness, but one that suggested that both attitudes were necessary to deal with the epidemic of violence. Newer representations of violence, including more blood and more senseless destruction, were confirmed and approved by men like Hoffman because of their access to the real. But this advocacy also showed that anti-stars were much like the stars of other eras in this respect.

Previous stars had been promoted with Horatio Alger myths, but such language was indispensable to the Rough Rebel's authority and credibility. A typical piece was headlined "From Odd Jobs to Superstar," citing portions of Hoffman's early 1960s c.v., including Macy's shirt salesman, short order cook, and janitor.[40] There was at least one other familiar type of Hollywood hagiography with which Hoffman pieces engaged at this time: the child of the industry. Other pieces highlighted his father's work as a studio set construction worker and his mother's choice of the name "Dustin" from a silent movie star. The Horatio Alger aspects and the industry child aspects tended not to be celebrated in the same articles. The humble origins story is more representative of a Tom Joad-like everyman without overt industry connections, presumably authentic enough for young audiences. This was a "lady doth protest too much" sort of positioning; the press *needed* to prove Hoffman's everyman *bona fides*. Eventually, this sort of everyman press was just what the industry rushed to commodify.

If Hoffman was no longer Benjamin Braddock, as many articles said, he was now situated closer to a Frank Capra hero, a man of the people. In March of 1970, Hoffman claimed he would never forget his brother's advice, which he quoted as: "If you ever hit it big, don't change your standard of living. If you do, you'll have to start accepting roles for the money, and then you're not your own man."[41] That's how this "own man" warned people that he wasn't just available to the highest bidder. Even his studio biography for *Little Big Man* cited with admiration and utter Kingian sincerity his "unwavering abhorrence for conspicuous consumption." Colin Westerbeck may not have realized that he helped burnish Hoffman's *bona fides* when he wrote, "The thing about a Dustin Hoffman that disgusts the old-timers is the fact that he doesn't even try to be a star. ... Nobody who has an office is going to be a star, let alone somebody who admits to the public that he has one. ... Hoffman just isn't the kind of person whose private life is going to sell copies of *Silver Screen*."[42] Hoffman couldn't have said it better itself. His studio bio named his "ultimate ambition": to produce and direct plays and films "of dramatic and social significance."[43] Taken together, these statements represented a discursive triumph of Kingian social engagement over Gamsonian irony in 1970. However, 1971 would bring a shift.

Straw Dogs: Textual analysis

Straw Dogs continued the themes of alienation of *Midnight Cowboy* and *Little Big Man*, but with a more severe critique of human nature that Hoffman abetted. Stephen Prince says that Peckinpah's main characters were always alienated:

> He uses mirror shots throughout his work to suggest conditions of alienation. Very often his characters see themselves in the mirror and it makes them uneasy. He was drawn to characters that are broken. For Peckinpah in fact the personality was fragmented. All of his principal characters are badly integrated people.[44]

Hoffman makes this "bad integration" clear in his rigid body language, which Laban would recognize as rather strong and indirect, indicating forcefulness without moral consistency. Hoffman here communicates alienation mostly *without* farce; his David is resolutely bitter. Prince says that "There is no moment when the tension abates,"[45] but there actually are some jokes in the script; for example, one of the workmen asks David if he has seen any of the riots back in the United States. David pauses for a moment and then says without a smile, "Just between commercials." This line is in the script (but not the book), a classic case of middle-class hip alienation that is no progressive challenge. Interestingly, Hoffman doesn't try to play it as a savvy joke, and instead he shifts on his feet and keeps his eyes indirect. Hoffman tries to play genuine, not hip, alienation; if Prince is right that the tension never abates, it's more because of Hoffman than the script. Opposing my central argument, Hoffman's performance truly enables critiques like Robin Wood's, when he says that "the disintegration of American society and the ideology that supports it is presented as total and final, beyond hope of reconstruction."[46] Only upon the film's release did critics twist the significance of Hoffman's performance.

Unlike Ratso Rizzo and Jack Crabb, David Sumner does have an ostensible goal besides survival: he is trying to complete an academic project, not that the audience is asked to understand or sympathize with it. But like Rizzo and Crabb, David sees terrible things and refuses to act. In *Little Big Man*, toward the last half-hour, Hoffman sits like Rodin's The Thinker on a rock in a desolate wilderness, and proceeds to trick Custer with a few mendacious words. In *Straw Dogs*, toward the last half-hour, Hoffman sits like Rodin's The Thinker on a rock in a desolate wilderness, and proceeds to undertake far more proactive violence. In Laban's terms, he is far more strong and direct now, implying rectitude as well as fallibility. According to Prince, the film is a parable about Vietnam: an arrogant American thinks he can impose his will on a foreign land. Hoffman certainly contributes to Prince's reading. While his Rizzo and Crabb seemed bewildered by events, David's constant rectitude makes passivity look like an affirmative choice. Another actor, or perhaps Hoffman himself, might have played David with a sort of constancy and work ethic throughout the film; because Hoffman chooses to shift in the third act, his turn toward proactive self-defense is also mocked (not least by his wife), which makes this film, of all the ones in Hoffman's oeuvre, the most thoroughly articulated message of being damned no matter what you do. Hoffman's thorough performance of hypocrisy turns moral ambivalence into moral corruption.

In Laban terms, Hoffman as David is strong and direct with his wife Amy, and more light and direct with the men in the first half of the film. Hoffman makes eye contact with them, but he smiles too much when they don't. His David is not comically deferential, like a Jerry Lewis type, but he is also not on their level. Hoffman as David scrunches his shoulders with them and shifts his weight warily, taking their measure without revealing himself. By contrast he is a tyro with Amy, exacting and methodical, with shoulders erect and almost never without a solid, forceful gesture suggesting his domination over her. Through the first hour of the film, Hoffman is wound tightly, taking each step as though on the balls of his feet, a sort of time bomb ready to blow. Through these carefully weighted gestures, Hoffman creates a portrait of a passive, thoughtful, isolated, and bookish man with genuine backbone and his own moral order, however twisted. The book and script could easily have been read as merely a 97-pound weakling, a mewling geek. Had Hoffman chosen to play him this way, the work crew would have been diminished into simple bullies. Hoffman's confidence makes their antipathy toward him less predictable, more layered, and more sinister, which pays off during the siege in the film's final third.

Peckinpah's film is more reliant on Hoffman's performance to communicate homosocial male–male privileging than *Midnight Cowboy* or *Little Big Man*. This script does not call for Hoffman's character to spend far more time with men than with women; instead, it calls for Hoffman to treat his wife and the villagers as problems. However, Hoffman's performance choices perpetuate the now-familiar exclusion of females, because David is more affable with strange men than with the woman he married. David doesn't share his feelings with men, but he doesn't share them with any women, either, and Hoffman's tightly wound performance suggests that he refuses to admit the need to share them with anyone. David accuses Amy of acting like a child, but the way Hoffman plays David, he is actually less mature, more spiteful, and less committed to the relationship than Amy. Hoffman extends the script's critique of his intellectual type by employing body language that isn't in the script, as when he sits in a chair with one leg folded to the point where his knee is at head-level and his foot on the seat. Did any star-actor in any film ever sit this way before the 1970s? The point that Hoffman's performance makes is that even this supposedly new man, this evolved intellectual, is a woman-hater.

This misogynist tendency is underlined by the fact that Hoffman's performance exemplifies Kingian sincere engagement, opposing Gamsonian irony. After bringing the injured Henry into his house, David calls around trying to find a doctor; when the work crew learns this, three of them barge into David's house. They get violent with Henry, demanding to know the whereabouts of Janice. As David pulls them off of Henry, clearly Hoffman is gaining strength—and thus moral force *qua* Laban. He is fighting for something, as he wasn't when they ogled his wife. As Amy comes down the stairs, the men explain the situation: Janice may be dead. David says he understands, but that doesn't justify violence against Henry right this minute. Here Hoffman retreats

Illustration 2.5 David (Hoffman) manipulates Amy (Susan George)

into his former strong but indirect mode, a slight Laban slash motion, as he uses the couch for ballast and pleads that the men would be better off looking for Janice. But in the next moment, Hoffman comes to a place of rectitude and never comes back. Norman says that this was never any of his business, that he doesn't belong here. As written in the script, Hoffman could have played this in a great variety of ways; he chooses to keep his jaw slack but his brow steady as he says "That's fine. Now leave." The men are sent away and later assault the house, throwing rocks through window after window. Hoffman doesn't play David scared, as the script would have permitted. Instead he seems almost relieved that he has a problem to solve, something he couldn't bring himself to do with his equations or with Amy. David is now careful, judicious, making moves like a chess master. If his jaw were up, David would be the sane man steadying a crazy man; if his brow were wide, he'd be a scared weakling sputtering. Yet neither is the case. Because of Hoffman's performance, David is making a slow transition into the morality of the other men. They already had more in common than they may realize. They all live according to their own rigid moral order. Because Hoffman's careful, measured body language establishes David as a man with some principles, it's around this moment that the film makes him into a hypocrite. The film thus suggests that there's a futility in maintaining *any* set of principles, on either side of the Atlantic: this is a deep and sincere alienation from even morality.

Sedgwick's homosocial subjects were not marked by ignoring women, but instead by setting themselves apart from even their lovers, by maintaining a moral rectitude that even their paramours would never quite understand. Hoffman goes out of his way to demonstrate this as David. When the men from the town begin to assault the house, Amy comes down and begs David to just give them Henry. Hoffman smiles the smile of the man with the royal flush, the one that knows so much more than the other; this is pure direct strength in Laban terms. David says matter-of-factly, "They'll beat him to death." When Amy says she doesn't care, David furrows his brow, examining her with yet more derision. He says, "You really don't care, do you?" Hoffman's manner convinces us that David's moral order is the right one; he can only be contemptuous of those that don't share it. He takes a few beats and says, "No. I care. This is where I live. This is me. I will not allow violence against this house. No way. Go on upstairs." Another actor could have made this a sort of hero's rousing speech, as when a character has finally come around to saving the world, but Hoffman's gestures and tone are of a piece with the same contempt he had for Amy earlier. In Hoffman's interpretation of David, he hasn't changed, he's just now treating the men the way he had treated Amy. This is underlined when she replies, "No please don't leave me," and he responds, "Just do as you're told." He cares more about a property he recently came upon than he does about his wife. It's easy to imagine a different masculinity presented by a different actor; Hoffman could have played all this like the beleaguered intellectual. Yet he never seems out of his depth with Amy. As played by Hoffman, David seems like the superior partner in an unequal relationship.

Though the film criticizes David's worldview, it never quite dissents from David's contempt for Amy. Never in the film does David take any responsibility for any of their problems. He blames them all on her, and Hoffman makes this appear "natural." Finally, as was perhaps inevitable, David physically assaults his wife. Amy hears Charlie begging her for Niles; she goes to the door to let him in; David pulls her away. He grips her wrists tightly in his hands. She says that if he won't give in, she's leaving. The script permitted Hoffman considerable leeway here, but he continues his measured strong directness (in Laban's terms). The look on Hoffman's face is surprise just for a flash, and then a contemptuous look that communicates that nothing she does could ever truly bother him. Let go, she does indeed start for the door, and then David slaps her down, as slow-motion emphasizes the moment. Hoffman is near-robotic now, instead of sympathetic (in the way that Nicholson or Gould, as we'll see, would have played it), as David pulls Amy's hair just as Charlie had when he raped her.

David pushes her into a chair and says, "Stay there and do as you're told. If you don't, I'll break your neck." Through Hoffman's assiduously corrosive performance David has believably become no better than Charlie. And the film has made a point of giving the audience no better alternatives.

One might say that Hoffman's entire star image is mobilized to change the effect of the story's ending from the novel. At one of the lowest points of the story, Amy screams for David and Charlie to stop Norman from raping her as he did before. Norman is ripping her sweater off as David and Charlie arrive and pull him off of her. As when Henry tried something similar, Hoffman alters David's rectitude and makes a Laban slash, moving quickly, until he sees that Charlie and Norman are in a stand-off. Now Hoffman reverts to stillness, but it's a slump-shouldered helplessness, continuing to align with the homosocial; Hoffman's body language suggests he will let the men determine what happens to Amy. Charlie points the shotgun at Norman while David, between them, looks onto the bed at his vulnerable, exposed, assaulted wife. We have seen how the iconic poster tableau of *The Graduate* was twisted to show Rizzo's restlessness and Crabb's warped fantasies; here, it's twisted almost all the way back to Benjamin Braddock because it suggests impotence, but a far angrier impotence than *The Graduate* implied. Hoffman and Peckinpah use star persona mobilization to increase the empathy of savvy audience members. The alignment with previous roles calls forth the frustration with all of Dustin Hoffman's passivity through all of his films up until this

Illustration 2.6   David (Hoffman) smiles the smile of the man with the royal flush

point. In *Who Is Harry Kellerman and Why Is He Saying Those Things About Me?* (released earlier in 1971), Hoffman whines to his therapist for what seems the entire film. In *Little Big Man*, Hoffman had a knife near Custer's back before Little Bighorn, but backed away from using it. Hoffman again and again refused to help himself throughout *The Graduate* and *John and Mary* and *Midnight Cowboy*. So when Hoffman as David Sumner finally takes a stand against the assault on his home, finally becomes proactive, despite all his brutality, misogyny, and naïveté, it is a welcome release. It is hoped that he will reconcile with his wife and subdue a pack of violent strangers, because of the Dustin Hoffman persona. As it turned out, the critics also saw the film through this same distorted lens.

Straw Dogs and 1971: Critical reception

Straw Dogs was received with markedly mixed reviews, some of which blamed Hoffman for failing to choose more enlightened material, implying (and thus assuring) star control of Hollywood projects. The press still named Hoffman as a unique talent, but asked more pointed questions about how he was using his power. In apparent response, Hoffman distanced himself more from his projects than he had in 1969, talking more like a classical-era Hollywood player.

First-time students of the period will no doubt be surprised to learn that when the BBC came to the Cornwall set of *Straw Dogs* in early 1971, the network spent most of its time not with the auteur Peckinpah, but with the star-actor Hoffman. The resulting half-hour featurette began with the song "The Sounds of Silence," extending the star image of Hoffman as Benjamin Braddock. The camera captured Hoffman joking about cauliflower as a star demand, shaving his own face, and prank-ishly checking on other cast members. These signified that not only does he look like an everyman, he really is one. Twice the interviewer said: "Dustin you are a family man." He asked Hoffman, "You really epitomize the young actor of the 1970s, how sensitive are you to this, how obvious is this to you?" Hoffman replied, "It was only obvious after *The Graduate*, because the part I played was a young man. Since then, it seems less obvious to me. ... Right now I'm almost thirty-four, so I don't feel that I represent the youth." Hoffman was unfailingly polite as he insisted on stripping away any artifice. This is all *very* different from the current popular myth of caustic, unapproachable Method actors like Sean Penn and Daniel Day-Lewis maintaining character at all times on set. (For reasons that are about to become very clear, Peckinpah might well have preferred to have employed a more unreachable Penn type.[47])

A cheerful, even obsequious male interlocutor complimenting Hoffman as the best possible representation of youth: here we see homosocial coding used to promote Hoffman's masculinity, which in turn was crucially the everyman Rough Rebel. The clearest statement that Hoffman wasn't David Sumner, nor interested in representing an alienated man at all times, came when the interviewer asked if he worried about only taking on character roles. Hoffman said, "I want to always come back different. Yes, I think I feel a kind of … I think of the audience as … it's a game in a sense, what can I do next, how can I surprise them, there is that element." Thus his films aren't for truly disillusioned audiences, but for those who can appreciate "a game." In accordance with this, he finished the piece by calling cinema "lightweight entertainment" compared to books and paintings, where an artist can do what he wants, take it or leave it. Because a movie may be "£20,000 a day" the problem is "you can't do it artistically." You could if you had nine months to spend on it, he suggested, but you don't have that, you have to get through it in two months. The BBC finished the featurette with the refrain from "The Sounds of Silence" that goes, "hear my words that I might teach you," continuing the association with Benjamin Braddock and the ironic, hip alienation of *The Graduate*. The message was that Hoffman is a nice guy who sees movies in the same distanced way as many of his antiestablishment friends, but thinks they're worth making and seeing anyway. In 1971, the *Los Angeles Times* agreed with Hoffman's self-positioning when he said he wanted to be "as artistic as possible," and called him "an artistic star."[48] This sort of discursive construction worked well for Hoffman himself and his future work, but turned out to be disastrous for *Straw Dogs*.

Upon the film's release in late 1971, critics discussed *Straw Dogs* mostly in terms of its commentary on violence; some found the film to demonstrate alienation *from* contemporary violence while others found that the film promoted violence. *Straw Dogs* producer Dan Melnick said that in the wake of the assassinations of Martin Luther King and Bobby Kennedy, everyone was very personally concerned about violence, and that this was an anti-violence film. Hoffman explained, almost defensively, why he chose the project:

> I was aware of a duplicity in myself. I was against the war in Vietnam, and yet violence also attracted me, and I thought that maybe I could put some of that into the character. I was attracted by the idea of playing someone who is running away from an external problem, who leaves America because it is becoming too violent, but who isn't dealing with the internal problem.[49]

Hoffman here suggests that his character's alienation from American violence may only lead to more violence, consistent with the film's hopelessness.

As with *Midnight Cowboy*, *Straw Dogs* was originally given an X-rating. But the studio and Peckinpah re-edited it to make it an R. *Straw Dogs* was released at the height of Oscar season, in the final days of December 1971, marking it as a prestige film. It entered a crowded marketplace of envelope-pushing "commentaries" on contemporary violence, including *A Clockwork Orange*, *The French Connection*, *Dirty Harry*, *Billy Jack*, and *Johnny Got His Gun*. When *Straw Dogs* was promoted, the tagline became "The knock at the door meant the birth of one man and the death of seven others!" This promotion, perhaps more than the film itself, encouraged audiences to see David as reborn through his violent ordeal. Taking the bait, critics did see it that way. One reviewer saw David's character arc and said, "To be passive is to attempt self-negation."[50] He had to be violent to be reborn, to be whole, to be the Hoffman we wanted from previous films. Hoffman would not always be seen as a nice guy in later decades, but in 1971 his nice-guy persona led many critics to favor the film—often for the wrong reasons.

Sedgwick eventually concludes that "sexual meaning is inextricable from social meaning—in the English case, from class."[51] In the case of press about Hollywood films, I would conclude that sexual meaning is inextricable from the discursive construct of the star persona, and the attendant expectations of who viewers want the persona and person to be. The problem of male–male privileging, and of David's mistreatment of Amy, was barely discussed by critics. Instead, reviewers contextualized this misogyny in terms of general violence. For Stephen Farber, Peckinpah accomplished much in his first contemporary film to give a woman a "fully realized" role:

> In perceiving violence as specifically sexual in origin, a means of corroborating a shaky sense of masculinity, *Straw Dogs* goes beyond other Peckinpah films and reveals a sardonic awareness of the psychological appeal of violence not present in the westerns.

For Farber, Peckinpah and Hoffman see all this and brutally challenged us to respond:

> It is David's pleasure that is shocking and 'dirty' to the liberals in the audience. But I think the more conventional approach of a *High Noon* or a *Wait Until Dark* is less honest and, in the last analysis, more

comforting. Peckinpah won't let us off [as] easily, he rubs our noses in the exhilaration of violence, forcing us to recognize David's—and our own—capacity for bestiality.[52]

The film's insistence on pools of blood is proof, for Farber, that the film did not sentimentalize violence. This aligns with *Life* magazine, who quoted Peckinpah as saying that his aim is "to rub their noses in the violence of it"[53] —similar to Nicholson's statement (next chapter) about attacking the audience. Opinions like these structure the Rough Rebel as the beast that admits himself, a man that we need to see being/becoming a man. Violence was proved necessary, represented by Hoffman. According to the headline (!) of the *National Observer*, "The violence ... seems altogether justified here." As for the rape, "not so much as a nipple is gratuitously exposed." The magazine's review concludes that "the triumph belongs to Sam Peckinpah. And triumph is not too strong a word."[54] After everything that happens in the first 90 minutes of the film, according to the *Saturday Review*, "Dustin Hoffman has to be either a saint or a total craven to pursue his policy of non-violence ... [the] picture comes alive when Hoffman ... kills off [six] marauders."[55] Stephen Prince claims that Joan Mellen, Joe Morgenstern, and Pauline Kael saw the film's message as: a small man can't satisfy a sexually alive woman without learning how to use violence. But Prince points out that this opinion is a distortion, and would only make sense if David were Peckinpah's hero and mouthpiece. The problem that Prince willfully denies is that that's exactly how critics mobilized the Hoffman persona. Prince also seems bewildered by the many critics who see Amy as a flirt, when in fact she is more committed to her and David's relationship than David.[56] This is also of a piece with love for Hoffman as a star; any woman turning away from their idol must be a bigamist. The privileging of Hoffman, abetted by his own performance, enabled the film's fans to engage in similar privileging, against the better judgment of directors like Peckinpah and critics like Prince.

Other critics were less charitable than Farber. Richard Schickel in *Life* wrote:

[I]t is preposterous to people a world exclusively with monsters and morons, just as it is ridiculous for Peckinpah to go around saying that all men are violent, that all are 'just a few steps up from apes in the evolutionary scale.' Any popular study in ethnology will show you that Peckinpah's people are, on the contrary, a few steps *down* from the primates. Even at My Lai, there were at least some individuals present to raise moral objection to that event (how else would we have heard of it?).[57]

Two scant years after *Life* had anointed Hoffman the anti-John Wayne, the same magazine aligned him with "monsters and morons": perhaps his first major comeuppance. Schickel holds Hoffman as responsible as Peckinpah, confirming and conferring star power.

Another critic who didn't understand Hoffman in the manner of the press packet ("anything but serious and studious") was Pauline Kael, who wrote:

Hoffman, notoriously a cerebral actor, projects thought before movement; he's already a cartoon of an intellectual. There's a split second of blank indecision before the face lights up with purpose. He never looks as if he just naturally lived in the places he's stuck into for the camera; he always seems slightly the outsider anyway, and his duck walk and physical movements are a shade clumsy. Whatever he does seems a bit of a feat—and that, I think, is why we're drawn to him. This role might almost be a continuation of his Benjamin in *The Graduate*.[58]

For Kael, Hoffman in *Straw Dogs* was even more out-of-place, even likelier to feel estranged from the normals. Taken in tandem with his role in *The Graduate*, he reeked indecision. The allusion to Benjamin also implied a more hip alienation, more Gamsonian irony.

Kael had far more to say about the film; she called it "spiritually ugly" and delivered her harshest thunderbolt (perhaps ever) when she wrote, "Sam Peckinpah, who is an artist, has, with 'Straw Dogs,' made the first American film that is a fascist work of art." Kael distinguished it from lesser current works like *Dirty Harry* and *Cowboys* because "it gets at the roots of the fantasies that men carry from earliest childhood." *Straw Dogs* was all the more dangerous because of the boy fantasies that it indulged—seething contempt for one's "pouty sex-kitten" wife, triumph over the bullies. This wasn't necessary violence in the manner of, say, a war; for her, the film "discovered the territorial imperative and wants to spread the Neanderthal word." If the message was only that a man should defend his home, that would be acceptable, but for Kael,

Peckinpah has not only pushed this to a sexual test but turned the defense of the home into a destruction orgy, as if determined to trash everything and everyone on the screen. The fury goes way beyond making his point; it almost seems a fury against the flesh.[59]

As mentioned, there had been several recent films with little but hostility for everyone and everything, but few were excoriated in such forceful, even defensive language. No matter how much alienation one wanted to portray, this level of violence indicated that something was deeply wrong with the movement and the man that Hoffman represented. And indeed, short years after this review, a *Straw Dogs*-level absence of redemptive qualities would fall out of Hollywood favor. Alienation proved to have its limits.

As it happened, Peckinpah read and responded to Schickel's and Kael's reviews. To Schickel he wrote:

> In the first place, the man who was running away from violence and commitment did everything he could to provoke it by his deliberate pacificity. Second, I doubt whether my ten year old son would go on a snipe hunt unless it was for a reason. What reason, but to test the fidelity of his wife. This is not the story of violence, this is not the microcosm of the world. This is a story of a bad marriage. ... I was astonished in your review that you didn't pick up that Dustin was the heavy. I obviously overestimated your perceptiveness of my own vision.

Peckinpah's letter to Kael is worth quoting in full:

> Dear Pauline, I read your review. Its ambivalence was complete, although I was distressed that you didn't pick up that David was inciting the very violence he was running away from. After the killing of Cawsey, he realizes exactly what he has done. I appreciate your concern and involvement, but I don't appreciate the description of the film as a fascist one because it has connotations which to me are odious. Shall I discuss this with my lawyer or are you prepared to print in public the "definition of the film." Simply, I think the term is in incredible bad taste and I intend to take issue with it. What do you suggest? How you can identify any element of my work in terms of fascism is beyond my belief and a red flag. Please let me hear from you. Sam Peckinpah.[60]

Peckinpah had actually fought fascism as a Marine in World War II. The problem identified in both letters is with Dustin Hoffman, not because of Hoffman's performance per se—his David was quite reprehensible—but because of his star persona, Schickel and Kael didn't know "that Dustin was the heavy." Had Peckinpah cast a less familiar actor, he would have run afoul of producer Dan Melnick, who said that a star of Hoffman's "caliber" was a "sine qua non" of the project.[61] Perhaps Peckinpah could have cast a star like Steve McQueen (whom he cast a year later in *The Getaway* (1972)), who had not spent his career repressing his violent tendencies, thus obviating audiences' rooting interests in *Straw Dogs'* third act? However, this might have risked losing the chance to comment acutely on pacifism. Could Peckinpah have done anything about press that fawned over Hoffman, or the BBC special that showed Hoffman to be a polite everyman on the Cornwall set, or the tagline that said "The knock at the door meant the birth of one man and the death of seven others!"? These things were probably beyond the director's control. Peckinpah had sought a deep Kingian social engagement, but was upended by the star system.

Hoffman had provided a performance of utter alienation, but even he distanced himself from it, making sure that people knew him to be hip:

> The irony was that ultimately David would have to face his own demons and his own repressed attraction for violence. That fascinated me, but I was also fearful that if this theme wasn't addressed in an explicit enough fashion, the film could be just knocked off as a "violent movie." And in fact, when we started shooting, it became clear that Sam was less interested in attacking these nuances than just shooting "Sam's movie."[62]

As with Nicholson and Gould in their 1971 films, Hoffman disagreed with his director over the redemptive nature of his character. Hoffman obviously distanced himself from Peckinpah here; taken in tandem with Nicholson's rejection of Peckinpah,[63] star-actor rejection seems to have had something to do with Peckinpah's increasingly marginalized career and style of violence after *Straw Dogs* (or at least, after *The Getaway* (1972) a year later). Hoffman would continue to rise as emergent even after Peckinpah receded as residual. This is complicated; one could argue that *Straw Dogs* was, in its way, a clever addition to the nascent Hoffman canon. Not to put too fine a point on it, onscreen, he proved he had a backbone. *John and Mary* (1969) might have proved that he could play a romantic leading man, but *Straw Dogs* went further. It proved that he could not only cavort with the young and nubile, but also manipulate, punish, and reject them. Outside these texts, however, Hoffman was already showing signs of the person who would later refuse to carry a gun onscreen.

This was most apparent in a profile of Hoffman in *Family Circle* from November 1971, titled "Do You Have To Go Through Everything

Before You Know It's Not Good For You?" Hoffman said that after his experience being addicted to pain-killing drugs following an onstage burn injury (in the mid-1960s), he would not endorse any philosophy that suggests trying everything once. Once a star that defended radical movements in print, he now saw and lived limits. The article ended by asking him about a bomb, then associated with a radical leftist activist group, that had destroyed his apartment 18 months before. Hoffman replied slyly, "You don't have to be *fanatical* about *anything* to know that it isn't good for you" (emphasis theirs). As a member of the middle class becoming a member of the upper class, Hoffman asserted his right to understand and represent the lower class: "No matter where you are, you're kidding yourself if you say you're not struggling."[64] Hoffman explained that being rich and famous is just as difficult as not being rich and famous. He was sounding more like a traditional Hollywood star, and Hollywood was in turn finding more about him that it could and would appropriate. As an actor he could play a man that enjoys killing, but in interviews like this one in *Family Circle*, the star came to say that he's a nice guy, maybe a little like you, disagrees with the war, agrees with parts of the counterculture, but lives a fairly traditional life. This interview, then, coming a month before the release of *Straw Dogs*, is a clear case of how the star system can overcome the director's intentions, the film's intentions, and in some ways the star-actor's intentions. Historians who write that an auteur cinema arrived in the late 1960s with films like *The Wild Bunch* (1969) need to clarify: these films worked to the extent that they complemented their stars' discursive constructs, and where they did not, they were rejected by the mainstream press.

To summarize this chapter, in his major films of 1969, 1970, and 1971, Dustin Hoffman was a major and often determinative contributor who, through his expressive, highly mannered techniques onscreen, and his interviews offscreen, demonstrated fluency with both genuine alienation and ironic distanciation. As Ratso Rizzo, Hoffman performed a convincing, lower-class futility in *Midnight Cowboy*. As Jack Crabb, Hoffman presented a more farcical absurdism in *Little Big Man*. As David Sumner, he updated his Benjamin Braddock character to demonstrate alienation through timidity, with little recourse to irony. His immersive, sometimes-Method performance style often suggested being trapped by disenfranchisement and disillusionment. However, his offscreen persona, of a happy, hip, socially traditional man somewhat muted this message of alienation, causing leading critics to misunderstand him. In addition, Dustin Hoffman onscreen and offscreen established what Eve Sedgwick would later call "homosocial" coding, meaning a male–male privileging at the expense of women. Because of Hoffman's efforts, male–male relationships were made more central to his films, and the actor–director relationship was also privileged offscreen. Hoffman was repeatedly verified in the press as the latest in hip freshness and the best way for Hollywood to respond to the counterculture. Hoffman, as much as any person, confirmed and promoted the Rough Rebel as the most laudable sort of star-actor, providing a model that many future star-actors would follow. One of the first of these was Jack Nicholson.

3
Jack Nicholson: The Realistic Romantic

This chapter situates Jack Nicholson's incipient star career as an attempt to appeal to young educated adults and, at the same time, maintain a considerable measure of Hollywood traditions. To an unexamined extent, Nicholson's performance style and interviews to the press at this time exerted a profound influence over the new movement of films. Nicholson's stature as an ethnic everyman, anti-hero, and unlikely star was a determinative signifier in his films, his ancillary discourse, and contemporary cinema more generally. Nicholson continued Hoffman's version of the Rough Rebel star image: not conventionally handsome, careerist, liberal but not radical, and privileging male–male relationships over male–female relationships. However, Nicholson's style of acting was less immersive and more natural, and his appearance was "rough" without being Jewish, both of which expanded the definition of the Rough Rebel.

In a post-*Graduate* environment, Nicholson wasn't reluctant to claim a somewhat ethnic label, and critics weren't reluctant to follow his lead. In interviews with the likes of *Playboy* and *The Saturday Review*, Nicholson enjoyed discussing "theocracy" in relation to his Irish Catholic upbringing. We have seen that reviewers avoided overtly Jewish labels with Hoffman, but in the case of Nicholson (then and now), critics mentioned his "Mick" charm and "Irish temper." Closer to Hoffman, Nicholson's influence can be understood particularly in terms of "ironical alienation"; to summarize the relevant part of Chapter 1, for Barry King, the (then) new star-actor demonstrates acting ability and "character" through differing sorts of performances onscreen while showing a consistent sincerity about social issues offscreen. For Joshua Gamson, however, the new star-actor represents "cynicism," and even "proud" "irony."[1] King does not reckon with stars that flaunt their ironic approach to the world; Gamson does not account for stars that attempt sincere engagement with social problems. In this chapter, I argue that Nicholson reconciles these contradictions, attempting a somewhat genuine disillusionment while also making clear his hip, ironic distanciation.

Hoffman and Gould also embodied a paradoxical mixture of alienation and hipness, but Nicholson, coming from a decade of Los Angeles-based films produced by Roger Corman, verified that the West Coast could still produce vital stars that represented this same hybrid. Dennis Bingham puts Nicholson's star image in quotation marks when he says, "'Jack Nicholson' promises the pleasurable breaking of rules and flouting of conventions."[2] But Bingham does not specify the origins of this pleasure, and I suggest it is because of what nineteenth-century writers called a "hail-fellow" quality on Nicholson's part: no matter how much he breaks rules and flouts conventions, he remains ally and friend to just about anyone. This was a different sort of Rough Rebel than his closest peers, expanding the possibilities for those actors and for filmmakers that used Nicholson as inspiration. Nicholson's performance style leaned heavily on techniques learned from Jeff Corey, resulting in a hybridization of playing himself and using certain formal exaggerations for pathos. One reason that I consider Nicholson in a chapter between Hoffman and Gould's chapters is that in many ways his performance style is somewhere between the immersive, Method-loyal Hoffman style and the "playing oneself" style of Gould. Nicholson's "hail-fellow" style showed that a slightly different sort of Rough Rebel persona could likewise be made to signify Hoffman's type of sympathy for the counterculture that stopped sort of activism.

The "hail-fellow" style enabled a common theme of Nicholson's films in this period, that of denial of the father. In *Easy Rider*, Nicholson as Hanson tells his jailers not to tell his old man he'd been in prison; in *Carnal Knowledge*, Nicholson as Jonathan tells Susan that his father "fails" as a job; in *Five Easy Pieces*, Nicholson as Bobby tries half-heartedly to reconcile with his dying father before giving up. It would be an over-simplification to align Nicholson with the counterculture simply because he refuses to agree with his father figures, as the hippies disagreed with their conservative parents. Gould's characters of the period are probably closer to the counterculture because they do not even consider fathers, content to explore their peers and themselves. The fact that Nicholson's characters even countenance their fathers in these films places him in somewhat liminal status that accords well with star-actor Nicholson's placement in Hollywood at this time. He is both of the town and against it, both loyal to the industry (always attending the Oscars, for example) and determined to change it, both interested in his (fore)fathers and in moving past them. Far more than Hoffman or Gould (who, for example, proudly declared their New York residency), Nicholson had a foot in both camps, in old Hollywood and the new ironic alienation. His characters' engagement with father figures confirmed this, and critical reactions confirmed this as well.

Many writers have commented on Nicholson's "killer smile," but a strong case can be made that his eyes and vocal timbre—Barry King's first and fourth performance codes, the facial and the vocal—are just as important. The eyes can project an intense listening quality, but when Nicholson is on about something, his eyes project a measuredly wild sincerity that almost dares you not to observe them. It is hard to describe the voice of Jack Nicholson; to imitate it, one uses a sort of nasal, high-in-the-throat register. It has something in common with Edward G. Robinson's voice, but Nicholson's voice doesn't suggest urban savvy as much as it does the idea that a little education can be a dangerous thing. His eyes, voice, smile, Laban-strength, and relaxed rebelliousness added up to something very new in American cinema. As we will shortly see, compared with the over-familiar "playing oneself" drudge of Peter Fonda's and Dennis Hopper's, people saw lightning in a bottle. Whether or not it was good acting almost didn't matter; his was an unfamiliar, gripping persona—associated with the new style of filmmaking and new attempts to appeal to young people.

Nicholson's "hail-fellow" style also tends to favor men over women, representing Sedgwick's "homosocial" coding in a rather different manner from Hoffman. Where Hoffman onscreen tended to dismiss women, Nicholson is closer to the figure of the wit and cuckolder that Sedgwick describes in her analysis of William Wycherley's *The Country Wife*. Where the onscreen Hoffman barely countenanced female opinion, and was arguably cuckolded in *Straw Dogs*, Nicholson's masculinity, at least after *Easy Rider*, seems to require that his wit and charm be praised by both genders, and he also goes some way toward sleeping with other men's wives. Sedgwick makes it very plain that this is still homosocial, still privileging men over women, but in Nicholson's case a woman's presence is more required—and thus, often, more humiliated. However, this was less the case in his breakthrough film, which excluded women more than it denigrated them: *Easy Rider*.

Easy Rider: Textual analysis

Easy Rider is about two men, Billy (Dennis Hopper) and Wyatt (Peter Fonda), who feel alienated from society and take to the road to find something better somewhere in America. It has been read by scholars such as Gilles Deleuze and David Bordwell as the nonpareil example of American disillusionment on screen, a metaphysical search for meaning. In the tagline, a man goes "looking for America and can't find it anywhere," but the most engaging thing that Billy and Wyatt do find is George Hanson (Nicholson). Hanson is also frustrated with society, looking for something better, but his attitude goes beyond Billy and Wyatt's simple disenfranchisement, and toward a more humorous distanciation from society. Before production, Fonda and Hopper had brought in Terry Southern as their third writer, Southern being most famous for *Dr. Strangelove* (1964). Nicholson provides a performance far closer than Fonda's or Hopper's performance to the spirit of *Strangelove*: bitter alienation leavened with biting farce. While Hoffman as Ratso Rizzo and as David Sumner is generally seriously committed to his estrangement from society, Nicholson as Hanson uses an array of devices to communicate both disillusionment and wit, hybridizing the Kingian sense of engagement with social issues and the Gamsonian sense of proud irony.

Dennis Bingham writes about Nicholson's "breakthrough performance":

> While Wyatt and Billy, obvious references to Western legend and all, are one-dimensional icons, Hanson conveys disillusionment crossed with the sense of being stuck between two cultures. He belongs neither to disaffected youth nor to the indifferent middle class.[3]

But Bingham does not really address how this sense of classlessness is mobilized for meaning. If Deleuze and Bordwell are right that this film is antiestablishment, then Fonda as Wyatt is numb, not letting society involve him for good or ill. Hopper as Billy laughs occasionally, but repeatedly returns to a sense of frustration and disappointment with society, something close to what the real Hopper presents in interviews. Nicholson, however, demonstrates both seriousness and a "hail-fellow" tendency, driving the film toward playful absurdism. This is seen in the threesome's first scene outside, when Billy and Wyatt announce they are leaving for New Orleans. Hanson unveils a business card from his pocket, and says "This is supposed to be the finest whorehouse in the South; these ain't no pork chops, these are US Prime!" His vocal intonation suggests a man about to shout (though he doesn't); he cocks his head and widens his brows, projecting strength but indirectness, a Laban "stretch"; while the camera is in medium shot, Nicholson's strain for effect makes it seem as though he could be standing on the tips of his toes. A few quiet lines later, he performs the line "Oh, I've got a helmet!" in a similar manner. It is very easy to imagine another actor playing these lines quite differently, in a more muted style like Fonda or Hopper, or in a more manic style from someone wishing to display anti-social insanity. Nicholson carefully leaves the viewer uncertain if he is truly alienated or more bemused at society.

For a movie called *Easy Rider*, its lead riders aren't all that easy. Billy is often frenetic, and Wyatt is perennially distracted, a dark cloud looming over his head. Nicholson may struggle with Hanson's Southern accent, but he nails the Southern attitude, a sort of gallows-humor, fatalistic, let's-have-good-times-anyway disposition. Before he gets on any bike, he's an easier rider than Billy or Wyatt. The film might have seemed *less* coherent for Nicholson's "hail-fellow" style—instead, it seems to adopt him as symbol of where it needs to go. In Nicholson's first scene, when Billy chastises Hanson for waking his friend, Hanson apologizes with a sort of Southern politeness. When Billy threatens Hanson for talking too much, Hanson loses the Texas charm. He regards Billy, yawns, and sticks his tongue out to the side in a sort of Laban slash. Hanson has his own priorities, and isn't going to be bullied by the likes of Billy. He is playfully "exterior" as Hopper and Fonda have not been, yet from this scene, it's clear he is oddly "interiorized" as well. Unlike Dennis Hopper, who plays Billy with all his cards always on the table, Nicholson hints at an interior life beyond the parameters of the story. If Hanson is judging Billy, Nicholson is careful to keep it to himself.

Nicholson maintains a careful duality of excess and control. When Billy asks for a cigarette, a guard named Bob says "You animals ain't smart enough to play with fire," to which Hanson interjects, "Oh no no no, that's all right Bob, that's all right, they're good boys, you can give 'em a cigarette." Nicholson could have played this bit with more pomposity, or projected authority. But Nicholson has made Hanson a bit of a good old boy himself, with the kind of authority that comes only when you get to know him. The three men engage in a bit of banter, with Billy trying to learn why Hanson got such special treatment. Hanson recognizes that the two men aren't local. He looks up, rubs his splayed hand over his neck, and says that it's good he found them before they got into trouble. He is a "character," in most senses of the word, a wild card, but he's also arguably settled into the background, a thing that anyone might find on the open road.

Through Nicholson's performance, George Hanson has a salubrious effect on Billy and Wyatt that naturalizes homosocial behavior. That's clear even without dialogue, in a montage as they ride the two bikes through Texas, Hanson sitting behind Wyatt. Nicholson symbolizes male–male comfort partly because he does not seem bothered in the least to share a motorcycle with another man (another actor could have easily played this differently). Riding with Hanson, Billy and Wyatt seem to cheer up on the road for the first time; the soundtrack plays a song that goes "If you want to be a bird," and he and Billy both extend their arms as though they're flying. The liberating effect is believable because Nicholson has made Hanson his own man, a devil-may-care sort of rogue that doesn't ask for love. Bingham's thesis, that Nicholson shows a "performed" masculinity, does not serve to explain Nicholson's masculinity in *Easy Rider*, which is never seen as problematic or difficult. Nicholson in fact makes male–male amity look quite unaffected.

Nicholson's final two scenes of the film demonstrate a propensity for Kingian alienation tempered with a Gamsonian social smile. The three men walk into a Southern diner, and the initial cue is through wardrobe: Hopper and Fonda wear sunglasses, while Nicholson does not, allowing his wild eyes to be seen. Another cue is through staging: Nicholson is

Illustration 3.1 Wyatt (Peter Fonda), Billy (Dennis Hopper), and Hanson's (Nicholson's) liberating effect on them

between Hopper and Fonda, which leads him to shift back and forth in his focus, making him appear more agitated. But in terms of perform-ance, Hopper and Fonda give nothing but their apparent selves, doing little but playing themselves, sitting in one place, being cool. Nicholson distinguishes himself. He is strong and indirect in Laban terms: he labors his breathing, he pulls back his shoulders then scrunches them up again, he alternates between sudden jokes and sustained agitation. Nicholson says, "We're in the establishment now, eh boys?"—a clear signal that these boys are not of the establishment and are not wel-come in polite society. If Fonda and Hopper had been alone to say such things, they might have come off as bitter misfit radicals, unlikely to engender sympathy. Thanks to Nicholson's performative good humor during the scene, the film *both* despairs of institutional solutions and maintains its perspicacious stoicism.

Nicholson's strong and indirect performance is oddly both crazy and normal, and his "hail-fellow" quality works to ameliorate everyone in the diner. Hopper asks Nicholson to repeat the comment about the estab-lishment, and he replies with a Laban slash (a sudden strong-indirect movement), and a lowered, conspiratorial voice of exaggeration, "I said, b-l-l-l-l-l-l-u-tang!"—the stammer or affectation of a genuine lunatic. Yet his exaggeration makes sense, because it's better to look crazy than to seem like a threat. It also suggests, in line with Gamson, that con-fronting society isn't as important as maintaining humor while getting along. Fonda finally says "Let's split," and Nicholson is the only one to put on his motorcycle helmet indoors, as well as the only one to mutter anything as they go: "Certainly real nice." Other actors could have played these lines, but other actors might have found it difficult to share sincere smiles with everyone in the diner. Nicholson as Hanson is both the crazy person and the one finding common ground. Neither King's nor Gamson's model quite allow for Nicholson's hybrid of aliena-tion and humor; Nicholson makes Hanson into everyone's lunatic.

Nicholson's final scene presents a Hanson the audience has barely seen: strong and direct, attenuated with eyeglasses and a Cheshire Cat smile. Hanson begins the scene as he and Billy and Wyatt sit around the night campfire: "You know, this used to be a hell of a good country. I can't understand what's gone wrong with it."[4] Here Nicholson is called upon to baldly state the themes of the film, but he is so centered and unlike his manic self in the diner that he complicates any overarching critique the film might intend. His Laban-strong and direct demeanor suggests that society may be rotten, but we can laugh at it and we'll be sure to be all right.

Illustration 3.2   Hanson (Nicholson) at the campfire

Billy (Hopper) and Nicholson (Hanson) banter about freedom. Hanson stays utterly still, looking knowingly into Billy's eyes, as he delivers his final pearls:

> Oh they're not scared of you. They scared of what you represent to 'em. ... What you represent to them is freedom. ... Oh yeah that's right that's what it's all about all right, but talkin' about it and being it, that's two different things. I mean, it's real hard to be free when you are bought and sold in the marketplace. ... Course, don't ever tell anybody that they're not free, cause then they gonna get real busy killing and maiming to prove to you that they are. Oh, yeah, they gonna talk to you and talk to you and talk to you about individual freedom. But they see a free individual, it's gonna scare 'em. ... It makes 'em dangerous.[5]

Criticizing being "bought and sold in the marketplace" is probably about as close as any Hollywood film has ever come to Marxist critique, exactly the sort of thing King had suggested, but Hanson finishes this by randomly flapping his arm. It's as though having your lunacy is more important than any particular knowledge about freedom. This is how the film establishes and then dilutes its antiestablishment themes.

In the following scene, Hanson is killed in his sleep by rednecks. Hanson was killed because of his personal dissonance between two worlds, the rednecks and the truly "free" men he spoke about. Nicholson's careful bridge between character and "normalcy," his weight and lightness, his strength and indirectness, helps to humanize this conflict and make the audience care about him by the time he is killed. In this way the tragedy of ambivalence and futility is made more poignant. Yet the fact that the film cuts directly from Hanson's murder to Billy and Wyatt eating in a velvet-draped restaurant somewhat undermines any fatalist message; of a piece with Nicholson's demeanor, as well as Gamson's general thesis, the edit suggests fun over mourning. J. Hoberman later wrote that the film "felt like a caper,"[6] and contemporary critics mostly concurred.

Easy Rider and 1969: Critical reception

Easy Rider was a hit film that became a phenomenon, widely credited then and now with articulating the feelings of a disenfranchised generation. Jack Nicholson received as much credit as anyone, and was often singled out as the film's best feature. Nicholson's performance in *Easy Rider* as George Hanson won several awards; in the press, Nicholson was anointed the sort of voice that America apparently needed to hear from. He was the human face on a new creative resurgence that integrated European style, counterculture ideas, and low-budget techniques from American International Pictures (AIP). Nicholson's feelings about and representations of disillusionment were promoted and received as the latest and greatest that Hollywood had to offer. Nicholson was the newest rebel to roll in on a motorcycle, an "anti-hero" who was taken to symbolize Hollywood's best representation of the counterculture. As a new star in the post-studio era, Nicholson in the press was both more ironic than King's model suggests, and more sincere than Gamson's model allows.

Easy Rider debuted at the 1969 Cannes Film Festival, where it was nominated for the Palme D'Or and received an award for best film by a new director. With this laurel in tow, the film debuted on American screens in the summer and soon became one of the breakout hits of the year. Eventually, it made about $40 million in North American rentals, on a cost of about $400,000, a 1:100 profit ratio that still stands as one of Hollywood's most impressive. Dennis Hopper would later claim that it was the first film produced outside the studio system to make a substantial profit. While most historians agree that the film provided a financial and stylistic model for many other productions in its immediate wake, Hopper suggested that *Easy Rider* was also something of a proto-film for the "independent" waves of the 1980s, 1990s, and 2000s. And Jack Nicholson was positioned as a crucial defining element of the film.

Nicholson was effusively praised in most reviews of *Easy Rider*; several critics went so far as to mourn Nicholson's character's passing. The *New York Times* called Hanson a "marvelously realized character" and went on to say that "Nicholson is so good, in fact, that 'Easy Rider' never quite recovers from his loss."[7] The *New Republic* found the film's "best performance—funny, utterly winning, and quite moving" to be Nicholson's, "who grabs the back of Fonda's motorcycle going past as if it were a raft that could save his life. There is a crazy sweetness in Nicholson that is pathetic without ever asking for pathos."[8] The image of Hanson on Wyatt's bike demonstrating "pathetic crazy sweetness" is a reasonable symbol of the Hollywood Renaissance, because the image is alienated, funny, and homosocial all at once. For *Esquire*, his "exceptional" performance was cause for reflection—"Once in a great while, when an actor you've been enjoying is suddenly killed off before the last reel, a whole film feels suddenly empty for his absence."[9] "Enjoying" is a key word in that sentence. Nicholson represented disillusionment, but also an enjoyment of life.

Critics made the point that cinematic rules were being rewritten, and Nicholson was situated as reliable. For Andrew Sarris, Nicholson's performance was the most praiseworthy element in a movie that occasioned a more than typical rumination on the state of cinema in America, a survey of films with similar themes of alienation:

> As it turns out, however, 'Easy Rider' displays an assortment of excellences that lifts it above the run and ruck of its genre. First and foremost is the sterling performance of Jack Nicholson as George Hanson, a refreshingly civilized creature of Southern Comfort and interplanetary fantasies. 'Easy Rider' comes to life with Nicholson's first hung-over entrance in a Deep-South dungeon. ... Peter Fonda, Dennis Hopper, and Terry Southern are credited with the script, and Dennis Hopper with the direction, but see 'Easy Rider' for Nicholson's performance, easily the best of the year so far, and leave the LSD trips and such to the collectors of mod mannerisms.

Sarris spent the review's final paragraph parsing arguments about the "nouvelle vague tricks and Bergman–Fellini–Antonioni mannerisms," calling them no more "voguish" than tricks from the 1920s and 1930s, and no less able to provide art and truth. Waving off "false cries of doom," Sarris concluded the review by saying: "It is not the medium that is most likely to get old, tired, and cynical, but its aging and meta-physically confused critics. This particular critic has never felt younger in his life."[10] Thus was Nicholson's status as avatar of youth and crea-tive innovation augmented by a powerful writer. Sarris clearly meant that even if the reach of Hollywood's pseudo-*nouvelle vague* exceeded its grasp, men like Nicholson would provide pleasure. In the midst of sup-posed disillusionment, we could rely on a star like Nicholson to make us happy with "fantasies" and not to advocate systemic change. Even in the summer of 1969, this mixed blessing foreshadowed Nicholson's star image and career that eventually privileged his skills with traditional melodrama over his participation in risky, experimental projects.

Peter Fonda saw Nicholson as more effectively communicating the film's disgust with society than he or Hopper could; he referred specifically to the line, "You know, this used to be a helluva good country. I can't understand what's going wrong with it." Fonda said, "He really is a patriot. He read that line ... with an authority that only comes if you believe in it. ... He read it like Henry. He's the Tom Joad, in a way, of our era."[11] This quote is striking because Fonda was gracious enough to anoint Nicholson as heir to the role immortalized in celluloid by his own father. Peter Fonda's sentiment here supports King's schema without caveats, an example of ostensibly sincere social engagement that Nicholson in fact did not always represent onscreen or offscreen. As noted in my first chapter, while Tom Joad had famously said "I'll be there," the post-Kerouac generation would instead be anywhere, main-taining a hip Gamsonian distance from problems and solutions.

As though to agree with Peter Fonda, Nicholson set a specific tone through his dozens of interviews following *Easy Rider*, demonstrating a sincere engagement that King would recognize and Gamson would not. Nicholson said he was looking for scripts in the future that involved deeply human characters embroiled in complex emotional situations. The characters that attracted him were "cusp characters" that under-mined middle-class values. "You've got to keep attacking the audience and their values," Nicholson told *Newsweek*. "If you pander to them, you lose your vitality."[12] In many ways, this statement about "attacking the audience" summarizes the radical potential of the new film move-ment. It's hard to imagine any star from twenty years before—or twenty years after—telling *Newsweek* the same thing. Nicholson lionized him-self the way many radical artists did, as difficult medicine that society needed to swallow. Elliott Gould said something similar to *Playboy* in 1970 when the interviewer said that most Americans feel threatened by radical movements: "They don't know what's best for them. They refuse to recognize the fact that things are always changing in our society."[13] Yet this hubristic tone arguably both alienated Nixon's "silent majority" and made anything short of radical revolution seem disappointing to the hard left.

With a different tone, Nicholson made it clear that he wasn't bringing socialism to Hollywood:

[W]hen you become an entity, unions become aware of you. You're a threat to their system when a picture like 'Easy Rider' becomes the top-grossing picture of the year. ... We had short crews, we worked long hours. People did favors. But you can't expect them to do favors forever. ... People outside the union are better. ... When I direct 'Drive, He Said,' I know I'll have to use IA, and it will make the film that much worse. Ultimately, they'll take it out of my ass for talking this way. But I'm only telling the truth.[14]

The solipsism is Gamsonian: instead of offering a healthy long-term prescription for industry stability, Nicholson would be sure to do what benefits him. Criticizing unions might have doomed a star in another era, but in this case, unions suffered, and Nicholson went on to become as large a star as any in the final third of the twentieth century. Again, because the media, then and now, hardly bothers to interview writers, directors, producers, or studio executives, star-actors like Nicholson, by describing their agenda, become determinative in setting the industry's agenda.

Nicholson's way of averring antiestablishment values was to make it clear he wasn't happy with the current state of the country. However, Nicholson didn't necessarily have any better ideas, not so unlike his onscreen representations. In one of his first two "star" feature articles, Nicholson claimed to want to run for President. He called the government corrupt and out of touch with humanity. He told *Philadelphia After Dark*, "In the 1920s, Dostoevsky could write that America is what paradise must be like. We're not there anymore. Our image has changed."[15] Here, Nicholson sounded quite a bit like George Hanson, but this newspaper didn't bother to say so. Instead the article concluded with: "Nicholson as President? I can think of worse choices—some of which have already been made. If you aren't certain just where we are now, go and see 'Easy Rider' and get a glimpse."[16] Elision of role and actor wasn't something that Nicholson rushed to contradict. Nicholson laid claim to being a member of a Silent Generation, saying that "silent people make better movies anyway, since film is a visual medium. I like spare things. I'm not articulate." He spent the rest of the article holding forth on everything under the sun. Prodded just a bit about this, Nicholson admitted: "I'm maybe the spokesman for the silent generation." Nicholson's silent/vocal contradictions arguably turned out to be fruitful, but his hypocrisy about careerism would have done better to have been addressed.

Nicholson, like his films, bore some of the traits that he was thought to criticize, simultaneously embodying and effacing the contradictions of his supposed disenfranchisement. Eighteen days after the *Los Angeles Times* gave *Easy Rider* another warm panegyric that included singular kudos for Nicholson, the same newspaper provided what might be called Nicholson's first "star" press, a piece headlined "Nicholson Leaves Obscurity in Dust." (When the article continued on another page, that next section was entitled "Jack Nicholson Rises to Fame"—self-fulfilling words if ever they existed.) The writer marveled first at Hanson, "a man of infinite raffish aristocratic charm and an acute sensibility." He complimented the lawyer played by Nicholson looking "as offbeat as he sounds." Nicholson offered that he didn't want the character to be "visually uninteresting," and said that he's "liked inconsistent characters" for a long time. Thus did the *Los Angeles Times* suggest that an "aristocratic" man could represent deviance without a problem.[17] Haskell later agreed:

> It is no accident that the role that put him over was that of the small-town lawyer in *Easy Rider*, a member of the Establishment, who could identify with the young. Unlike the cyclists/pushers, he could make the two-way passage from America to Amerika without losing his eccentricity and moral courage.[18]

What Haskell occludes is that eccentricity suggests, more than alienation, the comfortable class position of being able to laugh at it all. Gamson also suggests that ostensibly eccentric behavior is used to reify a knowing star image.

Nicholson was the best of the old and the new, a warmly received actor and star. In June of 1969, John Mahoney, in the *Hollywood Reporter*, named this supporting actor as a gifted creative artist who could productively remake half of Hollywood's most hallowed films:

> Jack Nicholson is one of the best young actors in town, long hidden in the underground and the quickie circuit, though to watch him work is to imagine how perfectly he could toss off remakes of the

massed filmographies of Henry Fonda and James Stewart and still retain a film presence that is his alone. ... Only a writer of his talents and improvisational gifts could create such a fantastic sequence as the one in which he describes his belief that "minutians in vast quantities are mating with people from all walks of life in an advisory capacity."[19]

Mahoney's critique shows more sensitivity to the idea of actor control than most reviews of decades past. I have already stated that, unlike their predecessors, the Rough Rebels found it advantageous to promote directors in the press; one reason was because that helped to remove power from studios and to establish themselves as fellow artists.

Director control was an area in which Nicholson mixed his messages, seeming like a different kind of man on different days, making it hard to understand his "real" self. Years after this period, Sharon Marie Carnicke wrote,

Many actors see their ability to adapt to narrative and directorial demands as the special expertise for which they are hired. Jack Nicholson argues that "your job [as an actor] is to give the director what he wants ultimately, no matter what it is" ... He notes his truncated performance in *The Passenger* (1975) "is exactly what [Antonioni] wanted" and that his exaggerated performance in *The Shining* was just what Kubrick wanted.[20]

Carnicke did not, however, mention that Nicholson was not above criticizing lionized directors. When asked about one of 1969's other hit films, he said,

Sam Peckinpah says *The Wild Bunch* is an indictment of violence on the screen, but I think he's mistaken. It's just violent. The events of his personal life in the last few years have turned his head around. He may have thought he was condemning violence, but he's really just used it.

To the extent that Nicholson's opinion came to dominate Hollywood, one would expect Peckinpah's career to recede, which is what happened.[21]

Jack Nicholson also sent mixed signals regarding classical-era directors. One piece said about him, "He idealizes directors. First there's John Ford then some of the others: Henry King, Fritz Lang, Vincent Minnelli, Frank Capra, George Stevens."[22] In another piece titled "Jack Nicholson

Has His Film Work Cut Out For Him," the writer quoted Nicholson as saying:

> Hollywood is still full of old directors. ... You see them at the Screen
> Directors' Guild meetings. They all want to work and they're all out
> of work. They don't know how to communicate with the audience.
> They can't get with it. People who can tell the truth in films are get-
> ting jobs.[23]

Nicholson even distinguished himself in a way that few new stars ever had, insulting the rather well-established director of one of his *upcoming* films, *On a Clear Day You Can See Forever* (1970), the director being Vincente Minnelli. He complimented Barbra Streisand but not much else:

> I don't know a movie that needs to cost $12 million ... it doesn't work;
> the scrim is bad. They could have shot it better—and for nothing—on
> a rooftop in New York. ... The fees are too high. ... Because of the films
> I had worked in before ... I have had a very free position. If I have an
> idea, normally it gets implemented. On 'Clear Day,' my ideas were not
> wanted for the character. They rejected those shoes. ... If I had dressed
> the character, he would have looked right ... in my own theory of act-
> ing, I must please the director, and I think Minnelli is good, but each
> night I was unhappy.[24]

In a 1971 interview, he said, "I was playing a hippie, and Minnelli asked me to cut my hair. Right then, I knew I was in trouble."[25] Although Nicholson contradicts himself, he is consistent about (his own) actor control, and his "theory of acting" that says he "must please the direc-tor" does seem to contain shades of Sedgwick's homosocial coding regarding a sort of productive unconsummable love affair that situates two males at the heart of control. As with Hoffman, this particular level of representation would have long-range effects.

Nicholson also demonstrated considerable perspicacity in a piece that began by calling his work in *Easy Rider* "one of the consummate acting jobs on film," and the man himself "a New Hollywood Renaissance Man." He said, "Eventually the industry is going to make all the wrong moves. They are going to try to make 10 more *Easy Riders*, and they'll sponsor a bunch of people just because they are young and they are not anything else."[26] Nicholson proved that he knew that simple disenfranchisement was insufficient, but he was hardly as ironic about it as Gamson would suggest. Quotes such as these demonstrate how a star-actor like Nicholson moves beyond totalizing schemas of sincerity or irony to produce a more polyvalent discursive construct. This construct arguably came into full flower in *Five Easy Pieces*.

Five Easy Pieces: Textual analysis

Five Easy Pieces began life as a vehicle for Jack Nicholson—even profilmically. Director Bob Rafelson had the "vision of Jack, out in the middle of a highway, the wind blowing through his hair, sitting on a truck and playing the piano." This was meant to indicate a man who has lost his sense of belonging to the world but not his sense of humor. Rafelson went to screenwriter Carole Eastman, whose *nom de plume* was Adrien Joyce, and asked her to "aim European, not Hollywood."[27] The lead character was named after Bobby Kennedy—meant to be a younger brother, suffering by comparison. Eastman's original ending killed Dupea by sending him in a car off a bridge in an echo of Chappaquiddick. Years later, when Gene Siskel asked Nicholson which of his roles most closely related to himself, Nicholson immediately named Bobby Dupea. "My character in *Five Easy Pieces* was written by a woman who knows me very well. I related the character to that time in my life, which Carole knew about, well before *Easy Rider*." He added, "So in playing the character, I drew on all the impulses and thoughts I had during those years when I was having no real acceptance."[28] Watching Bobby Dupea was meant to be the same as watching Jack Nicholson.

In *Five Easy Pieces*, Nicholson as Bobby is cut off from even his own desires, like some of the 1950s rebels, but the film gives him no genre-based solution, no way to be useful to society or himself. As Dennis Bingham says, "unlike the earlier antihero films, [it] posits an existential hopelessness more typical of European directors such as Antonioni or Resnais." Bingham is correct to identify the American Beat writers as influences, to see the text "as much of middle-aged male bohemianism left over from American literature of the 1950s as it does of 1960s counterculture." However, Bingham's analysis suggests only the Kingian codes of sincere social engagement, and effaces Nicholson's Gamsonian recourse to cleverness. Bingham usefully points out that Nicholson's performance in *Five Easy Pieces* "still reproduces women's diminished role under patriarchy,"[29] an observation that can be extended to Nicholson in *Easy Rider* and *Carnal Knowledge* as well. But Bingham observes this begrudgingly, as though Nicholson's Brechtian distanciation should help call our attention to misogyny. In fact, it is Nicholson's naturalistic behavior that reifies patriarchy in the most regrettable fashion.

The first half-hour of *Five Easy Pieces* establishes Bobby Dupea as a blue-collar common man, and Nicholson responds to the script with a very sincere performance of congenital oppression, in line with King's critique. Nicholson is light and direct in the Laban sense—flexible but forceful when given a reason. Nicholson looks utterly at home on a derrick, his hands running across the machines in a routinized fashion, his eyes dead as though this is all too familiar. Such verisimilitude would be difficult for a more established star or a better-looking newer star (e.g. Robert Redford). On the very authentic-looking oil-rig fields, Nicholson's performance is attenuated by high realism (of sets, lighting, costumes, makeup). Nicholson's everyman face, as much as his sincere, light-direct performance in the opening scenes, establishes any comment that the film can make about the working class. At one point, Nicholson offers almost a mantra of alienation in a matter-of-fact, light-direct tone when he says, "I move around a lot, not because I'm looking for anything really, but because I'm getting away from things that get bad if I stay," exemplifying sincere disillusionment in Robin Wood's sense.

An early scene brings the themes of the film into sharp relief, even as Nicholson's occasional Laban pressings show signs of becoming *too*

Illustration 3.3   Bobby Dupea (Nicholson) on oil-rig fields

exaggerated. When Bobby and his co-worker Elton are driving home, they come upon traffic, and Bobby is quick to lose his temper. As his car comes to a stop, Bobby shifts in his seat and in a Laban slash he almost spits, "some goddamn thing Elton, Jesus Christ!" He bangs on the steering wheel, establishing Bobby's short fuse. As cars honk at him, Bobby leans out of his car and unveils a moderate version of what would become a Nicholson staple, the tantrum against a stranger: "All right I heard you, why don't you flash your lights so we can see what else you got for Christmas?!" Dupea gets out of the car and walks around; Elton laughs while he takes the wheel. Bobby stands in the middle of all the stopped traffic and yells, presumably at everyone, "Ants! Why don't we all line up like a goddamn bunch of ants—the most beautiful part of the day—and get ourselves—" when he is interrupted by a dog barking out of a nearby car window. Bobby barks back at the dog, ferociously. His manic speech—delivered in hard-hat and faded blue clothes—shows sympathy for the conformity of work life and a desperate appeal for appreciation for nature. And when nature threatens him, Bobby growls right back at it. Here Nicholson's excess performativity (going beyond the needs of the plot) succeeds in laying himself bare. Like Hoffman's "I'm walking here" scene in *Midnight Cowboy*, Nicholson's extreme behavior is made to look less like outrageous posing and more like a quotidian vision of a crazy person—a car wreck, almost literally. Dupea doesn't seem to realize what the audience does—that the only real possible source of his anger is self-hatred. This duplicity is the heart of Nicholson's performance—both utterly self-effacing and deeply expressively romantic—and it goes a long way toward making his nihilism tragic.

Yet as the film continues, Nicholson goes beyond a Kingian sincere alienation, and allows a certain irony to color his performance. This is seen most famously in the sequence that includes the hitchhikers and the "no substitutions" scene in the roadside diner. The sequence argu-ably continues *Easy Rider*, with a role reversal: Nicholson is now in the driver's seat, figuratively and literally, and Palm is the hitchhiker with the random anti-society insights. The only time Bingham sees a char-acter "speak for the film" is when Palm Apodoca rails against "all the crap" of this society created by "Man." Yet we only meet her because Bobby shows some chivalry by picking up two women whose car has crashed. Palm reveals that she's going to Alaska because it's cleaner. This makes Bobby laugh as he says, "Cleaner? Cleaner than what?" He even pursues it, a smile on his face indicating he's having a laugh at them: "What makes you think it's cleaner?" He jokes with them that Alaska

has had a big thaw, and thus provides the keynote of the filmic movement, that alienation from society is best met with a laugh.

In *Easy Rider*, Billy, Wyatt, and George visit a small-town diner, get
called girls and monkeys, and leave without ordering; in *Five Easy Pieces*,
the "no substitutions" scene suggests what *would* have happened if
Nicholson had been allowed to order. Nicholson uses a careful light direct
quality, in Laban's terms a "dab" of calm, to make his eventual anger seem
more righteous. As Bingham says about the scene, "its effect comes from
the intensity of Nicholson's vocal inflections and the accelerating rhythm
of his diction."[30] Nicholson's voice is whisper-soft as he talks to the somewhat older waitress, asking her for a plain omelet with tomatoes, while
she explains that she can't allow substitutions. Bobby's voice is even and
his eyes are as dead as they were on the derricks; it's like he really doesn't
care what happens to him. However, when she says, "You want me to
hold the chicken, huh?", he raises his inflection as he replies, "I want
you to hold it between your knees." Because of Nicholson's steady strain
to maintain civility, he makes this scene signify futility even before the
waitress objects. She says, "You see this sign, sir?" She points to one saying
that they can refuse service to anyone, and says, "You all have to leave,
I'm not taking anymore of your smartness and sarcasm." Bobby says,
"You see this sign?" and with a sweeping exaggerated motion of his arm
from his left to right, knocks over all the drinks on the table and stands up
erect like a superhero. As written, it is easy to imagine another actor playing this scene with a more ingratiating quality, trying to at least be nice to
the waitress before he becomes upset with her; or alternatively as entirely
unaffected, caught by surprise by her intransigence. He makes the ending
a gesture beyond futility, and more of an ironic sick joke. In succeeding
years, Carole Eastman, Rafelson, Nicholson, and Henry Jaglom would all
take credit for writing the scene—and basing it on a real-life incident of
Nicholson's. Perhaps it goes without saying that Nicholson would have a
determining influence on things that came from his life.

This scene is definitive of the Hollywood Renaissance because, first, on
its most surface level it is antiestablishment. Bobby has to conform just
to get lunch, and he doesn't want to. Second, because of the age gap and
the line about "smartness and sarcasm," Bobby and his group are positioned as young upstarts. Third, the scene also validates sexually explicit
humor and at least one type of righteous violence, in a situation where
an old person just doesn't understand. Most significantly, it's ultimately
futile because they don't get their lunch and viewers never see them get
lunch anywhere, and after a lot of sincere agitation, the scene's ending
seems to attempt a big laugh. In other words, while previous and later

Illustration 3.4 The "no substitutions" scene, with the waitress (Lorna Thayer), Bobby (Nicholson), Rayette DiPesto (Karen Black), Terry Grouse (Toni Basil), and Palm Apodaca (Helena Kallianiotes)

generations of film characters, this far invested, might have found a solution that satisfied them, the alienation here is finally played as a joke. While the scene is a cry against the system, it isn't suggesting any better solutions, and Nicholson's performance, a hybrid of King's and Gamson's models, suggests that even rage against the system is at best funny.

Bingham distinguishes between two kinds of "antiheroes," one an immoral lead character to whom the audience is supposed to feel sympathy, and another "of whom the spectator is invited to disapprove." Usefully, he suggests that Nicholson exemplifies the latter in this film. Unlike the similarly aimless Jack Crabb, when anyone tries to break Bobby from his entropic routine, he gets irate. Nicholson often lets Bobby be unredeemable. In Laban terms, his generally gliding and passive gestures seem more contemptible as they become part of a determination to push away a woman pregnant with his child. Really, he is more and less than a man without a goal; he is a man trying to extricate himself from anything permanent. At the same time, throughout, Bobby retains an almost adolescent contempt for people that are more connected to the establishment, as in the "ants" rant and his contempt for Palm Apodaca. Because Nicholson performs Bobby like a drowning man too proud to take a life preserver, Bobby's misogyny is tied to self-hatred. More than many actors might have, Nicholson makes Bobby a man lost, forsaking everything. Bobby's fate is arguably more tragic than that of George, Wyatt, and Billy in *Easy Rider*, because Bobby will go on living in this way, ruining his own life and the lives of others.

Yet the film never turns wholly against Dupea, as seen most clearly in the climactic scene, Bobby's confession to his father, where Nicholson uses—even mints—his own careful blend of naturalism and overt gestures. On an overcast day, Bobby takes his father in his wheelchair out to the shore; the filmmakers could have easily set their denouement inside a house, even on a stage set, but Rafelson wisely surrounded the two actors with "reality," to vouchsafe whatever extremism Nicholson brought to the speech. From the first words, Bobby's voice is hesitant and sad: "I don't know if you'd be particularly interested in hearing anything about me. My life, most of it doesn't add up to much that I could relate as a way of life that you'd approve of. I move around a lot. Not because I'm looking for anything really, but 'cause I'm getting away from things that get bad if I stay. Auspicious beginnings, you know what I mean?" Nicholson later explained his approach to Bobby Dupea: "I was playing it as an allegory of my own career: 'auspicious beginnings.'" So committed was Nicholson to the idea of auspicious beginnings—with the perhaps-obvious corollary of inauspicious results—that he shoehorned the words into the script. Nicholson would not allow the audience to lose sympathy with Bobby in the third act.

In the scene, Bobby loses any hint of a smile and turns his head from side to side—it looks like Nicholson is searching for something sad. He says, "I'm trying to imagine your, your half of this conversation. My feeling is, I don't know that if you could talk we wouldn't be talking. That's pretty much the way it got to be before I left. Are you all right? I don't know what to say." And Nicholson loses his breath and cries. "Tita suggested that we try to but I don't know," and he cries more. "I think that she feel, I think that she feels that we've got some understanding to reach. She totally denies the fact that we were never that comfortable with one another to begin with." He wipes away his tears. "The best that I can do is apologize. We both know that I was never really that good at it anyway. I'm sorry it didn't work out." And he lowers his head. Fifteen years after shooting this scene, Nicholson he could recall the grass on the hill and the smell of the air. He told the interviewer that he used Stanislavski "emotion memory" in this scene; Nicholson wasn't above the Method when he needed it. According to Nicholson, "On take one, away I went. And I think it was a breakthrough. It was a breakthrough for me as an actor, for actors. I don't think they'd had this level of emotion, really, in almost any male character until that point."[31] This part of the interview is quoted without apparent irony or qualification by James Naremore in the canonical *Acting in the Cinema*, ignoring work like Montgomery Clift's in *From Here to Eternity* (1953). For Patrick McGilligan, this scene proved Nicholson to be "a Bogart with tears."[32] In a sense, Naremore and McGilligan helped turn the page on Hollywood's past, welcoming the Rough Rebel who could play a common man willing to lay bare extremes of pathos and emotionalism. Left unmentioned was that Nicholson's brand of vulnerability was utterly unseen around women.

At least Bobby wants to reconcile with his father; he shows no such inclination for his many female scene partners, and it is in those scenes where the sexism of homosocial coding becomes most apparent. In *Easy Rider*, Nicholson has limited contact with women; in *Five Easy Pieces*, he sleeps with them, manipulates them, and pulls them from their partners, all to show his contempt for them, as Sedgwick had described the homosocial behavior of Horner in *The Country Wife*. Bingham points out that Nicholson's deconstruction of masculinity only comes after a major construction of libido: "it might follow that a man as lost and confused as Bobby Dupea would be impotent, but Bobby pulls women into bed as easily as James Bond."[33] Nicholson as Bobby goes from woman to woman even though his girlfriend is pregnant. Most women in the story are attracted to him, including his homely sister. Yet Nicholson as Bobby seems happiest playing sports and card games with other men, and in scenes with women he seems edgy, as though looking for an exit. Nicholson's choices normalize the homosocial.

The general sexism of *Five Easy Pieces*, and Nicholson's performance of it, may be best exemplified by the scene of Bobby and Betty spinning around a room making love. The scene is both hyper-stylized and oddly realistic. The entire scene is one shot of flailing torsos and ecstatic faces, culminating when Bobby throws Betty on a bed and presumably comes inside her, smiling his widest grin of the film. Bingham writes, "After they climax (simultaneously) Bobby sits up, revealing a Nicholson grin and a T-shirt that reads 'Triumph,' the word referring to more here than the make of a motorcycle."[34] Nicholson wears a shirt while the actress playing Betty (Sally Struthers) reveals her naked breasts (how many films would follow this lead?), and the shot ends with the handheld camera finding Nicholson's boyish smile, the jouissance of both wit and cuckold. Much like Rizzo crossing the street with Buck, this scene is the movement in microcosm: raw, new, sexual, forbidden, appealing, and sexist.

Yet Nicholson also somewhat problematizes his character's sexism, occasionally going beyond what Sedgwick called her "formulations."

At one point, Bobby comes to his own house to find Rayette sitting looking catatonically at the wall, listening to lonesome-sounding country music. He is flat, non-expressive, his gait normal; he is on a sustained Laban glide, indicating strong indirectness, meaning that he may avoid things he doesn't like, but will stand up for what he believes in. When she's less than communicative, he snaps just a bit: "Okay I got your point, I hope you didn't strain yourself getting in here before I hit the back door." He sees his reflection in the mirror and doesn't seem to want to look, a mark of a lack of faith in oneself. Nicholson does let his voice crack as he says, "Come on DiPesto, I never told you it would work out to anything, did I?" Another actor might not have done the voice crack (it's not in the script). Nicholson, by doing it, establishes that not only does Bobby fail to get what he wants, he fails to get out of what he doesn't want. Seconds later, alone in the car, without warning, he spurts forth the most exaggerated moment in any of these films, a near-epileptic fit of rage. Bobby flails his arms and body all over his car seat, but Nicholson's grunts and squeals make clear that Bobby's frustration is mostly directed at himself. Bobby returns to the house, and asks her if she'd like to come, and she does. This is more indicative of the *best* of the movement: a declared lack of inner feeling, a declared absence of emotion, with a bare wisp of suggestion of salvation, almost certain to be lost at the next opportunity. This could align well with some of the better moments from films by directors like Michelangelo Antonioni and Federico Fellini (as Rafelson had declared he wanted), if it did not consistently come at the expense of women. However, in 1970, critics barely seemed to notice a problem.

Five Easy Pieces and 1970: Critical reception

The marketing for BBS's follow-up to *Easy Rider* used the Nicholson persona as extending disenfranchisement, describing Bobby as a man even more unable to find a home than Wyatt had been. The promotion for *Five Easy Pieces* drew on *Easy Rider*. The "Easy" in the phrase "Five Easy Pieces" was actually highlighted (perhaps five times thicker than the other two words) in the posters. *Easy Rider*'s tagline had said "A Man Went Looking for America And Couldn't Find it Anywhere," and now the tagline for *Five Easy Pieces* said, "He Rode The Fast Lane On The Road To Nowhere." While AIP promotions tended toward the scandalous and scatological, this particular publicity instead suggested the mass-marketing of absurdism or clever alienation. Critics went along with BBS, happy to celebrate Nicholson's diverse talents.

Stanley Kauffmann said that Nicholson

> plays the hero, Bobby, and proves that he is probably on the screen
> to stay a while—a long while. He has tenderness, fire of several
> kinds, spontaneous charm and—which he especially needs here—
> conviction of some depth. ... He is starting a screen life somewhat
> later than James Stewart or Henry Fonda or Gary Cooper did, but he
> may become something of an anti-urban myth-figure like them.[35]

This article was refreshingly honest that Nicholson was simply new
packaging on former star codes, but the idea of being an "anti-urban
myth-figure" could be read in several ways. Stars like Stewart, Fonda,
and Cooper were surely what Leo Lowenthal meant when he said
that stars cut off audiences from politics, yet they arguably had some
moments of social engagement. They did not have the "proud irony"
that Gamson writes about. Kauffmann's compliment suggests a discursive structure for Nicholson beyond disenfranchisement and beyond
irony, almost a star as a familiar friend, allowed to signify a wide variety
of meanings.

Jacob Brackman's review of *Five Easy Pieces* began by celebrating his
anti-star appearance: "Like Hoffman, Voight, Wilder, Gould, Sutherland
or Arkin, he seems spectacularly intelligent, and a *person*, relative to the
stars we grew up with." Nicholson was also seen as similar to the stars of
the films of the *nouvelle vague*. Many critics compared *Five Easy Pieces* to
European films in general and *Shoot the Piano Player* (1960) in particular.
For Brackman, *Five Easy Pieces* was

> the opposite of a genre film: What you least expected and therefore
> most hoped to see. Many critics have been using the word auteur to
> draw attention to tiny "individual" touches with which directors fla-
> vor "standard fare." By that measure, *Five Easy Pieces* is too original,
> too artful to even register on the meter.[36]

His point was that the film didn't need overt jump-cuts and fourth-wall
devices to make art. In a similar vein, the *Saturday Review* raved:

> Made by members of the same group that backed *Easy Rider*, this is a
> more probing film, staying real, while making distinctions between
> kinds of reality. Some have already begun to identify it with the tag
> of "road picture," seeing in it a new genre and one that is peculiarly
> American. Perhaps so, but it is more likely that a new generation

of film-makers has wearied of the studio, and what it finds outside inevitably colors the substance of its cinema.[37]

The film was all things to all people, against tired formalism and in favor of a new richness and substance that still respected old Hollywood in some ways. And Nicholson's style, whether over-mannered or ostensibly natural, was always characterized as a determining component.

Richard Schickel loved *Five Easy Pieces*, and wrote in *Life*, "If you see nothing else this year, you must see this film."[38] The film was similarly praised in many quarters, with Nicholson given primary artistic credit. For example, in a piece called "This Is The 'Pieces' That Jack Built," *The New York Times* complimented "the miraculous Jack Nicholson ... whose wonderfully agile characterization of the bedeviled hero communicates at once a profound intimacy with psychic pain and a vivid appreciation for the absurd in life and in himself."[39] When *The New York Times* has called you miraculous, you've probably arrived. Jack Nicholson and *Five Easy Pieces* were positioned as counterculture for those that didn't like counterculture, simultaneously classical and absurdist, with Nicholson as a "builder" of the movement. For the press, Nicholson's version of disenfranchisement now defined a generation, verifying the engagement that King discusses while eliding the ironic approach that Gamson discusses.

Five Easy Pieces was received as not only formally refreshing, but thematically superior to even the most radical counterculture films. *Variety* wrote:

> At a time when screenwriters are concentrating on the "now" subjects of sex and revolution, or experimenting with time distortion, simultaneous action and minimal plot, Rafelson and writer Adrien Joyce have stuck to a timeless theme—the search for identity—and have taken a strictly novelistic approach to their subject. And in an era when actors, more often than not, are treated as pieces of décor, Rafelson achieves his greatest success through a series of bold, subtly conceived portrayals. ... If Nicholson's 'Easy Rider' fans may be disappointed with this vehicle, his performance should leave no one dissatisfied. It is a remarkably varied and daring exploration of a complex character, equally convincing in its manic and sober aspects.[40]

This is a telling statement about how performance obviates the need for more radical filmmaking. Star studies shows that narrative is often sublimated to "rooting for" a star, to the point of preferring a bold performance to narrative closure. In only his second widely seen role, Nicholson was already this sort of star, already like the classical-era stars. Nicholson's arrival into the "select circle of American actors" was hailed by *Newsweek*, which awarded him his first national newsweekly cover in December 1970. The magazine extolled the actor who seemed to invest so much of himself in his roles and who "in his style and sensibility expresses the contemporary moment, in much the way Marlon Brando and James Dean radiated the resonance of the 1950s."[41] These reviews left little doubt that Nicholson represented an authentic masculinity, Hollywood's best possible response to youth skepticism. As a star, Nicholson represented just what the critics seemed to want—the newly "realistic," rough-hewn, morally ambiguous Hollywood, but not without parallels to men like Henry Fonda and James Stewart. Hollywood saw nothing in Nicholson that it couldn't incorporate—and the feeling was mutual.

Nicholson was neither strident nor entirely apolitical. In 1973, Molly Haskell wrote:

> Gould, Nicholson, and Redford are stars—as George Segal, Donald Sutherland, Bruce Dern, and Ryan O'Neal are not—through some mystical combination of talent, luck, and an X quality that harmonizes with a current mood. They don't flaunt it, baby, don't ride in limousines, but then limousines would finish them faster than a drug rap. They challenge the system, don't play the game, but then maybe the game has changed and they're simply playing according to the new rules.[42]

Haskell perceptively suggested that the key to "playing according to the new rules" was an ironic pose when one represented alienation. One of Nicholson's biographers named many people who failed to persuade Nicholson to be political, including Lynn Bernay, Don Devlin, Henry Jaglom, Jane Fonda, and Donald Sutherland. Nicholson would give joking reasons for not attending certain meetings. Nicholson may have been disillusioned and cynical, but rarely to the point of activism. Both onscreen and offscreen, Hollywood would follow Nicholson's lead.

In 1970, Nicholson's personality effaced some of his and his film's contradictions. *Movie Digest* said, "It is the measure of Nicholson's fine performance that he is equally at home in the world of the 'hard hat' as in the world of the pianist."[43] In agreement, the cover of *The Saturday Review* of September 26, 1970, celebrated "The Homeless Hero." The headline read: "Jack Nicholson is, without doubt, Hollywood's hottest new male star, but who is he really? HIPPIE? HARD-HAT? HERO?" This positioned Nicholson's star image as slippery yet representative, which suited Nicholson's career perfectly. In the article, Hollis Alpert named Nicholson as the "rootless, restless American in Bob Rafelson's film *Five Easy Pieces*. ... What better way to 'open up' a film story than to make its protagonist homeless?"[44] Yet Bobby Dupea isn't homeless, though he may be a wanderer.[45] Based on the home he grew up in, Bobby was in fact almost upper class, or at least on the high end of the middle class, not so unlike Nicholson himself. An actual homeless person that picked up *The Saturday Review* and somehow put together enough spare change to see the film might have felt a little disappointed to see himself ostensibly represented by a man with all the white male class privilege in the world. The press didn't notice a contradiction, and celebrated the unique representative powers of this "everyman."

Reporters even complimented Nicholson's fence-straddling. Rex Reed explained, "He has become the hero for two cults. ... The antiestablishment B-flick underground digs him because he's the proof that something good can come out of all that American-International garbage. And the over-30 crowd digs him too."[46] Marilyn Ross quoted Nicholson as finding such a dichotomy false: "I'm the type of person who would really resent the world if it came down to just two choices ... if that's the only kind of film they want to see then they're not too interesting an audience."[47] Nicholson's statement signifies less an attempt to move beyond Kingian sincere engagement and Gamsonian proud irony than to encompass both, to be a "hail-fellow" for different fellows. This was shown when Nicholson spoke to *Variety* in September of 1970 about his upcoming directorial debut, *Drive, He Said*. When the magazine asked why he was doing a university picture without riots or real revolutionary rhetoric, he replied, "I've been involved in exploitation films. I know when a cycle is over."[48] Yet at least three of Nicholson's biographers ascribed the box-office failure of *Drive, He Said* to Nicholson *failing* to know when a cycle is over, in this case the antiestablishment cycle of "campus unrest" films. And he also didn't seem to anticipate the somewhat feminist backlash that would greet *Carnal Knowledge*.

Carnal Knowledge: Textual analysis

Nicholson extended his alienated/ironic hybrid persona in *Carnal Knowledge*. Of the nine films closely studied here, *Carnal Knowledge* may represent the most direct take on masculinity and male sexuality; the film is about little else. In some ways it resembles *Bob & Carol & Ted & Alice*, with the same culmination of an abandoned partner-swap, but *Carnal Knowledge* doesn't allow a "cop out" (in the earlier film's terms) of a happy ending for its characters. Jonathan's ideology is that only his performance of masculinity *is* politically important. Like Hoffman in *Midnight Cowboy* and *Little Big Man*, Nicholson's character's goal is to not to have a goal, or to be a radical individualist. Somewhat like Bobby Dupea, Jonathan is fiercely committed to being uncommitted. As played by Nicholson, Jonathan winds up as disillusioned and nihilistic as any other Nicholson character.

Nicholson's vocal work is a key to his interpretation of Jonathan. In the first half-hour of the film, he affects a very working-class accent, more than he did even as Bobby Dupea. Nicholson invokes the stereotype of the dock worker, the sort of "ethnic type" that Humphrey Bogart and John Garfield played for years before rising to stardom. The script says "I give her to you" but Nicholson says "I give her ta ya"; the script says "Go ahead" but he says "Gah head." However, after the film's first half-hour, after Jonathan and Sandy have moved past college and into the working world, Nicholson reverts to his apparently "normal" voice (the one we know from dozens of subsequent Nicholson roles). This change isn't in the script, and based on screenwriter Jules Feiffer's statements, he had been trying to make Jonathan Jewish, not a working-class Ralph Kramden type. Coming the same year as Nicholson's campus protest film (*Drive, He Said*), Nicholson enables a somewhat surprising critique of elite universities. (Jonathan and Sandy attend Amherst.) One way of reading Nicholson's performance is that college—or Susan, his girlfriend there—has changed Jonathan and is complicit in making him the "ballbuster"-hating man he has become. ("Ballbuster" is Jonathan's preferred term for an objectionable woman.) Another way of reading his performance is that Jonathan was always a "ballbuster"-hater and that he was the snake in the Amherst grass, which might be a critique of affirmative action programs (in the 1950s, when the first part of the film is set, prestigious schools did attempt to recruit from outlying regions and white-ethnic groups). In either reading, Nicholson's performance makes clear that college is hardly a leftist paradise; likewise, Nicholson as a star is not always aligned with committed leftists.

As with Hoffman and Gould in 1971, Nicholson was asked to take his "anti-hero" status literally and play an educated yet reprehensible man. Where Hoffman was ruthlessly isolated as a distracted academic, giving audiences practically no hint of likeability, Nicholson as an academic is occasionally affable, leavening his aggression with winking smiles, more of a child that refuses to grow up. In Laban terms, Nicholson is sometimes strong and direct in the manner that Hoffman played David, but just as often allows a more ingratiating lightness and even indirectness in some scenes. Had Hoffman and Nicholson switched roles in 1971 (quite unlikely, considering Nicholson's derogatory statements about Peckinpah and the fact that Mike Nichols would not have wanted to look as though he were making a sequel to *The Graduate*) it is probable that Hoffman would have made Jonathan more detestable and Nicholson would have added some charm to David. Particularly because *Carnal Knowledge* as written is a relentless critique of male values, Nicholson's occasional Gamsonian flashes of irony serve to undermine the "anti" in "anti-hero," making the type less of a societal challenge and more of a playful upstart.

Early on, Nicholson is strong and direct, and may appeal to the audience by suggesting, meta-textually, that it is impossible to know anything. In an early scene, Jonathan and Susan sit at a booth in a bar, and Jonathan says: "Most girls I talk to, it's like we're spies from foreign countries, and we're speaking in code. Everything means something else. Like I say, would you like to take a walk, and it means something else." Susan demurely demonstrates that she understands about different meanings. Jonathan says, in his same working-class accent, "You're very sharp. I like that." She points out that *that* means something else. Thus is futility signified, complemented by Nicholson's performance of strong (yet naïve) confidence.[49]

Illustration 3.5   Jonathan (Nicholson) and Sandy (Art Garfunkel) in college

The inability to make a decision takes a more clearly female form in this film than in *Easy Rider* or *Five Easy Pieces*. Candice Bergen's Susan does a sort of Laban wringing in a jukebox joint where she dances alternatively with Sandy and Jonathan. She sits down with both of them and laughs hysterically, then grows slightly more sober, looking between them as if she's at a tennis match. A few film minutes later, as Jonathan berates her for not committing to him (Jonathan), and he says, a little unnecessarily, "You're really something," Susan bows her head as she says flatly, "I don't feel like something. I feel like nothing." After a few more exchanges, he walks away and then returns, as though he has swallowed all his pride: "Susan, I love you. Why can't you be more with me like you are with Sandy?" This is unusual, and could be considered a sudden Laban flicking gesture. For the first time since Nicholson's star status was established, he plays a person who is utterly vulnerable to someone who could hurt him. This doesn't last, but this juxtaposition almost suggests that Susan, by rejecting the clear-motivation Jonathan, made him into the indecisive, noncommittal Laban strong-indirect person that he is for the rest of the film (even though Jonathan forced the "love triangle"). *Carnal Knowledge* thus presents a woman as an Eve that delivers the period's apple of original sin—ambivalent futility.

Of the films discussed, *Carnal Knowledge* is probably the least concerned with politics as such. In one of the text's few moments of political awareness, Ann-Margret as Bobbie, his wife, tells Jonathan, "You wouldn't let me canvas for Kennedy." "Bobbie" may represent Bobby Kennedy, and if so Nicholson/Jonathan is preventing her from even enouncing herself. But this trope is quickly folded back into Jonathan's performance of masculinity; Jonathan says that he wants her to work, but she says he throws a tantrum if he calls and she's not home. Jonathan's masculinity takes precedence over politics. Jonathan says she's too tired to get beer, and adds, "You're more tired now than when you were working." Bobbie replies that she's in the house all day—per his request. They are a picture of a relationship in stasis, with both people refusing to do what they can to make it work. As she prepares to dress, she turns to him and asks if he wants to walk with her, and he says in that case he may as well get it himself. She frumps back onto the bed, saddened, not unlike Rayette in *Five Easy Pieces*. One clear reading is that the film criticizes this sort of woman for becoming passively domesticated. However, to Nicholson's credit, the man is hardly coming off any better: Nicholson's strong indirectness makes it seem like this is how Jonathan would be with any woman. Nicholson's performance as Jonathan is political in the sense that it goes beyond his previous alienation/irony dichotomy to represent, and even lionize, proactive futility.

Nicholson provides too many moments of pleasure for the audience to give up on him entirely. By the time Jonathan and Bobbie arrive at their big argument, *Carnal Knowledge* has aligned itself with Jonathan, and doesn't stop just because Jonathan insists on a life of indecision even while he criticizes Bobbie's life of entropy. Nicholson's eventual return to strong-direct movements suggest that the actor was holding back in *all* his previous efforts; Jonathan's ministrations against his wife are more exaggerated and tempestuous than even the "ants" speech in *Five Easy Pieces*. She says, "I know I sleep all day, I know I'm doing a terrible job, but you're not helping me any." He says "And who helps me?" Bobbie says she helps him. He says, with a Laban sustained press, "Your kind of help I can do without." She looks at him and says, with disbelief, "Can you? Can you really?" He is tying his tie and at this moment gives up on getting it right; by Freudian implication, he gives up on getting his phallus properly aligned. Now Nicholson lets Laban strong-direct sparks fly in full vent, implying that only he can be right. Jonathan says, "Ah, you'll do anything you can to ruin my day. I got up today feeling so good. You couldn't leave us alone. We were doing so well." He continues, a spatial explosion, his voice rising to a tub-thumping fever, "At one time, at one time it was great what we had. The kidding around, it can't have a natural time span? Affairs can't dissolve in a good way? There's always got to be poison. I don't see why, I really don't see why!" By now his hands are flailing, his fingers extended but taut. She purses her lips, tenses her body, and says "Jonathan do you want it over between us?" He replies, at the same heightened pitch, "Why does it have to be one way or the other?" She asks if he wants her to leave. He says, "I want you right here where you belong." She says, "What about you?" He says, "When I'm here, I'm here. When I'm not here, I'm, I'm there." She asks where. He almost spits, "Wherever." Has any onscreen man ever fought this hard for the right to do nothing? Profilmically, it's like Nicholson would prefer near-laughable volcanic anger to love or sentiment. This then stands for the bias of the star, the film, and the cinema of the period.

As he did in *Easy Rider*, but much more thoroughly, Nicholson as Jonathan makes Sedgwickian homosocial male–male amity appear natural; Jonathan invests all his trust in his best friend Sandy, and seemingly none in his female conquests. Jonathan conquers women mostly to one-up men, in line with Sedgwick's take on cuckoldry. The suggestive script of *Carnal Knowledge* might yet have struck a blow against hetero-normativity. Sandy calls Jonathan "sexy"; Sandy and Jonathan splash each other in a swimming pool; Sandy and Jonathan spend more onscreen time talking about sex with each other than doing it with others; Jonathan steadily finds it more difficult to get an erection. At one point, Jonathan says to Bobbie, "First Cindy, oh no not Cindy. How about Sandy? How about Cindy *and* Sandy?" (emphasis his) This throwaway line is the only textual suggestion of a threesome; the fact that it would be between two men and a woman confirms the male–male bonding as supreme. Bobbie turns to Jonathan and says, about her previous liaisons, "It got you hot." He says, "Something has to," suggesting that perhaps a man could make him more hot; lines like these (which are all in Feiffer's script) suggest that perhaps Jonathan is unsure of his heterosexuality.

However, the problem with a more queer reading is that Nicholson's performance is hetero-normative to the point of being anti-effeminate. The first third of the film is set in the 1950s, and it's easy enough to imagine one of the 1950s rebels (Clift, Brando, or Dean) as Jonathan, exuding a sort of slyly androgynous, seductive quality that could be said to attract any man or woman. However, Nicholson is not like Brando, Dean, or Clift would have been. Instead, Nicholson as Jonathan is so hyper-masculine that he seems to prove why Sandy and Bobbie have

Illustration 3.6 Sandy (Garfunkel) and Jonathan (Nicholson), gads about town

androgynous names. In Laban terms, his unrushed voice and smooth gestures are sometimes indirect but rarely weak (after the vulnerable scene with Susan); he's a cauldron of id that never needs to apologize. Jonathan is seen in the shower four times—perhaps finally getting clean, as Palm Apodaca had suggested in *Five Easy Pieces*—but Nicholson does not writhe or twist as he washes himself. This is part of his general confidence throughout the post-college part of the film; Jonathan never seems to have moments of self-doubt, quite unlike the 1950s rebels or even Nicholson's portrayal of Bobby Dupea. When Jonathan objectifies women, when he judges them entirely by their figures, when he says "believe me, looks are everything," Nicholson doesn't suggest a repressed homosexual that can't know himself (even if the script arguably does); instead he suggests a caddish heterosexual, closer to Sedgwick's homosocial cuckolder. And many subsequent dramatic films would do likewise.

Carnal Knowledge and 1971: Critical reception

We saw that the press around *Little Big Man* presented the film as a joint effort of Dustin Hoffman and Arthur Penn—the actor–director relationship (as friends, and artists) mobilized to appeal to audiences who were presumably skeptical of studio product like *Cleopatra* (1963). Something similar was at work with *Carnal Knowledge*. The main publicity poster of the film featured no images at all—perhaps it depended upon the prurient reputation the film would likely acquire. Instead, it was all words on a white background: names of collaborators, and the name of the film. The first line said "Mike Nichols, Jack Nicholson"; the next lines named the three other main actors along with the screenwriter Jules Feiffer, and the final line, in red instead of black, a standalone "Carnal Knowledge." This promotion suggests, in a manner unthinkable for Hollywood ten years before, that the actors, writer, and director are the main creators of a film—especially the director and lead actor. One article from 1970 said, "To those who believe that Nicholson was carried in on the crest of the 'New Wave' films, it should be clarified that he helped create them."[50] Nicholson couldn't have said it better himself. Asked about the creative process of *Carnal Knowledge*, Nicholson told one source that the operative phrase was "Let's run it by Nick and Nick."[51] The point is that this period marked a change in the way that films are marketed (and received, and in turn, made, because if you give actors and directors power, they're going to take it)—a change that we often take for granted today.

Carnal Knowledge received pointedly mixed reviews, and, combined with the harsh reception that greeted *Drive, He Said*, Nicholson faced backlash and serious controversy for the first time in his incipient career. The *Village Voice* attacked both of Nicholson's 1971 films, saying that the antiestablishment star of *Easy Rider* had done a political about-face, and that *Drive, He Said* posed an affront to the counterculture and student left. Reporting from the Cannes Film Festival, where *Drive, He Said* was apparently received with long, loud, boos, Mike Zwerin, the *Voice* correspondent, complained that

> the revolutionary character in the film ... the fact that this character becomes a freaked-out rapist ... can only lead good people ... to see all revolutionaries are crazy. A guy as hip as Jack Nicholson with his present power could get away with anything. And we cannot afford people like him "copping out"—and people like Fred Hampton get murdered by the cops.[52]

Yesterday Nicholson represented antiestablishment, today he *was* the establishment. Nicholson tried, as is his métier, to remain in both camps. He indicated that Godard would never make anything but a polemic until the Vietnam War was over, and said,

> I'm not that way. I feel as strongly about it but I think if you approach it that way, you do bore people and you don't achieve what you're after which is real change. I think if what you are doing is too naked you will alienate those who disagree and the people who already agree will fall in line with you.[53]

Not surprisingly, Nicholson lined up with Hollywood, or perhaps the other way around.

Nicholson's contradictions were well summarized by a star feature in the *Los Angeles Herald-Examiner* that was titled "A Realistic Romantic." Indeed, if Hoffman was the Artistic Star, his exaggerations designed for viewers to understand fables, and if Gould was the Urban Don Quixote, as *Time* said, the idea of a Realistic Romantic seemed to capture Nicholson's exaggerated/"playing himself" dichotomy almost too well. Nicholson said in the article,

> I'm a romantic. I see reality. I know how things are, I observe and know that. But I want them to be another way—something more. I'm a romantic because I allow myself to believe that things could be better, could be more than they are. Because I allow myself to want

that. Women, for instance. In my fantasy I've wanted the women I've known to be something more. I've let myself imagine that they have been. But I also see what they are. That's why I've never settled down with a woman.[54]

For this author, Nicholson is grounded in reality but reaches for fantasy. He sees the world shrewdly but with a light heart, melding cynicism with irony, even as he dismisses women. Nicholson's star discursive construct was becoming clearer and less flexible, enabling praise like the *Herald-Examiner*'s as well as less charitable readings.

In 1973, Molly Haskell usefully compared Nicholson to Dean in terms of generational politics:

> [W]hereas Dean, the archetypal adolescent—wounded, sensitive, childlike—stood for a generation on the brink of a cultural revolution, Nicholson is the more guarded and mature emblem of a generation which has lived through the upheaval, taken drugs, been on the "outs" with the authorities, but somehow survived. There is a certain cynicism, a defensive shell, that will prevent his ever opening himself up to us and becoming the sacrificial figure of identification that Dean was. In a world pervaded by stupidity and corruption, the line between the young and the old, the virtuous and the immoral is no longer quite so clear. Dean was the morbid but luminous expression of pure Oedipal longing, a primal drama he could freely translate into the anguished cry for a father's love in *East of Eden*, whereas Nicholson would play out the same role in *Five Easy Pieces* with more reserve.[55]

One can add that Nicholson probably had to be more reserved, or seem ridiculous. Nicholson represented both immature fatalism and a more mature approach to it, which included not always taking it seriously. In addition, Dean worked for female approval, but Nicholson seemed beyond caring about it, both on and offscreen, in accordance with the homosocial.

Carnal Knowledge was well in line with female-excluding themes of the time, which critics were finally beginning to notice. At least one influential source saw repressed homosexuality in Nicholson and Garfunkel's portrayals. Roslyn Drexler, in *The New York Times*, said that "*Carnal Knowledge* may be a study of latent homosexuality masquerading as two college roommates growing up." When asked about this, Nicholson scoffed at the idea of any layperson using such a term. He said, "You could probably project that implication onto Romulus and Remus or Abbott and Costello. I don't think that was really an intended statement of the work."[56] As Sedgwick might have predicted, Nicholson was careful not to reject homosexuality as anathema for everyone. However, unlike Dean, Clift, and Brando, Nicholson has never gone on record as saying that any kind of gay or bisexual behavior might be worthwhile *for himself*, and Hollywood has mostly followed this type of lead (actor).

The most important source to identify Nicholson's woman-hating was *Time*, which said in its review of *Carnal Knowledge*,

> As for Nicholson, it is no secret that he can take lines and make them assume almost any shape. But this is the first time he has been called upon to age 20 years in the span of two hours. It is more than merely his hair that thins; it is his amour-propre, his attitudes, his ego. Feiffer has composed a cartoon, but Nicholson has created one of the screen's few straight misogynists.[57]

It's not clear how *Time* meant "straight." But *Time* clearly blamed Nicholson for going beyond the script to show hate for women. When the press asked about Nicholson's views on women, he often quoted Wilhelm Reich, who advocated radical sexual freedom. Nicholson called Reich "the most important political writer and thinker of the last century."[58] Reich, reductively, put sex in the same place that Ayn Rand put personal happiness. Nicholson was proud to say that he was in therapy, because, as he said, therapy was where he could learn more about Wilhelm Reich. He spoke about sex as a universal curative. At another point that year, Nicholson said, "I want to make only X-rated films,"[59] signifying something like the popular image of Hugh Hefner turned into a movie star.

Nicholson's interview with *Playboy*, within a year of the release of *Carnal Knowledge*, became notorious for defining his masculinity in a way that he has since had to live down (or live up to). At least three of his biographers quote the line, "In a casual conversation with me, you could have a certain difficulty in separating my sexual stance from Jonathan's." In this casual conversation with *Playboy* he graphically described his sexual experiences; he denigrated and celebrated women repeatedly, in the same breath. He said, "A couple of years ago I told a reporter that for years I'd balled all the chicks I wanted to. Well, man, every chick I ever related to really resented that statement. ... I mean, no chick wants to be a part of some band of cunts." This wasn't an apology or a disavowal. Nicholson was already perceptive about main-taining his contradictions, whether regarding feminism and promiscu-ity, presentation and representation, exaggeration and playing himself, or alienation and wit. He tied dichotomies such as these to the job of the actor. He said his job was to keep people guessing, which is why he wouldn't do television talk shows. He knew that an interview like the one he was giving *Playboy* "will add as much confusion as to who I am as it will reveal truth." At another point he quoted a friend of his, "I can never tell if you're behind or ahead of the fashion."[60] Thus, Nicholson suggested that to maintain his liminal status as classicist and rebel, he would have to remain equivocal if not downright hostile toward women. This construction wouldn't surprise readers of Sedgwick's work on homosociality.

Jack Nicholson didn't see his character in *Carnal Knowledge*, Jonathan, as reprehensible, as he explained to *Playboy*:

> I moved Jonathan a great deal toward me. Mike Nichols and I agreed that this guy must not become a lascivious character, because that's not really what's being said. Jonathan is the most sensitive character in the picture. He's the one who doesn't recover from the original sexual triangle. He's never able to really trust girls after that. He winds up in a very ritualistic but honest sexual relationship with a professional, which is the best thing—not the worst—he can do for himself. ... [He's] given himself the best negative answer that he can come up with.[61]

Because Nicholson tries for empathy, the tone of the film feels less sure than *Straw Dogs*. "The best negative answer" might be a good way of summarizing the ironically alienated themes that dominated the new kind of films. The phrase straddles the line between farce and tragedy. If *Carnal Knowledge* isn't sure which one it is, that's partly because Nicholson's performance doesn't seem so certain either. In terms of being able to represent a man, Nicholson distinguished himself from his co-star Art Garfunkel. Garfunkel, like another folk singer, Arlo Guthrie in *Alice's Restaurant* (1969), did nothing to help the Kracauerian "non-actor" movement. If anything, Garfunkel proved that regular-looking untrained performers weren't really what Hollywood wanted, as evidenced by his career, which stopped cold for a decade after *Carnal Knowledge*. It was the hybrid of the exaggerated and the "playing him-self," as represented by Nicholson, that lingered, and put his sexism at a level of remove.

In *The New Yorker*, Pauline Kael invoked *Playboy* as she unveiled some of the harshest criticisms of *Carnal Knowledge*:

> It's as if *Playboy* had suddenly seen the error of its ways and now sold its remorse in the same crusading format. The effects are almost all achieved through the line readings, and the *cleverness* is unpleasant. It's all surface and whacking emphasis. The controlled hysteria of this desperate, surefire, hit-it-on-the-button comedy style has about the same relationship to humor that belting has to singing. ... The actors are badly served; they're served up, really. ... Nicholson [acts] up such a tormented, villainous squall that even his best scene— a well-written monologue about the perils of shacking up—seems to be delivered in full voice against cliffs and crashing seas.

Pauline Kael pointed out that Nicholson in *Carnal Knowledge* played the generation of Benjamin Braddock's parents, meaning that the "audience is already prepared to believe that they never could feel, never could relate."[62] Nicholson might have appreciated such a sentiment, if only to position himself liminally outside the counterculture. He said to one source, "I'm not that interested in the youth movement anyway. For one thing, I'm not that young."[63] Already, Nicholson negotiated a position for himself akin to classical stars, a discursive construct that could mean many things to many people. He represented the sort of alienated man that refuses to believe in solutions while also representing cinema as, perhaps, a placebo.

To summarize this section, Nicholson's hybridized performance of sincere disillusionment and caustic irony served as a determining characteristic of his films from this period. In *Easy Rider*, his George Hanson criticized "being bought and sold in the marketplace," yet he also laughed at the absurdities of life. In *Five Easy Pieces*, his Bobby Dupea appeared genuinely disgusted by people and institutions, yet when push came to shove Nicholson charged Dupea with a jokey sarcasm, as in the famous "no substitutions" scene. In *Carnal Knowledge*, Jonathan as written is a detestable "anti-hero," but Nicholson "moved him a great deal toward" himself, and played him more quixotically against anything but his own carnal desires. He demonstrated a talent to signify both alienation and irony simultaneously. As a broad summary, Nicholson's fence-straddling, "hail-fellow" quality served to diminish the films' social criticisms. His onscreen and offscreen trust of men to the exclusion of women also furthered the homosocial themes of the period. Critics celebrated Jack Nicholson as the best of both worlds in

1969–71—both counterculture and classical. Nicholson proved that the ethnic everyman could promote somewhat traditionally melodramatic Hollywood films while also exuding the antiestablishment values that were presumed to appeal to young audiences. Nicholson thus provided a prescription for future Hollywood projects. As palimpsestic as his star image may have been, it was still upheld as Hollywood's best, or perhaps second-best, response to an America beginning the 1970s. If any star-actor at the outset of the decade was more lionized than Nicholson, he would have to be Elliott Gould.

4
Elliott Gould: The Urban Don Quixote

This chapter situates Elliott Gould's incipient star career as an attempt to appeal to young educated adults while simultaneously maintaining and extending Hollywood traditions, much like Hoffman and Nicholson. However, Gould's performance style considerably differed from theirs, and it was this difference that proved consequential for successive films. Gould is both a continuation of the "ethnic everyman" figure pioneered by Hoffman and something of an expansion of the type, specifically an extension that bridges gaps between Hoffman's persona and the personas of classical-era stars. While Hoffman was understood as an exaggerated, mannered performer, Gould, by overwhelming critical consensus, was understood to be "playing himself." (In a characteristic comment, Gould said at this time, "My secret of being a formidable actor is that I seldom act. I'm always *me*."[1] (emphasis his)) Under Gould, the Rough Rebel figure retained its appeal to youth and to "ironic alienation," but expanded its parameters towards a more naturalistic acting style. Naturalism at this time was not favored in and of itself, as demonstrated by the fact that, in 1970, Gould starred in four films while the equally naturalistic Robert Redford, coming off of the smash hit *Butch Cassidy and the Sundance Kid* (1969), starred in none. Gould promoted a more everyman-inflected naturalism in 1969 and 1970, but by the end of 1971, curiously enough, considerably undermined it.

As with the chapters on Hoffman and Nicholson, I show how Gould signified ironic alienation and a certain "homosocial" tendency to exclude women. To recapitulate my schema, for Barry King, after the societal and industrial changes of the 1960s, stars found incentive to develop an "actorly image," which would engage with "the 'social issues' indicated [sic] by carefully selected narratives since these issues transcend particular films."[2] The star-actor would demonstrate acting ability and "character" through differing sorts of performances onscreen while showing a consistent sincerity about social issues off-screen. For Joshua Gamson, however, in this same period, "Cynicism, irony, and invitations behind the scenes engage. ... The irony is more than defensive; it is proud."[3] King does not reckon with stars that flaunt their ironic approach to the world; Gamson does not recognize stars that attempt sincere engagement with social problems. In this section, I argue that Gould, much like Hoffman and Nicholson, tries to reconcile these contradictions, attempting a somewhat genuine disillusionment while also making clear his hip, ironic distanciation even as both modes tended to privilege male–male bonds over male–female bonds.

Paul McDonald writes,

> Stars do appear to offer an unrivalled opportunity for product dif-ferentiation. At one level, various individual stars appear to share common characteristics, and the system of stardom differentiates performers according to type. For example, the "young male rebel" type is a category which would include stars of the 1950s, like Marlon Brando or James Dean, but also stars of later decades, such as Sean Penn or Christian Slater.[4]

But McDonald then explains that every star is actually unique, and so this monopoly becomes a source of struggle. If McDonald is right, it is all the more interesting that contemporary reviewers saw Gould as breaking Hoffman's monopoly on his type. One said,

> In the genre of Dustin Hoffman, Gould is the sort of actor one might pass on the street everyday without attracting attention. He doesn't appear to be an actor, much less a movie star which he seems des-tined to be. Glamorous he ain't. Gould is typical of the new actor. He believes in putting reality on the screen leaving patented gestures, style and mannerisms to a generation which is not his. "I try to behave naturally and not indicate anything," Gould said of his act-ing. "I love to take chances by not doing the predictable; it gives me an opportunity to do different things until I'm found out. I think I'm good, but I don't take myself seriously."[5]

One could argue that Gould was a more natural, less affected Hoffman, that if Hoffman was known as a performer, Gould was instead known as the real thing come to stardom. One could also argue that Gould was not all that different from Hoffman, and that he made sure that his branding included fans of Benjamin Braddock, who would, it was hoped, share both his suspicion for previous models and institutions and his sufficient humor to laugh about it all. McDonald's idea that these similarities might prove a source of struggle is a useful beginning point for understanding what Gould represented as a star after *Bob & Carol & Ted & Alice*.

Bob & Carol & Ted & Alice: Textual analysis

Bob & Carol & Ted & Alice is in many ways a bedroom comedy, but it should not be seen as apolitical, because its premise is to satirize contemporary mores. To a considerable extent, Gould as Ted is the "normal" one, the control in the experiment, the only one of the four eponymous characters not to subscribe to New Age or Freudian dogma. Before 1969, comedies often featured a somewhat swarthy, ethnic man in the supporting sidekick role, a "second banana" meant to be more exaggerated than the lead, to make the lead appear normal by comparison. Gould could have played Ted this way, as the square that doesn't get it, as overtly nerdy or marked as a misfit in the way of other character actors like, say, Tony Randall in *Pillow Talk* (1959). Here, due in large part to Gould's subtle, downplayed acting, the classic comedy formula is reversed. The more WASPish, chiseled-jaw type, Robert Culp, playing Bob, is the one who dismisses traditional values, leaving it to the apparent character actor, the less traditional-looking man, to hold the line against 1960s counterculture excesses. Although Gould as Ted is hip in the manner Gamson describes, he also maintains a Kingian sense of sincerity.

Alice, Ted's wife, describes Ted as nervous and uptight, but Gould doesn't really play him that way. Instead, Gould keeps his arms and legs loose and ungrounded. In Laban terms, Gould's light-direct manner is one of a flexible, moral man: he may modify himself to his situation, but he knows what he believes. In the long bedroom scene where Ted tries to make love to Alice, he says "I'm so nervous," but his tone changes so little that it sounds like an intentional lie (which would make sense). Scenes like these reveal Ted to be written as the sort of jittery, well-meaning everyman that, say, Jack Lemmon played in *The Apartment* (1960). However, Gould does not perform like Lemmon or Lemmon's type; while Ted does dance awkwardly and occasionally stammer for words, he still has a smooth integrity and a sort of irreducible core of probity. In this way, Gould makes Ted's masculinity less nervous and more natural, more of a man with no need for apology.

In the scene that precedes the orgy, Gould keeps his hands low and his face in a perpetual closed-mouth smile just short of a smirk. Gould as Ted says, "Hey you know I'm really getting drunk ... crocked." But Ted drunk is no expressive *tour de force*; he is ever sedate, ever controlled, without any sort of tics or posture changes. With this Laban smoothness, Ted represents the rock of stability that the rest of them swirl around. Because of how Gould maintains his ironic posture, the film maintains its wry tone.

Using a naturalistic Laban light-directness, Gould's speech patterns are precise but jovial, carefully enunciated but seemingly throwaway. In many ways altering the script, Gould's body movements and voice work make Ted very similar to the "playing himself" representations of comedies from earlier decades. Thus Gould as Ted signifies the sort of man, somewhat like Dean Martin or Rock Hudson, who is letting all this silliness happen but maintaining a core of traditional morality. He is not as overtly ironic as Gamson's model of "post-studio" star suggests. The newly negotiated joke is that Gould behaves like Martin or Hudson, but his appearance is not the same. When the shaggy Gould becomes the last resister of the period's Dionysian imperatives, writer-director Paul Mazursky extends and expands the same joke that Mike Nichols played by casting Dustin Hoffman as the lead of *The Graduate*: here's the educated ethnic face of the counterculture (with an appearance comparable to Bob Dylan, Mario Savio, Jerry Rubin, or Allen

Illustration 4.1   Ted (Gould) in bed with Alice (Dyan Cannon)

Ginsburg), tempted to experiment, but all he really wants is some sort of domestic normalcy.

For a supporting role played by someone with the face of a character actor, Ted breaks Hollywood tradition by always being less animated than the other three. In one scene, Carol and Alice sit on the couch, and Alice, now deliriously happy and saucy, now expressive, begins to grill Bob about any new affairs since the last one the group discussed. Ted says "Honey, it's none of your business," in a quiet but forceful voice. After Alice peppers Bob with a few more questions, Ted crosses to his wife, saying "What are you writing a gossip column or something?" and he sits by his wife. James Naremore identifies expressive incoherence when the actor is performing something for us while the other characters are not really aware of it, like obvious guilt over an affair. But Gould barely signifies this, even when one goes back to look for it; Gould is doing none of the traditional tics of someone hiding something, the averted eyes and nervous laughter and so on. His eyes are perhaps slightly wider than usual, but he is mostly light-direct and comfortable. As Bob speaks elliptically about someone having an affair, Ted actually throws a party nut at him, but so mildly that the other characters don't appear to notice. He says "Come on Alice, that's enough," and perhaps the "playing himself" was also not to reveal Ted's indiscretions too early, because the line reads as simply a reprimand of Alice's nosiness. At the same time, he is utterly blasé as he eats, the naturalistic comfort in his own skin verifying his everyday status.

As written, Gould's relative "normalcy" can only make sense (meaning, only be funny) in terms of preserving white, middle-class, heterosexual privilege. Gould continues to behave in the smooth, unaffected (if perhaps repressed) style that Steven Cohan describes regarding 1950s stars in *Masked Men*. As the group leans toward orgy, Ted reacts to Alice's hysteria, picking up Alice's skirt as he goes, "Alice you're flipping! Will you put your clothes back on? Will you put ..." In Laban terms his tone is direct, but his body language is less weighted. Thus his rebuke is sharp but still somehow not freighted with unshakable conviction. Instead, through his passive, ungrounded manner, he seems to hold space between id and superego. Because of the flat, calm, non-exaggerated way that Ted says "Well, I do feel aroused, I can't deny that" while Carol disrobes him, Ted is confirming that an orgy would simply be a calm, measured, even conservative thing to do. Ted smiles like a child as Carol takes off his shirt, and as the four of them begin to walk into the bedroom, he says wryly, "First we'll have an orgy, then we'll go see Tony Bennett." While the other three fool around, Gould goes to the bathroom, showing off his hairy chest, feeling his weight, his movement, in Laban terms never diverging from the direct lightness, demonstrating that nothing could really change his world. As they all climb into bed, Ted tries to defuse the tension with conversation about the stock market. As Gould plays Ted, he is above it all, the establishment mobilizing the antiestablishment for a bit of fun.

Gould's light-directness, then, serves as a crucial ideological indicator. As the one who makes jokes about transcendental ideas and keeps them at a safe distance, Gould as Ted represents the film's institution-friendly perspective. The ethnic outsider remains he who is alienated, but in this case, he's alienated from his friends that are trying to become part of, or at least learn from, the counterculture. One key feature of *Bob & Carol & Ted & Alice* is that it is a satire of the pre-baby boom generation, who were too young to have served in the war but too old to fit into the "don't trust anyone over 30" generation. Hoffman, Nicholson, and Gould—along with the other men becoming star-actors at the end of the 1960s like Beatty, Hackman, Redford, Sutherland, Wilder, etc.—were in fact born in the 1930s, but many of their early films elide that fact, asking audiences to accept them as counterculture avatars. In *Bob & Carol & Ted & Alice*, Gould, in establishing his persona, takes the unusual step of representing the establishment. It is easy to imagine another actor making a show of feigning such representation, but Gould's naturalistic, light-direct style communicates complete comfort in being

Illustration 4.2 Ted (Gould) climbs into bed with Carol (Natalie Wood), Bob (Robert Culp), and Alice (Cannon)

bourgeois and upper middle class, eschewing a more critical approach. Gould's "playing himself" performance of Ted personifies alienation *from* the counterculture even as he jokes about its excesses.

It might be said that Bob and Ted encompass oppositional political readings. Bob and Ted are the names of President John F. Kennedy's two brothers, aligning the two lead men with the most celebrated and *au courant* of white ethnic liberal heroes. However, Gould's easy, seemingly effortless mantle of class comfort and respectability seems to better represent the Silent Majority. (Richard Nixon coined the term "Silent Majority" for his constituents a few weeks before *Bob & Carol & Ted & Alice* began principal photography.) In the light-direct and naturalistic manner that Gould performs Ted, he represents any enfranchised professional of the late 1960s that engages with, but remains dubious about, the counterculture. He performs the film's apolitical nature, as symbolized by a brief speech by a cameo player who tells the story of walking into a voting booth and deciding not to vote because he "wanted something more out of the day that [his] vote could have afforded" him. Gould smiles at all of it, resisting only over-indulgence, in the manner of many 1950s stars, but also in the manner that Gamson describes post-studio stars.

Like *Carnal Knowledge*, *Bob & Carol & Ted & Alice* is in many ways about the masculinity and sexual mores of the generation just before the baby boom. While many contemporary films took advantage of newly lax censorship to show young people exploring sexual freedom—like *I Am Curious (Yellow)* (1969) and *Zabriskie Point* (1970)—*Bob & Carol* took the unusual step of making its central characters into parents of young children, to emphasize their generational limbo. Alice says "Now it's sex, sex, sex ... shouldn't it just happen? It used to just happen." Ted tells a young sexy woman whom he assumes to be promiscuous, "We feel differently about sex than your generation." Ted is the only one of the four main characters not to seek advice from a man; Bob and Carol's entire narrative results from the male guru's influence in the film's outset, and Alice has a six-minute scene with her male psychiatrist. By contrast, Ted does not seek advice at all, and in a poolside scene he chastises Bob for using a double standard (Bob wouldn't want Carol to do as Bob does). In many ways, Ted exemplifies the flexible yet basically moral rectitude of many 1930s-born Americans; Gould's Laban light-direct mannerisms bring the script's conception to life. In the scene where Ted advises Bob that Bob is living by a double standard, Gould's thick, pitch-black body hair almost overwhelms the screen for more than a minute, in a way that no hirsute torso did in a Hollywood film before. If Gould's hairy chest and back can be called a motif, surely it symbolizes the warts-and-all realism of this era. If the film let this unsightly hair be visible, it will let other unsightly aspects be visible. This suggests the everyman as guarantee of authenticity, well in line with Gould's nascent star image.

The film is not as homosocially coded as a film like *Midnight Cowboy*; certainly, Bob and Ted are seen relying on their wives for their happiness and fulfillment. However, in the poolside scene, Bob encourages Ted to sleep with other women, and it is here that a homosocial trust opens up to the exclusion and humiliation of females. As Ted, Gould represents a new man who diligently tries to meet his wife's needs, right up until the point where they conflict with his. Gould walks a fine line between serving Ted's needs and Alice's; in his vocal tone and body language, he seems happier with himself than he is with Alice. It's true that, in the script, Ted never says he's sorry to Alice. But another actor might have made this seem contemptible, and Gould, by playing his morally upright self, naturalizes this dismissal of a woman. Ted winds up having an affair, while all his wife Alice gets is scorn from her therapist. Gould as Ted insists on a sort of childish smile, by which he projects passiveness, as if he is only swept up in events and going along for the ride, like many of Cohan's 1950s stars. By the end of the film, male and hetero-normative privilege is asserted, and despite Ted's poolside advice to Bob, Ted got away with the double standard. Boys will be boys, and girls will suffer, "recuperating the homosocial" as Cohan put it.

One might have thought that a film called *Bob & Carol & Ted & Alice*, promoted with two men and two women in bed together, would come close to an examination of at least bisexuality. However, Hollywood's first film with two couples together in bed made sure to squelch the barest hint of non-heterosexuality, and Gould is entirely complicit with this. The script never suggests any attraction between Bob and Ted, but it's easy to imagine other actors playing it that way, by lingering on each other's faces, by furrowing their brow at strange new feelings, or by some sort of subtle half-wink or half-smile during mutual dialogue. Not only does Gould not bother with this sort of performance, he goes beyond the script just to prove how straight Ted is. This is seen in Gould's first scene, when Culp as Bob echoes the words of his transcendental retreat, "We really do love you," and Gould replies "We love you too." Gould lowers his shoulder just a bit and flutters his eyelashes, the classic coding of the straight man insulting effeminate behavior. The scene ends similarly, after everyone has opened up about their very enounced feelings, with Gould as Ted announcing a new very important feeling; he brings his shoulders down, juts out his lip very slightly, holds in his breath, and then allows a devilish smile to break as he says "I feel ... you should pay for the check." In Laban terms, his light-direct manner is one that will never countenance looking foolish, and Gould convinces that this includes hetero-normative behavior. Unlike even the stubborn Jonathan played by Nicholson in *Carnal Knowledge*, Gould's body language does not indicate that Ted has changed in any way by the end of the film. At any point, Gould could have chosen to have Ted look at Bob and at least giggle; if that happened, the editors didn't include it. In the orgy culmination, after some awkward kissing, everyone seems to call it off. They just open their eyes and look at each other, Ted as innocent and bewildered as any of them. As the film concludes, all four of them leave the hotel; they hold hands with and look lovingly at their spouses. Gould as Ted was and is hardly the nervous person Alice described; instead, he was right all along. Gould looked like something new but acted like something very familiar: he claimed heterosexual leading man coding for himself. As it happened, the critics were complicit.

Bob & Carol & Ted & Alice and 1969: Critical reception

In 1969, the press generally praised *Bob & Carol & Ted & Alice*, and named Gould as a crucial and representative element. Gould's newly minted discursive construct was described almost as the counterculture come to life on the big screen. Gould was also associated with some of the most praised talent in other fields. *The New York Times* aligned Gould's taste with critical artists:

> Gould plans to make movies out of Bernard Malamud's "The Assistant," Jules Feiffer's "Little Murders," and Arnold Weinstein's "The Days and Nights of Beebee Fenstermaker." Elliott is especially excited about "Murders," not only because he will probably act in it (he had the lead in the short-lived Broadway version), but because Robert Benton and David Newman are doing the script, and Jean-Luc Godard will direct.

After associating Gould with canonized edgy talent, the *Times* quoted Gould at his most hubristic:

> I'm the hottest thing in Hollywood right now. ... By the end of the year I'll have made four movies. Four movies in one year—that's not bad, right? I always knew there were things going on in me, that

I had something to express. I don't take the success seriously, though. But I'm pleased for my friends. There are a lot of people I want to be able to help—actors, writers and directors. And now I'm finally in a position to.[6]

The truth was that he made four movies partly because he was one of the only actors in 1969 to sign a multi-film deal, and he was now tied to the weakened studio system in a manner that would not suit his image as an apostle of freedom. Gould could hardly say "Four movies in one year—because I have to finish this Fox contract I probably shouldn't have signed in the first place." Instead, he contributed to publicity that, as we'll see, pretended not to be publicity. He was the rising star as anti-star, the actor-artist as a badge of authenticity, a way to show that Hollywood was now "getting it."

Elliott Gould's face became familiar to gossip columns when he attended the Oscars in April 1969 with his then-wife, Barbra Streisand, on the night that she won Best Actress for *Funny Girl* (1968). The next six months saw some degree of press speculation about Gould and Streisand's apparent legal separation. Gould's most extraordinary sign of "arriving" was probably an article from *The New York Times* dated October 5, 1969, headlined "Now Who's the Greatest Star?" *Bob & Carol & Ted & Alice* had only just opened the New York Film Festival, and wasn't even yet playing in New York, but the nation's paper of record was already racing to displace a star, Barbra Streisand, that it had spent most of the decade building up. It was as though *The New York Times* was afraid of getting left behind the latest crazy fad, the newest thing for the youth audience.[7]

In another article written well before the release of *Bob & Carol & Ted & Alice*, James Bacon in the *Los Angeles Herald-Examiner* introduced the most common narrative about Gould as an emergent star, namely how he might avoid becoming Norman Maine to Barbra Streisand's Vicki Lester (art imitated life when Streisand remade *A Star is Born* in 1976). Bacon's article was just one of many at this time to imply homosocial coding, by implication reversing more familiar feminist logic: Bacon implied that behind every successful woman was a man. Bacon listed the many projects that Gould has in development, and marveled at Gould's apparent luck:

He's playing male leads because he came to Hollywood at the right time. Twenty years ago—even five—he would have been cast as a heavy. But this is the Lee Marvin–Dustin Hoffman era in the movies. So Elliott plays romantic leads, mustache and all.[8]

The effect is to suggest that Gould is someone that the counterculture can trust. These articles show that Gould benefitted from a remarkable amount of "star build-up" (a term the press then decried) before *Bob & Carol & Ted & Alice* had even come to theaters, remarkable because Gould was marketed precisely as the sort of star that didn't conform to the old star-making rules. The authors of the promotional articles showed no traces of appreciating that irony as they constructed Gould's star image.

Upon release, *Bob & Carol & Ted & Alice* was universally understood as a response to the counterculture, and celebrated as an updating and revisiting of sexual taboos in a confusing time of sexual revolution and post-Hays Code cinema. The *Hollywood Reporter*'s headline called *Bob & Carol* the "'Go-See' Movie of the Year,"[9] and two other influential reviewers secured the film's place as a summarization of daily life, and by extension, Gould as representative of the current mood. Gould's key role was received quite warmly, as all involved had anticipated since the producers chose to showcase Gould's long scene in industry previews early in the year. By the time the press got around to reviewing Gould in *Bob & Carol & Ted & Alice*, they did indeed find him the same sort of brilliant, unaffected, realistic actor that they had already discursively constructed. One said, "Gould, in his second screen appearance, blossoms as a young comedian of subtle resources and compelling talent as Ted, the diffident philanderer."[10] His acting skills were even favorably contrasted to the other members of the cast: "Where the others slip too often into caricatures he never stops being a real up-tight person insecure about everything including the smell of his breath."[11] And: "Culp is his usual, breezy self, but is somewhat upstaged by Gould, whose facial expressions match the wit of the screenplay."[12] The general tone was summarized thusly: "Gould, the one most on an even keel sexually, decides to go along only after much prodding. Plainly his heart is not in this sort of thing. ... Gould, playing a somewhat oafish character, scores heavily in his second movie role."[13] Gould was clearly positioned as a thriving man of his time.

For reviewers, alienation in *Bob & Carol & Ted & Alice* took the form of seeing the absurdity of contemporary life and showing that you "get it," meaning societal disillusionment with farce attached. In this regard, Gould clearly excelled. In *The New Yorker*, Pauline Kael's review of the film took several thousand words to explain why some reviewers attack a movie for being entertaining, how filmmakers tried and failed at revue humor in recent years, and why, despite some problems, *Bob & Carol* was "the liveliest American comedy so far this year." Though the film to her resembled a 1950s farce (as did *The Graduate*), "this movie is made up of what was left out of the optimistic Doris Day comedies." Like Schickel, she felt "we" respond to comedy like this, which she aligned with Mike Nichols' and Elaine May's routines, because "We laugh at the tiny, almost imperceptible hostilities that suddenly explode, because we recognize that we're tied up in knots about small issues rather than big ones." For Kael, Mazursky took the best aspects of TV and made them work on film, which is "a bit more unusual than it may seem." She made it clear that Gould was the essence of real: "[W]e *like* Gould—not just because of his performance but because of an assumption, which is probably false, but which this kind of acting imposes, that he is what he's playing."[14] Kael in this period often spearheaded the assault of the Hollywood Renaissance on previous norms by dividing audiences into those that "got it" and otherwise, and here she clearly distinguished the film as an admirable upstart. And she promoted Gould's "playing himself" as the correct sort of performance, one that saw absurdity and chose to laugh.

Gould aligned well with Hoffman and Nicholson as sympathetic to the general anomie of the counterculture. The *Los Angeles Times* called Gould "kind of existentialist himself."[15] In one interview, with the subtitle "Today movie heroes have to be real—and he is," Gould explained:

> I used to look at the films of the 50s, and see the kinds of people that the movie companies, the Establishment, would project, to create a certain kind of glamorous image, and I used to think, "Oh my God, there really are those special people. I could never look like that, and I could never act like that," because they acted in a certain specific, staccato, definite kind of way. But life isn't definite, and I think people are getting much more curious and sophisticated now, and want to see them*selves* personified, rather than creations of Hollywood.[16]

Gould thus positioned himself as an amalgam of new realism and general discontent with society, in fact asserting that the two are mutually inclusive. Another article agreed:

> He has become more "natural" in appearance (sloppy, some would say) as she has become more sophisticated. ... The five-day growth of beard was necessary for his part in "Mash"—but not the yellow oilskin windbreaker, striped sweatshirt, and khaki slacks. He is a man, as he reminded me, who is "very opinionated." "Things for effect," he said, "are questionable. Actors dress for effect. Actors date for effect. It all suddenly becomes real to them and they're affected. I'm sort of awkward. Real awkwardness is grace."[17]

Awkwardness was grace, the deviant was the normal, and the unaffected, anti-institutional man was the real man. *The New York Times* called Gould "Portnoy personified,"[18] associating him with the lead character of a book that had only come out that year. *Portnoy's Complaint* would go on to become Philip Roth's most successful novel, the story of a tense, bottled-up man who expresses his extreme sexual frustrations to his psychoanalyst. Many promotional articles mentioned that Gould was in psychoanalysis. Gould represented the more "normal" person in an abnormal time of sexual licentiousness, a Rough Rebel that everyone could understand and laugh with. He was a triumph of everyman humor, and of marketing.

By Gould's time, a key discursive strategy for appealing to educated youth was to talk candidly about acting in a way that previous generations hadn't. Gould told the press that he approached one of his first scenes on *Bob & Carol & Ted & Alice*, where he had to eat abalone out of shells, like a Method actor, but after eleven takes, he realized that being a Method actor wasn't as effective as he'd heard. Gould said he smoked actual pot during a scene where the characters were smoking pot, but for this, Gould credited hearing the news that day that Nixon had defeated Humphrey in the 1968 presidential election.[19] Gould created a star image of dualisms, being both Method and flexible, and being a pot smoker that waited until he had a reason to smoke it. Gould's assiduous star image construction was worthy of any build-up from the studio era. For example, Gould talked about the moment of filming the orgy. As the actors sat in bed waiting for direction, Mazursky apparently said to them, "Just do what you want. Whatever feels right."[20] Gould told the reporter than when he heard this, it scared him. This seems a bit unlikely, but helps to cement Gould's "everyman" *bona fides*. *Time* played along when it wrote,

> When Gould got ready for the orgy in *Bob & Carol* by dousing himself with deodorant, gargling and climbing into bed in his undershorts and executive-length socks, millions of sexually unliberated men and women not only laughed at his unease but were moved and comforted by it.

Gould said,

> I recall there was some degree of manipulation going on for the four of us to physically interact ... but I couldn't do it. Bob would have liked to have, and I think that Dyan was hysterical enough to perhaps go on and use her hysteria, but the anchor there was Natalie.[21]

Yet Gould made it clear that his reverence for Natalie Wood kept the scene from spilling over into something that might have been too ribald. Thus Gould was careful to convey respect for both the previous kind of Hollywood cinema, as associated with Wood, and respect for middle-class traditions, including a rejection of homosexuality and infidelity in one swoop. With these statements, Gould conveyed that he was not just another crazy hippie, and that, somewhat like Hoffman and Nicholson, he respected both sides of the so-called generation gap. Hollywood would never get any closer to making "counterculture stars" than it did with Hoffman, Nicholson, and Gould, and statements like these demonstrate that their shrewdness and careerism were absolutely complicit in compromising Hollywood's version of that culture.

Gould's *bona fides* as a man were also asserted. Just as *Time* had used its first cover photo to put Dustin Hoffman apparently in bed with Mia Farrow, the *Los Angeles Herald-Examiner*, in a promotional article for Gould, "Gould Blossoms As Actor," featured a photo of Gould in bed with Natalie Wood, his torso hair on full display, in a shot all the more notable as publicity because it's not actually from the movie. As in Hoffman's case, the photo was probably unimaginable in the Hays Code era. Also as in Hoffman's case, an icon to the prior generation (Farrow being ex-Mrs. Sinatra, Wood having starred in *Rebel Without a Cause* (1955) and *West Side Story* (1961)) was matched with a new kind of young ethnic anti-star, at least partly to show how hip and swinging everyone was. For the first half of 1969, Gould was best known to Americans as the husband that accompanied Streisand to the Oscars; now, reports had them separated, and another legend was already in bed with him (or at least his star image). Gould managed to tie rebelliousness to disdain for the marriage contract: "Me, I don't believe in any standards. I believe in doing what you want to do."[22] This sort of celebration of freedom at the expense of loyalty to a romantic partner is well in line with the Sedgwickian homosocial.

Star libidinousness aligned well with articles that promoted *Bob & Carol* as a film where the synergy of the actors combined to great effect. To *The New York Times*, Natalie Wood made fun of her former diva behavior:

> When you start out ... you have great fun making them put all that in your contract: "I want so-and-so or I'm not playing!" ... There's a time for that. I've had mine. ... The whole "star" business seems so far away. ... I'm [into] the really reals, they're what I believe in.[23]

Gould's then-wife, Barbra Streisand, visited the set, just as *Funny Girl* was becoming a smash success, to ask Wood about how to get these kinds of perks put into her contract, distancing her from Wood's "really reals." Who were the really reals? The interview isn't clear on that point. But presumably they were the avatars of authenticity, the everymen like Gould who didn't have anything like the kind of perks Wood described. Wood, like Elizabeth Taylor in *Who's Afraid of Virginia Woolf?* (1966), was de-glamorizing her star persona in a way that would have been very unusual in the 1950s, and even more so today.[24] Many scholars write of "masculinity in crisis," but this is far less true of Gould's nascent stardom. According to articles like these, Gould's swinging, ironic, disaffected version of masculinity was thriving. In his rave in *Life*, Richard Schickel made it clear that this film shone an unparalleled light on the zeitgeist:

> There are scenes in B&C&T&A that will come to seem, in memory, the perfect measures of our contemporary domestic desperations in this "transitional" era. The best of them is an in-bed quarrel between Ted and Alice that may be the longest—and is surely the funniest—such scene in Hollywood's history. It summarizes so many issues that cause us anguish and anxiety—the statistics of Kinsey and Masters, the psychological by-products of the pill and the pursuit of prosperity, the half-digested advice we have received about the new ways men and women are supposed to relate to one another. It is a great scene—at once hilarious, discomfiting and, finally, a little sad and more than a little thought-provoking.[25]

Schickel made it clear that Gould signified the new man as well as anyone, basically confirming to the hip that this film would not insult their intelligence. Like other reviewers, Schickel saw *Bob & Carol & Ted & Alice* as a perfect summary of contemporary insecurities between the sexes, and Gould in particular was widely praised as the sort of man we could all relate to. Perhaps onscreen masculinity might have been in some sort of crisis, but as a star, Gould represented the new masculinity at high tide. Somehow, this tide rose even higher in 1970.

*M*A*S*H*: Textual analysis

In his light-direct Laban combination of righteousness and looseness, Gould represents the alienation and farce that is central to *M*A*S*H*. Of all films of the period, *M*A*S*H* asks to be understood as starring a cast

of "everymen." No film before or since has used the word "introduc-
ing" as many times in the credits (sixteen), a sort of badge of untainted
Bazinian realism. The overlapping dialogue is also a newer mark of
authenticity. Onscreen, Gould as Trapper John appears unwashed and
doesn't strain to be heard, fitting into this new milieu seamlessly. Less
than two years before, another war film, *When Eagles Dare* (1968),
featured Clint Eastwood and Richard Burton and their female co-stars
in coiffed hair and spotless makeup after jumping out of airplanes.
Gould, as we have come to know him, would never have fit into such
a film. Through his understated, light-direct, playing-himself naturalism, Elliott Gould represents the normal man in a representation of
war that was equal parts realism and farce. If director Robert Altman's
many statements are any indication, the shooting script was mostly
improvised by actors given a great deal of freedom—thus we are invited
to conclude that Trapper is chiefly Gould's creation. As Trapper, Gould
offers indices of both moral authority and whimsy, hybridizing King
and Gamson's models, while capturing and extending the film's central
absurdist theme.

Gould specifically performs the key theme of alienation paired with
humor. After Gould as Trapper hits Burns, Colonel Blake says he's under
arrest and must be confined to his quarters. Trapper uses a strong-direct
Laban thrust as he says "Oh Henry are you kidding?" A moment later, a
younger officer begins to tell Trapper that he's under arrest, and Gould
just walks past him, saying, "Oh come on, cut it out Vollmer." He
might have almost skipped past Vollmer; instead, in Laban's language,
he is weighted, grounded, suggesting a man with deep convictions.
Though Trapper flouts authority, he establishes himself as something of
an authority. His arm gestures and vocal tones are utterly natural, suggesting "playing himself," and Gould's somewhat intellectual persona
projects the air of someone who knows at least as much as the guy
telling him what to do. This aligns Trapper/Gould with the progressive aspects of the counterculture. J. Hoberman later wrote that Gould
was the "first to sport the luxuriant Zapata mustache popularized
by the righteous outlaws of SDS,"[26] and indeed, in the time between
the filming of *Bob & Carol* (October–December 1968) and *M*A*S*H*
(May–August 1969), the Students for a Democratic Society had become
infamous when they invaded the Columbia administrative offices. But
the SDS was sincerely progressive (aligning with Barry King's definition), not absurdist; Gould, by contrast, took "radical chic" to a farcical
and sometimes problematic place. Altman later said, "I think Elliott did
a lot of thinking about Groucho Marx when he was doing this film."[27]

Indeed, Gould improvises the line "Say the magic word, make a hundred dollars" in a voice just like Groucho (the line is from Groucho's talk show "You Bet Your Life"). Groucho Marx could and did make fun of anything and everything, but was hardly known for intractable antipathy toward society. Gould provides deterministic assistance in taking the film from what might have been progressive disenfranchisement to a more playful absurdism.

Another example is seen when Gould wears an Uncle Sam hat and naturalistically enjoys himself as the troops sing his praises. Because of Houlihan taking offense at Trapper's violent outburst, as Colonel Blake explains it, Blake must postpone Trapper's promotion. Houlihan is then positioned as emasculator of Trapper, and Gould more than rises to the challenge. The postponed promotion barely lasts a scene, and minutes later, the company enters the mess hall carrying and embracing Trapper as their new chief. Conspicuously *including* some company women, they sing "hail to the chief" with changed lyrics: "Hail to the chief, he's the best of all the surgeons, he needs a queen to satisfy his urges, Hail to the chief, he's the best of all the trappers, he needs a queen to sit upon his lappers." Gould had many vocal and gestural options here; Trapper looks at Houlihan and says with a devilish gruffness of entitlement, "No, no, no, that one. Bring me that one over there. That one. The sultry bitch with the fire in her eyes. Take her clothes off. I want that one, yes, yes. Take her clothes off, and bring her to me now. Now." It's difficult for today's readers to really appreciate the power of the word "bitch"; it wasn't common in Hollywood prior to 1970. Gould's "playing himself" is very convincing as a lascivious man happy to use his power to put a woman in her place. None of the company audibly rejects Trapper's request (though Houlihan leaves the area), and thus the objectification of Houlihan stands, until it gets worse. As Molly Haskell said later, "As funny as the twosome are, there is a cruel, elitist streak to their games. The humor is not so much that of subversion of meaningless routine as of the tricks smart schoolboys play on their less adept comrades."[28] Haskell here identifies the Sedgwickian homosocial, men at play to the exclusion of women. On one level, it's all in good fun, which is part of what makes the misogyny less overt and more corrosive.

In Laban terms, Gould is light and direct even as he smiles like the Cheshire Cat (not unlike Jack Nicholson). He might have been more weighted, or more forceful, to suggest a sort of desperation. Instead, his casual whimsy suggests that Trapper is rightfully to the manor born. His Kingian moral authority suggests that the aggrandizement of Trapper

Illustration 4.3   Trapper John (Gould) sporting the "luxuriant Zapata mustache"

is natural, even fair. Instead of antagonizing the establishment, Gould suggests that he would enjoy a new establishment with him as the leader. Gould uses his light-direct performance to make Trapper personify the idea "the king is dead, long live the king." Gould's Laban gliding suggests that however much people may rebel, they still want a leader who will wear old symbols. Gould makes his eyes shifty in a confident way, and says imperiously, "No food, no food, sex, I want sex, sex, bring me some sex." It is easy to imagine an actor playing this with sarcastic exaggeration, or alternatively, using a bewildered sense of humility, but Gould's comfort suggests that Trapper is at ease with being made king. As played by Gould, Trapper enjoys flouting authority at every turn, but unlike, say, Dean in *Rebel Without a Cause* (1955), he's also determined to impose his own Dionysian standards on everyone else. Through his sly, almost fey gestures, Gould is like a counterculture dauphin, and the audience is clearly meant to sympathize. He mutes progressive critique by suggesting his own ascendance. He is neither as sincere as King suggests nor quite as insincere as Gamson's examples.

Gould's command, "Take her clothes off!", is foreshadowing: scenes later, when Trapper gives the cue to drop the wall of Houlihan's shower stall, the loyal men obey and Margaret is naked and humiliated in front of the camp. According to several sources, this really was a prank on the actress playing Margaret (Sally Kellerman), thus her horrified reaction to her naked exposure is quite genuine. Gould triggers this with a fey gesture, a dropping of a handkerchief. His Laban light-direct manner is specifically somewhat like a dauphin, imperious and catty, very different from how other actors might have approached the same role. This is also seen in the scene set in the mess hall the morning after Trapper has humiliated Margaret by broadcasting her lovemaking to Frank Burns on the camp public address system. After bumbling into her with pronounced exaggeration, Trapper acts stereotypically effeminate when he says, "Well, what's the matter with her today?" to Hawkeye. In *Bob & Carol*, this lisp lasted only one line, but here, Gould carries on for about half a minute the caricature of the swishy homosexual fashion designer that reserves special animus for females, particularly when he follows up with the sinuously spoken line, "She's a bitch." It's as though Hollywood's old censorship rules were merely repressing a hatred for women that could now take full flower. Gould makes this sarcastic misogyny appear quite natural, even inherent to the war. It turns out that it was anything but. J.M. Kenny later interviewed real Korean War doctors, and claimed that every doctor reported that such mistreatment of women could never have happened in real life.[29]

I have now stated repeatedly that the Rough Rebels were not seen to represent repressed homosexuality in the manner of the 1950s rebels, that while Brando, Dean, and Clift were sometimes understood as bisexual on and offscreen, Hoffman, Nicholson, and Gould (and their colleagues not extensively profiled here, like Alan Arkin, Richard Benjamin, Gene Wilder, Gene Hackman, and Warren Oates) did not tell the press of any bisexuality and did not perform it onscreen. Although it is tempting to say that Gould's occasionally lispy line readings as Trapper only reinforce dominant heterosexuality, it must be admitted that more is at play in *M*A*S*H*. Like *Midnight Cowboy*, the film certainly privileges male–male companionship over male–female companionship, but also like *Midnight Cowboy*, it seems to go a bit beyond the Sedgwickian homosocial to position heterosexuality as a problematic construct. The script includes the almost lyrical line "If a man isn't a man anymore, what's he got that's worth living for?" spoken by Painless, the dentist who has half the men in camp (but not Trapper) lining up to sneak a peek at his large penis. Painless says "I'm a fairy," and Hawkeye "cures" him by getting the local sexy nurse to sleep with him. This is indeed hetero-normative, but the film manages to call the entire episode into question, emphasizing the artifice and silliness that attend these "conversion" shenanigans.

Illustration 4.4 Hawkeye (Donald Sutherland) and Trapper (Gould) – "something about a relationship between men"

Aiding this artifice is a very special friendship that seems to blossom between Hawkeye and Trapper, rendering reports of their offscreen alliance against Altman no surprise. Donald Sutherland later referred to their pairing off:

> We were trying to be as true as we could be, and together I felt that Elliott and I captured something about a relationship between men, and it's hard for me to have relationships with men, I thought that we were able to capture something that was evocative of the spirit of fellas in service.[30]

At the end of the film, when Hawkeye gets orders to leave, he lingers with Trapper, as though not sure if a handshake goodbye is really enough. As throughout the process, Altman and the script gave Gould considerable latitude; Gould chose to keep his body language subdued, his voice low, and his light-direct manner suggestive of a spurned lover. In an earlier scene, when the duo gets "a chance to go to Japan with your golf clubs," Gould grabs his friend by the arm and says "Come on Shirley" in a throwaway line that was almost certainly improvised. Gould does not, as he easily might have, play that line with a put-on swish. Instead his voice appears to be in his normal register (based on many of his other roles and TV interviews), like a real lover. By maintaining this naturalistic milieu through what Laban might have called "smooth-smear" gestures, Gould and Sutherland show something more than just heterosexual best friends, almost more than Sedgwick's homosocial codes.

In other scenes, Gould's "playing himself" style abets a nuanced take on masculinity as a sort of game. In the scene where Trapper calls Houlihan a "sultry bitch," when the camp throws him a party, Gould audibly sings the words in unison with them, "He took his orders and shoved them up his rectum." In another scene, when Burns attacks Hawkeye, Gould as Trapper says in a strong, indirect manner, "Watch out for your goodies, Hawkeye. That man is a sex maniac, I don't think Hot Lips satisfied him. Don't let him kiss you Hawkeye." On one level, Trapper is insulting Frank by calling him gay, but the fact that Gould lets his eyes shift around suggests that he is only doing this for approval, and that such insults are only part of studied artifice. In another scene, Gould as Trapper tells the story of the stallion Man of War being put out to stud when he retired, and after having 120 to 130 foals, "When he died they did an autopsy and they found out he was a raving queen. ... No that's a little-known fact, but it's the truth." Gould might have played this line with an obviously false sarcasm or frat boy bluster, but he actually sounds more quietly sincere. Through this sustained Laban light-direct sincerity, Gould helps make *M*A*S*H* less of a straightforward assertion of patriarchy, and more of an exploration of many facets of male power and preferences. Critics, however, tended to miss this nuance, and instead focus on Gould as straight everyman and characteristic symbol of *M*A*S*H*.

*M*A*S*H* and 1970: Critical reception

Gould was named in the press as representative of the thematic and formal aspects of *M*A*S*H*. This was best symbolized by the many posters that used Trapper's devil-may-care Hawaiian shirt. His everyman, "unlikely-looking" credentials helped sell the film's claims to absurdism. Gould helped introduce America to an acute yet whimsical form of alienation that would, in its adapted-for-TV form, win more awards than any other sitcom in American television history. As a broad summary, it's fair to say that the press received the characters' signification as: people need us to be serious, and we sometimes will be, but the whole thing is crazy anyway, so let's all goof around as much as we can. This was something of an encapsulation of the cinematic movement in general.

Gould was strongly identified with both the "authenticity" (the preferred word of Charles Champlin in the *Los Angeles Times*) and the generally swarthy, rebellious themes of *M*A*S*H*. For *Variety*, Gould *was* the movie:

> Elliott Gould, Donald Sutherland and Tom Skerritt head an extremely effective, low-keyed cast of players whose skillful subtlety eventually rescue an indecisive union of script and technique. In Gould as the totally unmilitary but arrogantly competent, supercool young battlefield surgeon, a reluctant draftee whose credo is let's get the job done and knock off all this Army mack, the film finds its focus and its statement, after an uneven start. Problem is the mixture of realism with the old style broad comedic technique that has lately scuttled a succession of unfunny comedies.[31]

The article clearly meant to refer to the combination of blood-soaked patients and jokey banter as problematic, but by identifying Gould as the film's "focus and statement," the article rightly suggested that Gould represented his own problematic combination of "realism" and "broad comedic technique." Altman said that the operating room blood scenes "gave that film credence," adding, "You have to pay for your laughs."[32] They also gave Gould's star image credence as someone who knows pain enough to joke about it, someone who is right to blend disillusionment with superciliousness.

Generally, however, critics agreed with Fox's promotional material, which said: "[T]hey are the best surgeons in the Far East and they are hell-raising lunatics who make a shambles of army bureaucracy. ... Underlying the ribald, irreverent humor is the story of how men survive the tragic waste of war and how, in the midst of such destruction, they strive, sometimes ridiculously, to cling to their sanity and humanity."[33] Sure enough, reviewers fell in line with establishing the antiestablishment nature of the enterprise: "MASH gives a more effective and realistic picture of an aspect of war than all the heroics of a John Wayne."[34] Another: "'M*A*S*H' is irreverent of many things: war, sex, bureaucracy, military decorum, but never of the unquenchable spirit of its people ... [the film] retains an extraordinary sense of actuality through the use of improvisational delivery which gives latitude to a carefully wrought script."[35] And *Life* perhaps best summarized the style and themes when it wrote that *M*A*S*H*

> represents the first time in our movie history that soldiers and doc-tors spoke as surely they must under the pressure of war. ... But the good guys are not just a bunch of merry pranksters. They are best understood, I think, as Robin Hoods of rationalism, robbing from the rich stockpiles of madness controlled by the people who manage wars and doling it out in lifesaving doses to the little guys caught up in the mess. Vicious in their persecution of the pompous, they have a wonderful tenderness with outcasts and innocents.[36]

Gould, as a leader of the "Robin Hoods of rationalism," was a fly in the ointment, an upstart against the system, but often closer to ribaldry than rebellion.

Reviewers lauded Gould's performance as a key aspect of the film's greatness. One said, "If Elliott Gould keeps selecting and performing in films the way he has thus far, people may start going to pictures just because he is in them."[37] (The incredulity is what makes it "anti-star" press—star-making for a presumably cynical age.) Another: "[T]he performers, most of whom are newcomers to me, are superb, starting from the top with Sutherland, Gould (who really does seem to be Hollywood's comic hope, just as the publicity says), Tom Skerritt."[38] Yet another: "Trapper, pungently played by Elliott Gould, is a fur-bearing slob with the skills of a Christiaan Barnard and the instincts of a por-nographer."[39] Gould hardly raised any objections to being identified with the antiestablishment nature of his characters, and indeed often welcomed it. *Motion Picture Exhibitor* agreed that M*A*S*H was "Gould's show" and established his anti-institutional credentials by identifying him with literary greatness and representational power:

> Elliott Gould gives his best performance to date as the eccentric, cyni-cal surgeon, a characterization which will remind many of Yossarian in Joseph Heller's novel, "Catch 22." Gould carries on his own private guerrilla war with the establishment in an effort to preserve some enduring human values in a world seemingly gone mad. He is ably assisted by Donald Sutherland and Tom Skerritt, both of whom give sensitive performances. 'M*A*S*H,' though, is Gould's show. In the first three films of an already distinguished career ("The Night They Raided Minsky's" and "Bob & Carol & Ted & Alice"), the young actor proves himself to be a very funny man. In 'M*A*S*H,' his comic role

is embellished with serious overtones as his sardonic exterior only thinly disguises a basically sentimental emotional personality. The image of a shivering Gould huddled up in his sleeping bag is a haunting one. For some, it will sum up the "angst" of 1950's America.[40]

Mike Nichols complained on the DVD commentary track of *Catch-22* (1970) that his film adaptation of the famously antiestablishment Joseph Heller novel was repeatedly compared unfavorably to *M*A*S*H*, dooming its box office.[41] Here the media anointed Gould as *Catch-22*'s Yossarian, the disillusioned captain who sees life for the farce it really is. Gould was now Portnoy *and* Yossarian, the modern subversive that is too clever to truly advocate revolution.

Some critics pointed out that the system remained not all that challenged, like Richard Corliss:

> [T]he film is no more anti-war than "The Graduate" was anti-bourgeois. ... Neither group [of characters] is even vaguely political, and neither film is remotely radical. Indeed, 'M*A*S*H''s heroes are experts at beating the system, not changing the system. ... And the air they exude is less the crackling atmosphere of an SDS meeting than the stale beer smell of a Sigma Nu frat party. All the sideburns, swish gestures and scatological jive can't conceal their panty-raid sensibilities.[42]

Corliss saw that absurdism was not true resistance. The idea of beating the system but not changing the system became the key theme of the new films, crucially enabled by Gould's performance.

Richard Schickel in *Life* celebrated the hetero-normative nature of *M*A*S*H* without irony when he wrote, "They manage a miraculous cure for a dentist who is suicidal over an imagined loss of virility,"[43] and John Mahoney in the *Hollywood Reporter* was only slightly less sanguine: "If one could stop laughing long enough, he would have to admit that the overly pious, the officious, the prudish among the film's company of surgical workers fall victims to some very cruel jokes, but that is as natural to the comedy as it is to the survival of the men and women who perform their jobs with pride and efficiency."[44] In a sign of how widely hailed *M*A*S*H* was, only months after its release did an article in a major periodical discuss its sexism, in a piece called "I Admit It, I Didn't Like M*A*S*H":

> 'M*A*S*H''s trio of "heroes" (Andrew Sarris's words) are also bully boys ... like hip vampires, they'll go for the jugular only when they see it

exposed, preferably on a redneck ... the characters [are] not caricatures, they're meant to be real. ... In what other movie have we been
expected to sympathize with the torturers, however likable, and hoot
at the victims, however venal? ... But, the movie argues, the Swamp-
men are performing therapy on Hot Lips. And sure enough, Nurse
Houlihan is soon liberated, by sleeping with one of the heroes. The
effects of this liberation are not entirely positive, however: a woman
who, when repressed, displayed a tremulous but innate dignity, suddenly becomes an idiot when freed. The movie's idea of redemption is
to turn her, and all the other women in the outfit, into affable imbe-
ciles who are only to be trusted with passing the scalpel, cheerleading
at a ball game, and acting as acquiescent bedmates.[45]

This article from *The New York Times* may have been the first media
source to make clear that the masculinity featured in the new style of
films was often hostile to women. A letter to the editor, nearly a year
later, reacting to Vincent Canby's Top Ten list for 1970, made the same
point:

Women in "M*A*S*H" are regarded not as people but as collections
of sexual parts to be patronized and humiliated for laughs. That the
blatant misogyny of this film has been so blandly accepted by the
critics is scary; that Canby should call it "unequivocally funny" is
obscene.[46]

A reader was ahead of most critics in seeing the movement's misogynist
nature.

While Hoffman's roles were often distinguished by their differences,
Gould's prior associations were simply noted in reviews for *M*A*S*H*:
"Elliott Gould, of Bob & Carol & Ted & Alice, is a heart surgeon here—
possibly the most amusing heart surgeon ever."[47] "Elliott Gould, fresh
from his huge success in Bob & Carol & Ted & Alice, is the best—and
best-known—in a bunch of zany medics." Another: "Gould, with Bob &
Carol & Ted & Alice, has already become a big name, but his fine performance here shows that his hilarious Ted was no fluke."[48] It was the lack of
differentiation between parts that distinguished Gould from Hoffman
and, to a lesser extent, from Nicholson. This lack eventually harmed
Gould's career. However, with four films in theaters (*M*A*S*H*, *Getting
Straight* (1970), *Move* (1970), and *I Love My Wife* (1970)) toward the end
of 1970, Gould was certified by Quigley as the Number One Star of the
year.

In 1970, Gould had what can only be called an *annus mirabilis*; even as some of his films stalled at the box office, still his every move and gesture were seen as representative of the new kind of movie star. *Playboy*, whose headline called him "antiheroic," explicitly identified him with "reality" over "fantasy":

> In short, he is no one's vision of a matinee idol. ... At a time when the public is demanding reality rather than fantasy on the screen, his spectacular rise exemplifies the changing thrust of the motion-picture industry. Twenty years ago, Gould's quirky virility and radicalized appearance would have made him, at best, a movie heavy.[49]

Gould verified the ordinary over the extraordinary, as *Time* made clear in its September cover story on him:

> He embodies an inner need to be hip at the risk of seeming silly, the struggle not to give in to the indignity and/or insanity of contemporary life. ... Gould is more than just a synergistic reaction between the era and the audience ... he is a prime example of the kind of film star who needs a wave length more than a makeup man. ... The way he looks is part of the Gould effect. It is not so much that he seems so ordinary as that he seems so little like a star. His clothes, whether custom-made suits of crumpled fatigues, never quite fit; his hair could use a trim.[50]

Time quoted Jules Feiffer, who aligned Gould (and Arkin and Hoffman) with a "new mythology," and Mel Stuart who claimed that "inserting a personal quality over the role" was a thing of the past, though *Time* was perspicacious enough to question this, claiming that audiences identified with Gould's personal quality. Even as Gould's precise performative nature was contested, his type's dominance was not.

Time compared Gould to John Garfield (Sklar's third City Boy), because of their "distinctly urban identity," unfavorably comparing Garfield's strut to Gould's stumble, but favorably comparing Gould's reduction of his antagonists to "absurdity." The clear implication was that Gould represented a realism that Garfield never quite attained. *Time* anointed Gould the Urban Don Quixote, "the archetype of the urban man struggling to stay afloat in a swelling sea of neuroses."[51] Without captions, the article's photos from his five most recent films all showed Gould seducing or getting in bed with a nubile young female. It seems unlikely that any *Time* cover story on any previous star ever featured quite so prurient a layout. *Time* confirmed the Rough Rebel as Don Juan. If the ethnic everyman might have been considered a fluke after *The Graduate*, this *Time* story can be considered the discursive triumph of the type: Elliott Gould as the dominant sort of star and man.

Garfield was not the only former star to suffer by comparison. The *International Herald-Tribune* wrote incredulously:

> Gary Cooper would have been recognized. Clark Gable would have been recognized. ... There is no question that Elliott Gould is a superstar. But the word no longer means what it used to mean. The old superstars were so handsome they were almost beautiful. Look at Tyrone Power. Look at Errol Flynn. Elliott Gould is not pretty. The old superstars were usually assigned their roles by superproducers such as Jack Warner or Harry Cohn, all of whom are now dead, even those still living. The roles were mostly identical. Year after year, decade after decade, Gary Cooper said "Yup" and "Nope." Although Hollywood thought this great acting and awarded prizes, it really, objectively speaking, isn't so hot, is it? The new superstars, Gould, Sutherland, Dustin Hoffman, and the others, are first and foremost ACTORS. In every role they even look different—very different.[52]

But they didn't, not as much as this article claimed. In Gould's case, his mustache could be eliminated, but his hair length and color pretty much remained the same. Likewise, Gould hardly made a show of "ACTING" as Hoffman did. When press articles play with the facts in this manner, their bias toward reifying stardom is made more evident. The *Herald-Tribune* chose specifically stiff-jawed classical-era stars, ignoring more diverse leading talents of decades past, for the same reason.

Unlike Hoffman and Nicholson, but like his media supporters, Gould downplayed previous so-called everymen. In contrasting his image to them, Gould suggested to *Hollywood Citizen-News* that, by comparison, they were hardly upstarts compared to him. The article read:

> Now you can hardly go to a movie without seeing him in it; even if [he] isn't in it. He looks like he belongs in it. He fits perfectly the hippy intellectual that is in vogue. He is almost its image, symbol. He is smart enough to say: "If these were the days of Bogart, Grant, Cagney, Robinson, I wouldn't stand a chance. But these are the days of Hoffman, Voight, Benjamin. I'm 'in' with them" ... He has been for the past three to five years in analysis. ... He is a very casual dresser, ordinarily wearing a sports shirt. Usually of rough material. A sweater,

slacks, moccasins and carrying a handbag made of deerskin and fashioned by an Indian.[53]

Here Gould constructs himself as pointedly even more authentic than the previous City Boys, and if that seems a stretch, his clothes are more rumpled than theirs. This aligned with *Cosmopolitan*'s feature on Gould: "In the new movies peopled by the new superstars, costumes no longer look and hang like costumes, they look and hang like clothes the characters might happen to own."[54] Actually, movies had always used the actors' clothes (at times), a classic "lady doth protest too much" signal that this was a triumph of publicity over fact, presenting Gould as the everyman that young adults without a large wardrobe budget could relate to.

In late 1970, now that Gould was something of a swinger, *Playboy* was the next logical interview. To *Playboy*, Gould actually embodied the opposite of his statement to *Hollywood Citizen-News*, and tried to unhistoricize his rise:

Playboy: Trapper John in M.A.S.H. epitomizes, as you do, the kind of believable antihero currently in vogue among younger audiences. Do you ever think about your good fortune in arriving on the scene at this propitious time?

Gould: Categorizing the time we live in by the actors who are playing roles is horseshit. I think that whenever I came into prominence had to do with my finding of myself. It may sound egocentric, but I think I could have made it any time in the past 30 years. In fact, it may have been more exciting to have done work like I'm doing when people were less conscious of labels like "antihero." Or any labels, for that matter. If I have to be labeled, the label should be "realistic actor." But, God, labelling is so commercial.[55]

These contradictory quotes show that Gould was inconsistent on former stars, and inconsistently demanding the label of realism even as he played the antiestablishment card of shunning labels. In the same interview, he spoke of a recent time doing mescaline at Disneyland and seeing the park for the "crassly commercial" place that it was. He also spoke of driving home from Disneyland "still smashed." Gould showed no trace of awareness that these comments might lose him some of the "Silent Majority" fans that he presumably wooed when he played Ted.

In fact, in the same article, Gould dismissed such fans:

Playboy: According to many polls, the majority of Americans don't really want fundamental social change and, in fact, feel threatened by radical movements.

Gould: They don't know what's best for them. They refuse to recognize the fact that things are always changing in our society, that nothing stays the same. Unfortunately, that head-in-the-sand attitude gives license to chauvinistic bullies like the hard-hats for beating up those they disagree with—especially the young. As a result of such perverse treatment, we're seeing a vast fragmentation between the generations and an incredible consolidation of young people who refuse to be fucked around with any longer. I'm with 'em all the way and I think they can tell that from the kind of movies I've made. Unlike their parents, they want to be provoked, get involved—even when they go to see a film; they want to come away with something more than a good time. Their parents are happy with placebos like Airport, which is doing terrific business. They want to be conned. They want to be finger-fucked. They don't want to know what's going on.[56]

With this, Gould engaged a new sort of alienation: alienating most of his potential audience. Hoffman mildly agreed with radical movements, and Nicholson elliptically favored "attacking the audience," but neither said that a majority of Americans "don't know what's best for them" or "want to be finger-fucked." In fact, this quote complicates my thesis, because instead of being able to attribute Gould's later box-office failures to a perceived lack of talent or range, audiences may well have shunned Gould because of his offscreen enounced values.

His disposition toward his ex-wife revealed another unhealthy aspect of alienation. In 1969, as noted, Gould was careful to only say polite and complimentary things about his estranged wife, Barbra Streisand. In 1970, with all his success, one might have guessed that he would be even more gracious, but instead he said: "I had the responsibility for a family, and it was crucial that I know what the intentions of the people advising us were because my mate didn't."[57] When asked how her fame affected him, at one point he replied in the third person: "It might have been when he had to wave by-by to his Loved One every morning when the Brink's truck carried her away."[58] Thus did Gould do his part to diminish a woman in favor of his own rising stardom—if not a marker of the homosocial, then certainly a marker of increasing sexism. His misogyny and alienation from a broader fan base came to a tipping point in the following year, 1971.

The Touch (Beröringen): Textual analysis

Gould offers a slightly less naturalistic performance style in *The Touch*, and indeed this performative shift helps determine a different sort of message. In *The Touch*, Gould as David Kovac represents what Europeans often see as the good and the bad about Americans—direct, emotional, unpretentious but presumptive. As the protagonist and unique American element, Gould varies his established mien of "playing himself" to be somewhat more direct and weighted, in Laban terms, than he had been before. Gould's general uninflected steadiness stands for a staid plain style, an American directness that the film compares to the more perspicacious Swedish attitude, a contrast that serves to criticize David, and by extension, America. It is useful to compare Gould to Hoffman in *Straw Dogs*. Both were ABC Pictures productions; both films brought their Rough Rebels to the cold, stony landscapes of Northern Europe to work with all-European casts; most importantly, both asked the American to play a "heavy." (Also, Ingmar Bergman had wanted Hoffman for *The Touch*.) But while Hoffman's David asked for no sympathy, Gould's David occasionally does, with smiles and mannerisms seemingly beyond the script. Far from making Gould more sympathetic, Gould's guile makes David's failure to understand himself and his effects all the less forgivable, and all the more biting a critique of the United States. Gould is indeed alienated, but this time, finally, alienation is not leavened with irony. In Hoffman and Nicholson's studied 1971 films, the star prevented audiences from seeing the character as a villain. By contrast, Gould, known for "playing himself," is understood as a malevolent force, indeed understood and rejected.

In some ways, *The Touch* has no business in this study, because it's not even a Hollywood film. However, the case of Gould and Ingmar Bergman's tumultuous alliance reveals much about the potential and limits of the nascent American cinematic movement. Now that the estimable Bergman has an American star-actor for the first (and only) time, he is intent on criticizing American power, and Gould aids and abets this critique in ways he may not even be aware of. Bergman's critique includes the title *The Touch*, a reference to David's failed extensions; his sister eventually reveals that he suffers from a sort of premature arthritis in all his extremities. This is of a piece with the character Karin describing David, "No one has helped me more, no one has hurt me more": a critique of American power in the Vietnam era, of good intentions that have become imperial and corrosive. Gould does not convey any physical deformity (which might have made him more sympathetic), but instead excels at the presumption and condescension that can make Americans intolerable. He keeps his shoulders slightly slumped but his head erect, a sort of intense intellectual posture. His overarching forcefulness, according to Laban, ironically serves to question his authority.

Like Hoffman's David, Gould's David is alienated from American society yet also preserves its trappings; unlike Hoffman, Gould isn't entirely consistent with his gestures and expressions, making his morals look like matters of convenience or caprice. In the only scene where Gould's David tries to break up with Karin, he tells her, "Go to hell. Go back to your mediocre bourgeois, that's where you belong." In Laban terms he is heavy, suggesting labored authority and probably specious reasoning. His shoulders are slumped but he holds his head high and his eyes ablaze with barely controlled fury; he spits the words not with desperation or urgency, as he might have, but with an imperious manner that suggests he has already planned three moves ahead. Thus Gould suggests that David has considered the bourgeois and will never compromise with it. In a letter narrated in voice-over, Gould talks about "returning to the outside world" with what sounds like genuine bewilderment. However, in a later argument with Andreas, David scoffs at Andreas' quite comparable use of the term "outside world." (Andreas says he doesn't know why David is so aggressive, another reference to imperialism.) David goes on, in a pedantic voice, "I think you better talk to Karin. I think you should take advantage of her loyalty. I think you should make yourself touching and helpless, talk about the children, about all your years together. You have the upper hand Andreas, don't worry." David goes from criticizing Karin's "mediocre bourgeois" tendencies to recommending these tendencies to Andreas with a weighted sureness that, in Laban terms, undermines his certainty. He is neither consistently sincere in King's sense nor consistently wry in Gamson's sense. Because Gould alters David's tone, his body and voice irregularities make him worse than a hypocrite; instead, David doesn't even know what he believes.

Like David in *Straw Dogs* and Jonathan in *Carnal Knowledge*, Gould's David in *The Touch* is every inch the new socially conscious man even as he values his own needs over the needs of others. Unlike any of the other male characters featured in this study, Gould's David has little use for homosocial male–male companionship. Sedgwick's "formulations" are not as applicable here. Through Gould's strong-direct, hostile performance, Gould indicates that David's dismissal of men is less about overriding heterosexuality and more about his alienation from everyone. Hoffman's David wanted to be alienated; Gould could have played his David that way, but instead his David doesn't even seem to realize how far he is from help, how much he needs someone. In a rare moment of quiet vulnerability, he admits, "I don't know what to do with all these churned up feelings." But neither Karin nor the film follows up on this cry for help, and the rest of his performance reduces any potential sympathy.

While Gould does not privilege the homosocial, he clearly manifests sexism. When Hoffman's David strikes Amy, it is of a piece with his moral delusion, but when Gould's David strikes Karin, it's more like a flail of collateral damage, the problem with getting too close to such an unstable person. In another scene, Gould's David is drunk and stoned, yet doesn't put on any affectations of slurred speech or swagger or the like. Gould chooses to play him as an angry spiteful lover. David yells at

Illustration 4.5 David (Gould) clings to Karin (Bibi Andersson)

Karin, "What are you doing? Huh? What are you gonna make the beds and tidy up? What are you going to do? You're going to go out to do the shopping and buy a roast for dinner? Or what are you going to do? Are you a domestic service agency or what the hell are you? Can't you come to me now? Can't you come?" He shows absolute contempt for her life as a housewife, daring her to be more feminist. Gould could have played these lines like a drunk lapsing into nonsense, or even as an arch tease, but instead he chose to play them with burning vitriol. After a moment, Karin capitulates; once again, as in *Straw Dogs* and *Carnal Knowledge*, forceful misogyny is rewarded. David's tone changes when she arrives, but he never apologizes throughout the film. However, unlike *Carnal Knowledge*, the film is clearly against him.

Bergman's critique of America is immeasurably enabled by Gould's hopelessly bitter performance. If one thinks of Gould as a clear avatar of the new cinematic movement—he appeared on the cover of *Time* as Bergman's script was finalized—Karin's rejection of David represents Bergman's comment on the Rough Rebels and new trends coming out of Hollywood. If Bergman agrees with his character Karin, then it seems

Illustration 4.6   Karin (Andersson) in focus while David (Gould) is out of focus and out of touch

as though Bergman concurs with disillusionment, but the bias toward endless futility and self-loathing can't be reconciled. Andreas expresses the same sort of meta-comment when Karin announces that she needs to leave for London to finalize things with David. Bergman scholars often cite Max Von Sydow as the director's voice, and here, for the first time in the film, Von Sydow loses the twinkle in his eye and his temper: "Take your responsibility and bear it, make your decision, and for once, take the consequences. This drama has been going on for nearly two years, now I'm tired of it. I don't want to be another act. Suffering must have an end. It cannot go on indefinitely. I don't want to be poisoned by hatred, spite." Two years (a time not otherwise made necessary by any part of the narrative) could be the time since Nixon claimed he would end the war in Vietnam, but it could also be the time since the "Hollywood Renaissance" achieved critical mass (with the summer of *Easy Rider*, *Midnight Cowboy*, and *The Wild Bunch*) or even the time of Gould's incipient stardom. It's as though Bergman reprimands Gould and American cinema for being too indecisive and fatalistic and refuses to be "another act": another film of the more embittered style, like Antonioni's *Zabriskie Point* (1970). By film's end, if Bergman is commenting on Kinder's "new American realism," then Karin, representing European art movements, in essence says: we're not going anywhere and we're not changing for your sake. And as Gould plays David, in contrast to how Hoffman or Nicholson might have approached the character, David is in clear denial about this truth. Gould's performance of David Kovac represents an alienated America that does not know what it wants and tends to ruin what it claims to love. In turn, and as a consequence, Gould ruined the esteem he had had from critics.

The Touch (Beröringen) and 1971: Critical reception

Paul McDonald writes,

> [S]tar texts ... take place in particular and historical circumstances ... stars seem to be objects of fashion and changing audience tastes. A star who at one time entertained enormous popularity because he or she was seen to be "of the moment" may very quickly become stale in the public imagination.[59]

This may never have been truer than in the case of Elliott Gould in 1971, when his star image lost its luster in the least uncertain terms imaginable.

The 1970 *Time* cover story that anointed Gould the Urban Don Quixote had also included a quote from Ingmar Bergman, who had nothing but praise for Gould: "I'll tell you exactly what I found in Elliott. It was the impatience of a soul to find out things about reality and himself, and that is one thing that always makes me touched almost to tears, that impatience of the soul." He aligned such childishness with, impressively enough, Mozart and Picasso and Stravinsky. He also said that it would be a "catastrophe" for Gould only to make films, because he would excel with the works of Shakespeare, Ibsen, Strindberg, and Molière. Is there a more prestigious canon? Bergman concluded:

> Elliott Gould is one of the absolutely real actors. ... He has this certain atmosphere, a certain mind, a certain sort of imagination, a certain thing you feel that the body of the actor is an instrument, and that he is conscious enough and talented enough to play on it perfectly—the whole time.[60]

It's hard to imagine stronger praise, particularly considering the source. In September 1970, then, this Rough Rebel was anointed a Crucial Artist, his discursive construct at apotheosis.

The same cover story quoted Bob Kaufman, writer of *Getting Straight* and *I Love My Wife*, in an apparent joke:

> When he's on the set, Gould thinks every director is Fellini. When the picture is finished, he's already David Lean. But by the time it's released, he's Mervyn LeRoy. Let's face it, one day Elliott's going to say that Bergman's a jerk.[61]

Indeed, Kaufman could not have been more right. Gould began to sour on Bergman about a year after Kaufman's statement, just before the reviews for *The Touch* came in. Gould told the press that he called Bergman even though he doesn't "ever call anybody." Bergman said he couldn't come over, not unlike the Karin character in the film. The difference was that Bergman meant it, and this was apparently enough for Gould to launch a tirade:

> One of the things that puts me off is the "honor" of working for Bergman. So an American actor went and worked with this brilliant man! I don't think he's terribly important anymore. As far as young people and the revolution that's going on here, well, I've seen *The Touch*,

and I told Ingmar it is really quality, but I'm not that impressed. ... I'm just disappointed by perhaps his limitations. ... I know I could show him things he never dreamed of. On the other hand, maybe this film with an American actor, in English, with American money is his passport to do other things. Don Giovanni! I would really like to do that before I do Othello.[62]

In hindsight, it is easy to criticize Gould for biting the hand that fed him, for hubristically projecting himself into projects that never wound up happening, and for continuing to praise any sort of revolution over Bergman's work. Bergman's next three films (*Cries and Whispers* (1972), *Scenes From a Marriage* (1973), and *The Magic Flute* (1975)) were almost universally considered masterpieces. But Gould's bridge-burning here also went some way toward severing part of the movement's potential, an alliance with innovative European masters.

Perhaps Gould's corrosive comments would not have mattered if *The Touch* had succeeded, but it didn't. *The Touch* was a box-office failure both in the United States and abroad. It had a few critical partisans, but most critics disparaged the film in general and Elliott Gould in particular. Often, Gould was compared with his co-stars Bibi Andersson and Max Von Sydow, and found extremely wanting. The reviews of Gould's work in the film suggested almost a personal grudge against him, a fury suggestive of a betrayed lover or a victim of deception. One year after his "hard-sell publicity build-up" (as *Playboy* called it), critics were ready to rip him apart for not being everything they had said he was. For Richard Schickel, Gould represented the problem with the absence of studio machinery and the presence of increased star-actor agency; the faster the rise, the faster the potential fall.[63]

Unlike Hoffman and Nicholson, all of Gould's major roles were characters with advanced degrees. Here, critics found his ostensible expertise utterly implausible. One taunted: "I, for one, never believed that his archeologist could find a cuff-link in a messy bureau drawer, much less an ancient shard on a hillside."[64] Another stormed: "Gould is beneath contempt: His catfish mouth emits a cutesy baby talk; he has only three expressions—childish eagerness, childish fury, childish hurt—and he uses them as glaring primary colors. His voice is monotonous, his accent much too crude for an archeologist—in fact, one doubts that he could dig up a telephone cable."[65] Gould was still playing himself, but the downside was now apparent: this "self" was no archeologist. These and other reviews suggested he wasn't smart enough to do it. If smart was being taken away from his "playing himself" star image, this man who had only played high-level professionals had no other persona on which to draw.

The *New Republic* summarized the problematic nature of the whole enterprise when it ended its pan with these words:

> Yankee, go home. Sweden for the Swedish. Bergman films for Bergman and his ensemble. The mistakes they have made up to now have been daring, have been their mistakes. *The Touch* is a detour up a bland alley.[66]

This could be read in several ways. One is as a warning to Bergman not to engage with Americans any further, to return to previous satisfactory all-Swedish representations. Another reading would laud Bergman for an intentional alienation from Americans by the end of the film, agreeing with Bergman that Swedes have their own problems and are best to leave alone Americans and their anomie. Neither reading particularly favors Gould. It's as though David had no right to any disenfranchisement, or that he didn't deserve to find a home anywhere. Unfortunately, because of Gould's naturalistic technique, these impressions transferred on to Gould, who appeared as though he deserved to be rejected. Now that Gould was no longer laughing at disillusionment, people were disillusioned with him. We have seen that writers elided facts to celebrate Gould at the expense of the stars of previous eras, assigning to Gould distinctions he never really merited. Now, by contrast, one review found Gould unrealistic and suffering in comparison with other character actors of earlier eras:

> Elliott Gould looms out of theme and context in this Bergman-written "love story" that seems part Diary of a Mad Housewife, part Brief Encounter, and part "My Lover, the Psychopath." He completely shatters the realities his co-stars create. ... Gould [is] simply incredible. He cannot look Miss Andersson (or anyone, I would suggest) in the eye and say "I can't bear all these churned-up feelings" or "I didn't know it would be like this." A Leslie Howard or Charles Boyer of the early forties he's not. He is the embodiment of the contemporary American, with a glint of cynical humor ever present in his eye, and schmaltz comes haltingly—or dubbedly—to his lips ... all he displays is foul temper and insensitivity.[67]

The dark side of the ironically alienated Rough Rebels was now in full view, and almost fully spurned. If an appearance unlike Cary Grant or Gary Cooper had been promoted as an advantage, if this made the Rough Rebel figure possible, Gould was now encountering its disadvantage: deep lack of sympathy for an unlikable character.

Crucially for this new symbol of manliness, reviewers made it clear that it wasn't just that Gould was ineptly performing an unlikable person, but that Gould was unlikable, and that Andersson's character could never have found him attractive. One said: "He is just plain ugly company, a bad lover, a selfish friend. How is it possible that Bibi Andersson could ruin her life for him?"[68] Another:

> Her attraction to David is entirely possible and probable not perhaps as David is played by Gould but as David may have been conceived by Bergman. To accept it fully would not be a question of Gould making the character more attractive—more Lelouch as one might say—but more natural. His effort as an actor shows in the face of the other actor's ease.[69]

Another wrote that "the bearded, stormy Gould is as disheveled within as without, his apartment a disaster area of daily refuse ... as though he has to ratify some kind of preamble to their affair before she dares to think herself worthy."[70] The clear implication was that she shouldn't have to debase herself, that Gould's David wasn't worth the effort to bring him back to self-worth. Another sneered:

> In this company Gould really is an intruder. Intended (I think) to be brash, he is only gross, and there is all the difference in the world. ... Gould fails to make himself believable as a lover. He's neither the roguish seducer nor the wounded boy, but only an ill-mannered boor. ... The summarizing difference is that Gould is always an actor consciously acting, earnestly trying but failing to make the character seem anything but a stillborn fictional idea.[71]

Jerry Lewis was probably never held in such angry contempt. Because of reviews like these, the idea of "playing oneself" fell far out of fashion in Hollywood. Arthur Penn and Mike Nichols would not again cast nonprofessionals like Arlo Guthrie and Art Garfunkel, and Gould would find it hard to find work.

Outside the text, Gould was curiously absent. Few promotional or star interviews survive of Gould from 1971, even when it came time to promote his first co-produced feature, the poorly received *Little Murders*. Apparently, the press got enough of him in 1970, and Gould, not bound by a studio contract as prior generations had been, was seemingly uninterested in doing press. Richard Schickel did write *about* Gould:

> Another reason why the star system is likely to continue its decline is that, as with every other cultural commodity, so with the stars—our attention span is shorter than ever. Thus we now see show-business phenomena like Elliott Gould, who has gone from discovery to stardom to decline in eighteen months—an entire career compressed into a wink of history's eye.[72]

Gould now represented the intrinsic problems with the evolving star system.

In March of 1973, *The New York Times* ran a headline that said "What Ever Happened to Elliott Gould? Plenty!" The article said that Gould "plummeted from the exalted position of superstar to has-been in the absurdly brief span of two years." According to the *Times*, Gould returned from Sweden in mid-1971 to begin shooting *A Glimpse of Tiger*. However,

> Even before the cameras began to roll, there were rumbles of wrongdoing. It was rumored that Elliott had threatened to thrash his trembling co-star Kim Darby, that he had exchanged blows with director Anthony Harvey, that he was freaked out on drugs and subject to spectacular outbursts of emotion, that he had pulled a disappearing act, that he was no longer the lovable looney we had taken to our hearts ... he merely agreed to cancel the project and pay the production costs.

Gould responded to these charges without denying them. He concluded, "The price I paid was a lot of badmouthing and no jobs for two years." The article explained that *A Glimpse of Tiger* did eventually get made into a big hit, *What's Up, Doc?* (1972), starring Barbra Streisand in Gould's role, directed by another highly praised newcomer named Peter Bogdanovich. In 1970, Gould's ex-wife seemed to be residual (in Raymond Williams' language), but now that Gould was the residual one, he once again showed mistrust for his partner when the *New York Times* asked when he'd be marrying his beau Jennie (whom he brought with him to Sweden when she was 18, and who by that point had had two kids by him): "The relationship Jennie and I have never has to end, and if I'm in California, it would be natural for me to stay with Jennie and the children."[73] Gould did not say that he saw his two years without a Hollywood job and his continual distancing of women as related.

To summarize this chapter, Elliott Gould was a prominent, determinative contributor to his major films of 1969, 1970, and 1971. Gould performed ironic alienation in a manner that differed from Hoffman and Nicholson. Gould seemed to "play himself" in a "naturalistic" manner and was celebrated by many press critics of the time. As Ted in *Bob & Carol & Ted & Alice*, he represented the relatively alienated establishment, bemused at the counterculture and lampooning its hypocrisy. As Trapper John in *M*A*S*H*, he seemed to adopt the style of the genuinely antiestablishment Students for a Democratic Society, only to undermine any solutions other than those that lionized himself. As David in *The Touch*, he represented disenfranchisement from historical problems in Europe and contemporary unrest in America. Generally, he poked fun at authority and at newer solutions as well, and could often be sexist. His performance style was naturalistic to the point where Pauline Kael spoke for many reviewers when she said that he seemed to be what he was playing. Kael meant this as a compliment, and indeed Gould was received as Hollywood's best possible response to the counterculture, a key figure for Hollywood's appeal to young educated adults. However, for reasons ranging from playing an unsympathetic man naturalistically to offscreen hostility toward his ex-wife and toward Americans who want "to be finger-fucked," little more than a year after appearing on the cover of *Time*, his career seemed all but over. In a manner that focused more on natural wit and less on virtuoso performance than Hoffman and Nicholson, Gould represented the Rough Rebel: an often misogynist ethnic everyman who is so alienated that he refuses to find solutions to problems. Perhaps in part because this refusal seemed especially genuine in Gould's case, by the end of 1971, critics turned away from him while continuing to embrace (if a bit more ambivalently) Hoffman and Nicholson. The Rough Rebel remained a potent force, but its wings had been clipped.

5
Conclusion

Dustin Hoffman, Jack Nicholson, and Elliott Gould represented Rough Rebel star-actors in 1969, 1970, and 1971. These Rough Rebels were understood as the greatest of young star-actors and as excellent responses to Hollywood's twin crises of creativity and capital. Because of the Rough Rebels' agency, their styles of performing, and their star images carefully constructed to appeal to young adult audiences, some of the most seminal films of the period were frequently dominated by their versions of alienation, by their ironic reactions to that alienation, and by their dismissive attitude toward women. Hoffman, Nicholson, and Gould, to a heretofore unexamined degree, made these films what they were, and prevented them from being something else.

Hoffman and Nicholson's more precise, mannered, labored, exaggerated approaches were eventually praised over Gould's more naturalistic style; had other actors been cast in the same roles, those actors would have privileged other representational aspects. Hoffman and Nicholson and Gould's characters were all understood as disillusioned in the manner of characters in recent novels, but this also meant not overthrowing any system, and Hoffman and Nicholson's offscreen comments made it clear that they wanted to succeed in and maintain the movie business. In this way, they helped encourage audience members to feel the same way. Gould was more rebellious, and eventually more marginalized. Hoffman, Nicholson, and Gould, coming in the wake of an inclusive, ethnically inflected counterculture, verified a new everyman sort of masculinity, but their masculinity was not as inclusive of women as other men might have been. By 1971, all three men were perceived, in varying ways, to have overstepped somewhat, and their methods and abilities were called into question. Through their performances inside the texts and their interviews outside the texts, Hoffman, Nicholson, and Gould established both possibilities and limits of the so-called Hollywood Renaissance, casting a wide shadow over future American cinema.

This study has shed new light on a portion of Hollywood history, which perhaps deserves a slight postscript. The critical and popular under-appreciation of *Straw Dogs* may have had something to do with the fact that Hoffman seemed to go missing for about a year, never to play any of the fictional roles he'd mentioned to the press before. Hoffman would return with three ostensibly "true stories"—*Papillon* (1973), *Lenny* (1974), and *All the President's Men* (1976). For a star-actor who had theretofore exclusively done fiction, perhaps biography would prove easier to defend. Though he remained immersed in roles, he was attenuated by far less overt misogyny and violence than *Straw Dogs* had signified.

After the critical hostility toward *Carnal Knowledge* and *Drive, He Said*, Nicholson seemed to retrench. Among the parts Nicholson turned down in the early 1970s were a leading role in *The Sting* (1973),[1] Napoleon for Stanley Kubrick,[2] and Jay Gatsby in *The Great Gatsby* (1974). Nicholson said, perhaps surprisingly, "Creatively, they weren't worth my time." He seemed to want people to believe that he favored riskier fare. Although Nicholson liked to brag of his "adventurous" choices when picking the films he made immediately following *Easy Rider*, his calculations were not strictly merit-based. His next films—*The King of Marvin Gardens* (1972), *The Last Detail* (1973), and *Chinatown* (1974)—were written and directed by friends whom he could trust with his hybridized acting style.[3]

As directors sculpted their visions around Hoffman and Nicholson's personas, their versions of alienation and irony still inevitably served as determinants. Hoffman and Nicholson's type of "anti-hero" basically came to define sober, dramatic films of the 1970s, a sort of gritty anomie that despaired of solutions while offering a sometimes witty, over-labored plaintive cry in the lead male performance. This describes award-winning films like *The French Connection* (1971), *The Last Picture Show* (1971), *Deliverance* (1972), *The Candidate* (1972), *Serpico* (1973), *Mean Streets* (1973), *Save the Tiger* (1973), *The Conversation* (1974), *The Parallax View* (1974), *Dog Day Afternoon* (1975), *The Day of the Locust* (1975), *Three Days of the Condor* (1975), *Taxi Driver* (1976), and *Network* (1976), not to forget the aforementioned prestigious mid-1970s films of Hoffman and Nicholson themselves. Over-reductively, Hoffman and Nicholson—and to some extent Gould—provided the "blueprint" of wry alienation that these films mobilized. I have written that Gould's falling out with Ingmar Bergman diminished chances for cross-pollination between European and American artists, and thus it's worth mentioning that Jack Nicholson did indeed go to Europe to star for Michelangelo Antonioni in *Professione: Reporter (The Passenger)* (1975), and Nicholson also worked to bring Roman Polanski and Milos Forman to Hollywood to direct, respectively, *Chinatown* and *One Flew Over the Cuckoo's Nest* (1975). These were fruitful collaborations; but for Gould, there might have been even more.

Two films stand out from this period—in terms of accolades and in terms of using this "blueprint"—the Francis Ford Coppola-directed *The Godfather* (1972) and *The Godfather Part II* (1974). Coppola's masterworks, as canonized as any popular art and endlessly referenced as American artistic pinnacles, are unimaginable without the minor revolution spearheaded by, more than anyone else, Hoffman, Nicholson, and to some extent Gould. It was these star-actors who proved that the white, non-beautiful, Method actor could elicit plaudits. It was they who proved that a deeply alienated, ethnic-based masculinity could prove as potent (and homosocial) as any other. (Hoffman and Nicholson both auditioned to play Michael Corleone; indeed, Pacino told *Inside the Actor's Studio* that Coppola used Hoffman's stardom as an example in his fight with Paramount to cast Pacino as Michael.) If the *Godfather* films had been made before 1968, they almost certainly would have starred actors that were prettier and less mannered/labored than Al Pacino and John Cazale and Robert DeNiro (among others). These films would be unrecognizable to us today. We can never know if they would have served as first examples of popular Hollywood art, but it seems unlikely.

Why did Hoffman and Nicholson continue to succeed and Gould didn't? Why did the Artistic Star and the Realistic Romantic remain in demand even as the Urban Don Quixote did not? It's possible that Hoffman and Nicholson were simply more talented, their publicists more assiduous, their agents more successful than Gould's. It's possible that Hoffman did well to contract with United Artists, and Nicholson to hitch his star to BBS, while Brodsky–Gould never quite had the same success or savvy or simple luck. It's possible that Gould overexposed himself while Hoffman and Nicholson were careful not to star in more than one picture a year. But it is equally useful to understand their divergent careers in terms of their behavior offscreen and onscreen during this period.

Offscreen, the flourishing careers of Hoffman and Nicholson and the stalled career of Gould seemed to signify discomfort with radical movements, excessive use of drugs, and hostility toward women. In their discursive constructs, Hoffman and Nicholson had always muted any pretense toward revolution, had sometimes praised older Hollywood, had been careful not to be too closely aligned with SDS or the Black Panthers, and had made it clear that they wanted to work above all. Additionally, Hoffman had been victimized by apparent student-radical violence, while Nicholson had devoted his life to Hollywood for ten years before becoming famous. While Hoffman didn't really do drugs and Nicholson certainly did, Nicholson, unlike Gould, wasn't known for letting drugs affect his on-set work or for driving stoned or for letting drugs show him the corrupt nature of beloved American institutions. Unlike Gould, Hoffman and Nicholson pointed out their own age, and that they didn't have much time left to play young roles. While Nicholson did advocate "attacking the audience," neither he nor Hoffman rebuked a majority of Americans for not knowing what's best for them or for wanting to be "finger-fucked" by Hollywood; neither said of protesting kids that they were "with them all the way." The turn away from Gould, then, is hard not to associate with America's turn from radicalism after Kent State and the end of new troops going to Vietnam. Filmgoers apparently still wanted artists, but not ones that favored a vaguely defined "revolution" over the likes of Ingmar Bergman. Even prior to this period, the Rough Rebels had seen Hollywood embrace the more institutional Paul Newman over the more radical Marlon Brando, the more institutional Sidney Poitier over the more radical Harry Belafonte. Perhaps Hoffman and Nicholson were simply part of a continuum of accommodation, but in 1969 radical politics seemed uniquely mainstream in a way that it was not before or since.

Following this period, the most successful star-actors express careerist sentiments along the lines of Hoffman and Nicholson and generally do not become radicalized. When they do become outspoken—like Martin Sheen or Tim Robbins—they often find their careers marginalized.

On the subject of offscreen misogyny, neither Hoffman, Nicholson, nor Gould was fastidiously loyal to the women raising their children at this time, and they all made a few questionable statements. However, while all three actors savagely humiliated their leading ladies onscreen in 1971, only Gould was accused of similar behavior offscreen. Gould was the only person for whom a studio (Warner Bros.) collected on an insanity clause because of alleged threats to a female co-star. And Gould was hardly penitent about it: "That's *her* problem; she's been frightened for a long time."[4] Gould was not exactly a casualty of feminism; it would be erroneous to say that after 1971 Hollywood realized it had gone too far. It would probably be closer to the truth to say that after the smash success of pornographic films like *Deep Throat* (1973), Hollywood realized it needed to distinguish itself, including more complete roles for women, and that Gould had hardly proved himself necessary to such a vision.

As a corollary, only Gould was in position to bite the hand (Streisand's) that fed him to success, and the fact that he did, and that her career flourished after his career fizzled, is perhaps more exception than rule. Streisand was her own sort of Rough Rebel, but her surge in the post-1971 period can also be seen in terms of an increased emphasis on polish and technique in the wake of a surfeit of cheap imitations of *Easy Rider*. Like Hoffman and Nicholson post-1971, her onscreen exaggerations and offscreen distance from radicalism were adopted into somewhat traditional, precise (though more overtly skeptical, compared with mid-1960s) storytelling, while Gould's non-exaggerations and radical sympathies found no place for most of the 1970s except in the relatively transgressive films of Robert Altman.

Based on the scathing reviews of *The Touch*, critics did not favor Gould's "playing himself" technique harnessed to drama. Trained, character-based acting seemed to win out over verisimilar naturalism. Of course there always have been and always will be star-actors in Hollywood that seem to "play themselves," but in the wake of the spaghetti western cycle and the increasing prestige of cinéma vérité, there was reason to think that documentary-style performances would gain new credence. However, after the critical rejection of Elliott Gould (and others, like Art Garfunkel in *Carnal Knowledge*) contrasted to the critical approbation given to Dustin Hoffman and Jack Nicholson, verisimilar "non-acting" was basically invalidated among artistic-leaning Hollywood. In prestige productions, predilection toward Method acting and highly mannered performance continues to this day.

Post-1971 Hollywood would decisively feature well-trained actors able to play exaggerated character roles—like Hoffman, Nicholson, Gene Hackman, Richard Dreyfuss, and the casts of the first two *Godfather* films—and generally reject the more naturalistic, verisimilar actors like Gould, Sutherland, Hopper, and Peter Fonda. To some degree, Nicholson problematizes this with his hybridized style, but his crying at the climax of *Five Easy Pieces* (which James Naremore named as unprecedented) was very much an exaggerated Method moment, and may well have solidified his status as a star-actor. As quoted in a comment in praise of Gould, *Cosmopolitan* said that the new character-faces were, in contrast to all those years with Gary Cooper and Errol

Flynn, first and foremost ACTORS—in their capital letters.[5] Ironically, the triumph of this line of reasoning eventually worked against naturalistic actors like Gould, who might have been better off in the days of Cooper and Flynn.

The Hoffman–Nicholson brand of everyman absurdism was certainly in ascendance in the early 1970s, but, by decade's end, had somewhat retreated. It's a bit too easy, and over-simplified, to blame this retreat on the larger industry reaction to the successes of *Jaws* (1975) and *Star Wars* (1977). Rough Rebels were in decline for reasons that may not have been directly related to the resurgence of the blockbuster. Gould could no longer spearhead his own projects, and Hoffman and Nicholson chose to branch into somewhat more formulaic material and a markedly less confrontational tone with the media. Hoffman's "softer" *Kramer vs. Kramer* (1979) won Best Picture and Best Actor at the 1979 Oscars, while Nicholson, perhaps chastened by his association with a disgraced Roman Polanski, no longer praised "attacking the audience," and instead used his clout to make more generic exercises like *The Shining* (1980) and *The Postman Always Rings Twice* (1981). Many of the actors that came in on their wave, like Richard Benjamin, Alan Arkin, Bruce Dern, and Warren Oates, never quite achieved their level of control and power. Gene Hackman and Donald Sutherland did, but generally also demonstrated a survivalist instinct to star in whatever projects studios suggested.

Perhaps the most celebrated legatees of Hoffman, Nicholson and Gould of 1969–71 were Al Pacino and Robert DeNiro, who might also be fairly called Rough Rebels. Like Hoffman, Pacino and DeNiro represented integrity partly by eschewing any television appearances (including the Oscars) in the 1970s. For various reasons, Pacino projects fell apart as often as not, and by the mid-1980s he was unable to exert determinative power. As for DeNiro, he was thrust into an unprecedented situation when a man named John Hinckley shot and wounded the new President, Ronald Reagan, and immediately blamed it on DeNiro's character (Travis Bickle) from *Taxi Driver* (1976), just after *The Deer Hunter* (1978) had been shown to cause the suicide rate to spike. DeNiro, in typical Rough Rebel fashion, had skipped the ceremony when he won for *The Godfather Part II*, but he did indeed come to the postponed (because of Hinckley) Oscars for 1980. When he won for *Raging Bull* (1980), in the context of the blood on the streets, he almost had to be conciliatory, and he was: "I hope I can share this with anyone that it means anything to and the rest of the world and especially with all the terrible things that are happening. ... I love everyone." If the Rough

Rebel movement was practically dead in early 1981, this mea culpa, clearly neither hip nor alienated, was the final nail in the coffin.

We have seen Richard Schickel and others blame the Rough Rebels, or at least the industrial changes that they signified, for a diminishing of the power of stardom during the 1970s. It's as though anyone can become a star now, and thus stars don't mean what they did in the days of Gary Cooper and John Wayne. But I hope I have shown that this is not entirely the case. Perhaps anyone can become a star (particularly in the reality-TV era), but it takes training and talent to maintain stardom, not just "playing yourself." Perhaps the most significant legacy of Hoffman, Nicholson, Pacino, and DeNiro is that some kind of clear proficiency with different kinds of performance is now usually required to maintain a long career in American movies. Although there are Hollywood stars that serve as rare exceptions to this in the post-1970s period, most careerist star-actors have done a lot of training. Spencer Tracy may have once said that an actor is only required to "Know your lines and don't bump into the furniture," but few American star-actors seem to subscribe to that today, and that is one clear and positive legacy of the Rough Rebels.

Dennis Hopper claimed that *Easy Rider* served as an early influence on the American independent cinema of the late 1980s and 1990s. Though Hopper was known for dubious claims, the Rough Rebels did show that low-budget films with talented, trained, "everyman" actors signifying alienation could find an audience. It is hard to imagine films like *Blue Velvet* (1986), *Matewan* (1987), *sex, lies and videotape* (1989), *Barton Fink* (1991), and *Reservoir Dogs* (1992) without "gutsy" everyman performances at their center. While John Cassavetes and European auteurs also served as influences, it was the Rough Rebels that proved that performances like theirs in films of the 1970s could be broadly successful. By the time of this "Sundance" generation, however, Hoffman and Nicholson had moved on to a part of Hollywood that had little to do with independent film.

Unlike Gould, Hoffman and Nicholson continued to influence Hollywood even if their films became somewhat less ambitious. Hoffman's Oscar-winning performance in *Rain Man* (1988), decried as a self-absorbed, over-expressive "stunt" by Pauline Kael, seemed to validate a whole new subspecies of roles: the sentimentalized disabled person as a pinnacle of acting virtuosity or a 1990s equivalent of playing Hamlet, as seen in films like *Awakenings* (1990), *Scent of a Woman* (1992), and *Forrest Gump* (1994). As for Nicholson, no one else could quite be him, but he certainly helped to change Hollywood again when he negotiated for 15% of the gross on top of his $6 million salary for playing The Joker in *Batman* (1989). Nicholson's eventual and unprecedented $50 million paycheck for the film put Hollywood stars in a new stratosphere, powers to be groveled with for another generation. Whatever Richard Schickel may have written about star diminishment, the impact of these two roles invaluably assisted a trend toward treating successful star-actors as deities to be catered to both onscreen and off, and treating their films as star vehicles to the exclusion of other performers and filmmaking styles that did not complement the stars. In some ways, this was a return to classical Hollywood; in other ways, it was a heretofore unknown capitulation to stars (who typically did not control production in the 1930s) that often compromised the final products.

This book hoped to glean something about character actors and lead actors, in fact about character actors *becoming* lead actors. In my case studies, character actors spoke for a cinematic movement's authenticity and provided representation for disenfranchisement through commercial media. It is not clear how character actors becoming lead actors might be understood in other times and in other places. At least since Ancient Greece, there have been supporting roles and leading roles, and it seems likely that even then, the leads were played by symmetrically featured people who conveyed moral rectitude, while supporting parts were probably performed by more off-beat players. Film studies is hardly the only discipline to speculate about why some audience members embrace the men (and occasionally women) that seem to represent the best of a society, and others embrace the off-kilter, the cultish, the losers. Media studies, more than some disciplines, has often shown a preference for the latter—countless dissertations devoted to *Star Trek* and *Buffy*, to horror and science-fiction and avant-garde, while scholars of drama admit to feeling part of the so-called "radical middle." This book has shown that, at least in this case, when the ostensibly deviant moves to the apparent middle, the middle loses a lot of its radical aspects.

Future researchers would do well to contrast character and lead actors, to contrast the "cultish" and the "mainstream" impulses in film acting, to note the emergent, dominant, and residual within any culture of film acting and the audiences that respond to it. It is easy to enthusiastically embrace the deviance of, say, Peter Lorre in *M* (1931) and easy to denigrate the more mainstream acting of, say, Robert Donat in *Goodbye, Mr. Chips* (1939). It is more difficult to attempt to show how dominant ideology can be challenged yet reified when the off-beat moves to the center. Actors deserve their place in considerations of evolving representation. This study is only an attempt to read some details of their onscreen and offscreen life and see how those details represented evolving codes of alienation and masculinity. Other details might have been chosen to illustrate other points (and in fact were in previous drafts). I have offered what I believe to be readings of Rough Rebel behavior most relevant to film history.

This book has only provisionally offered Laban Movement Analysis and other codes as a way of "reading" cinematic acting, and would welcome other systematic methods of reading the vast array of signs proffered by actors in films. Other scholars would no doubt have chosen other methods. Performance is a slippery business, subject to all sorts of mis- and re-interpretations, and the conclusions offered here can never be more than tentative, based on previous scholars and contemporary literature but always aware that a given sign can be read a thousand ways.

This book offers a counter-history, or at least supplement, to histories that focus on film directors' approaches to the material. Star-actors have been a convenient and very visible determinative force, but my book also suggests that other talent might benefit from more scrutiny: producers, writers, camerapersons, editors, musicians, even casting directors. Film history textbooks tend to acknowledge the limitations of teaching history as a succession of ideas of a few men who held the title "director," but with that caveat they tend to go right ahead and teach it that way anyway. We all know what bears repeating: films are not literature or any other art form potentially produced in solitude. Films cannot be seen as products of anyone's single mind; their collaborative nature must be emphasized and even celebrated.

If a scholar wanted to make the case that Hoffman, Nicholson, and Gould were as determinative and influential over their films and future films as any of their directors—including Robert Altman, Mike Nichols, Arthur Penn, and Sam Peckinpah—I hope this scholar would use some of my findings as a starting point. The Rough Rebels may well have paved the way for the young directors eventually known as auteurs (and, in two cases, saviors of the industry) that came immediately after them: for example, Peter Bogdanovich, Francis Ford Coppola, Martin Scorsese, George Lucas, Steven Spielberg. The Rough Rebels at least contributed to the directors' discursive constructs, partly by praising directors in a manner that previous stars hadn't, and partly by validating the idea of brash "everyman" upstarts against the system, onscreen and off. This was seen especially in the "buddy film," whose codes can be somewhat extrapolated to the actor–director relationship, and indeed were in the press particularly in the cases of Dustin Hoffman and Arthur Penn, and Jack Nicholson and Mike Nichols. As of this writing, the power of the mainstream "auteur" director in Hollywood stands at high tide, with the recent successes of films heavily promoted as directors' visions by the likes of James Cameron, David Fincher, and Christopher Nolan. The Rough Rebels' discursive triumph of the everyman has helped these directors.

A lingering question persists, as it does behind many histories: did the times create the men, or the men harness the times as no one else could have done? If Hoffman, Nicholson, and Gould had never been born, would we have invented them? This book hopes to have at least demonstrated that if men like Warren Beatty, Robert Redford, and Steve McQueen had played the roles in the studied films, the films would have been quite different; but this book can acknowledge the idea that if, say, Alan Arkin, Gene Hackman, and Gene Wilder were to have played these roles, perhaps the received significances would not have been all that different. Hoffman, Nicholson, and Gould are finally historical agents, unable to transcend their time and place, and perhaps not the only people who could represent their brand of absurdist, ironic alienation. Still, speculation regarding substitution can only go so far: these *are* the hallowed films, and they *were* the men who, in Nicholson's phrase, moved the films toward themselves.

In conclusion, taken together in their films from 1969 to 1971, Dustin Hoffman, Jack Nicholson, and Elliott Gould embodied a hip, gritty disenfranchisement from society that mocked problems as well as solutions and that excluded and often denigrated women. These three men were mostly widely praised for the rough figures they were and the rebellion they represented. They may seem strange in retrospect, but in 1969 and 1970, their star images were constructed as just what Hollywood needed, as a wise and carefully nuanced reaction to young college students' taste, the counterculture, and other cultural trends. As very visible synecdoches, Hoffman, Nicholson, and Gould shared significant credit and blame with directors and writers and producers for the meanings of the films. At Hollywood's financial nadir, during a crucible period that would send ripple effects through succeeding decades, Dustin Hoffman, Jack Nicholson, and Elliott Gould represented Rough Rebels.

Notes

1 How to Represent a Rough Rebel

1. Lane, "The Current Cinema: Hot Stuff," pp. 90–1.
2. Kanfer, Cocks, and Winfrey, "The Moonchild and the Fifth Beatle," pp. 10–15.
3. Hughes, "Arthur Penn 1922– : Themes and Variants."
4. Uncredited, "The Good Guys Wear War Paint."
5. Uncredited, "Carnal Knowledge," p. 66.
6. Neale, "'The Last Good Time We Ever Had?' Revising the Hollywood Renaissance," p. 90.
7. McDonald, *The Star System: Hollywood's Production of Popular Identities*, p. 108.
8. Kinder, *Close-Up: A Critical Perspective on Film*, pp. 221–2.
9. Bingham, *Acting Male: Masculinities in the Films of James Stewart, Jack Nicholson, and Clint Eastwood*, pp. 6–7.
10. Sklar, *City Boys: Cagney, Bogart, Garfield*, p. 9.
11. *Merriam-Webster's Collegiate Dictionary: Eleventh Edition*, pp. 1037 and 1084.
12. Wood, *Hollywood from Vietnam to Reagan*, p. 29.
13. Krämer, *The New Hollywood: From* Bonnie and Clyde *to* Star Wars.
14. Sedgwick, *Between Men: English Literature and Male Homosocial Desire*, p. 19.
15. Claydon, *The Representation of Masculinity in British Cinema of the 1960s*, p. 137.
16. Sedgwick, *Between Men*, p. 35.
17. Quoted in Harris, *Pictures at a Revolution: Five Movies and the Birth of the New Hollywood*, p. 163.
18. Haskell, "Gould vs. Redford vs. Nicholson: The Absurdist as Box-Office Draw," p. 45.
19. Several reviews and star interviews from this period mention Nicholson's Irish charm or his "Mick" attitude. Eventually, in 2007, Nicholson told *Parade*, "I've a very Catholic Irish grandmother, one of the Lynches. She is the root of the family, although my *immediate* family were failed Irish Catholics ... My family were tough-minded people who didn't go much for what they called the 'shanty Irish' or professional Irish. But they were *Irish*, and it manifested itself from an early age." "Interview with Jack Nicholson." *Parade*, December 2007. http://www.parade.com/celebrity/articles/071204-jack-nicholson.html, accessed February 22, 2013.
20. Gleason, "American Identity and Americanization," p. 129.
21. Segal, *The Americans: A Conflict of Creed and Reality*, p. 157.
22. Negra, *The Irish in Us: Irishness, Performativity, and Popular Culture*, pp. 18–19.
23. Naremore, *Acting in the Cinema*, p. 43.
24. Quoted in Harris, *Pictures at a Revolution*, p. 375.
25. Quoted in ibid., p. 279.
26. Quoted in ibid., p. 329.
27. Glazer and Moynihan, *Beyond the Melting Pot: The Negroes, Puerto Ricans, Jews, Italians, and Irish of New York City*, p. 4.

28. Greeley, *Why Can't They Be Like Us? America's White Ethnic Groups*, p. 166.
29. Tietje and Cresap, "Is Lookism Unjust? The Ethics of Aesthetics and Public Policy Implications," pp. 31–50.
30. Such as the one by Alan Slater at University of Exeter, discussed by Gosline, "Babies Prefer to Gaze Upon Beautiful Faces."
31. Martin, "The Phenomenology of Ugly."
32. Anderson, *The Sixties*, pp. 69–75.
33. Gitlin, *The Twilight of Common Dreams: Why America is Wracked by Culture Wars*, p. 71.
34. This might also be characterized as the difference between modernism and postmodernism.
35. Sherrill, "New Troubadours," pp. 11–13.
36. Armbruster, *The Forgotten Americans: A Survey of Values, Beliefs, and Concerns of the Majority*.
37. Gitlin, *The Twilight of Common Dreams*.
38. Rosen, *Popcorn Venus: Women, Movies & the American Dream*, p. 341.
39. Bingham, *Acting Male*, pp. 113–14.
40. Norman, *What Happens Next: A History of American Screenwriting*, p. 240.
41. Quoted in Biskind, *Easy Riders, Raging Bulls: How the Sex-Drugs-and-Rock 'n' Roll Generation Saved Hollywood*, p. 23.
42. Cook, *History of the American Cinema—Lost Illusions: American Cinema in the Age of Watergate and Vietnam, 1970–1979*, p. 345.
43. Quoted in Harris, *Pictures at a Revolution*, p. 268.
44. Hansen, "Introduction," p. xxv.
45. Williams, "A Lecture on Realism," p. 64.
46. Dennis Hopper, commentary track on 1999 DVD re-release of *Easy Rider* (originally released 1969).
47. Uncredited, "Bonnie and Clyde Captivates Public, Starts Significant Trends," p. 2.
48. Sklar, *Movie-Made America: A Cultural History of American Movies*, p. 301.
49. Kanfer, "The Shock of Freedom in Films," pp. 15–24.
50. Biskind, *Easy Riders, Raging Bulls*, p. 27.
51. Wilson, "How to Fail and Yet Win."
52. Graves, "The Graduate," p. 64.
53. Gussow, "Dustin," p. 41.
54. Biskind, *Easy Riders, Raging Bulls*, p. 54.
55. Williams and Hammond, "Introduction."
56. Sklar, *City Boys*, p. 13.
57. Gamson, *Claims to Fame: Celebrity in Contemporary America*, p. 44.
58. Ibid., p. 45.
59. King, "Articulating Stardom," p. 162.
60. Gamson, *Claims to Fame*, p. 54.
61. King, "Articulating Stardom," pp. 163–4.
62. Uncredited, "*Playboy* Interview: Elliott Gould," pp. 60–8.
63. King, "Articulating Stardom," p. 158.
64. Pudovkin, "Film Acting," p. 36.
65. Engel and Siddons, *Practical Illustrations of Rhetorical Gesture and Action, Adapted to the English Drama*, p. 4.
66. Ibid., p. 15.

67. Ibid., p. 356.
68. Baron and Carnicke, *Reframing Screen Performance*.
69. Schwartz, "Torque: The New Kinaesthetic of the Twentieth Century," p. 101.

2 Dustin Hoffman: The Artistic Star

1. Wood, *Hollywood from Vietnam to Reagan*, p. 29.
2. King, "Articulating Stardom," pp. 163–4.
3. Gamson, *Claims to Fame: Celebrity in Contemporary America*, p. 54.
4. Goldstein, "*Midnight Cowboy* and the Very Dark Horse Its Makers Rode In On," pp. D1–2.
5. Harris, *Pictures at a Revolution: Five Movies and the Birth of the New Hollywood*, p. 361.
6. Kanfer, Cocks, and Winfrey, "The Moonchild and the Fifth Beatle," p. 12.
7. Had Hoffman come along in an era less obsessed with youth culture (e.g. the 1940s), perhaps he'd have felt less obliged to do something new. How was Hoffman supposed to live up to this dressing-down of the previous generation? The first thing he could control was his own acting technique, and the first alternative, the one that he had practiced for years on the New York stage, was the Method. He almost couldn't help but try to have the career that Dean and Clift never had.
8. Burke, "Rosemary has a New Baby," p. 17.
9. Michaelson, "Dustin Hoffman Savors the Bittersweet Taste of Success," p. 21.
10. Chapman, "The Graduate Turns Bum."
11. Simon, "Rape Upon Rape."
12. Gertner, "Review: *Midnight Cowboy*," p. 9.
13. Uncredited, "Midnight Cowboy," p. 36.
14. Graves, "Dusty and The Duke: A Choice of Heroes," pp. 5–15.
15. Wilson, "Dustin Hoffman (Superstars: Will *Midnight Cowboy* Spawn Another?)," p. 37.
16. Graves, "Dusty and The Duke," p. 8.
17. Biskind, "*Midnight* Revolution," p. 318.
18. Iain Johnstone, "*Making Straw Dogs*," BBC featurette made in 1971, presented on 2003 DVD release of *Straw Dogs* (originally released 1971).
19. Lenburg, *Dustin Hoffman: Hollywood's Antihero*, p. 50.
20. Oppenheimer, "Dustin Hoffman: From Odd Jobs to Superstar," p. 50.
21. Wilson, "Dustin Hoffman," p. 39.
22. By "unafflicted," I am assuming that I am hearing Hoffman's "normal" voice—an assumption that I make based on scores of media interviews with the actor and my own brief interview with him.
23. LeBlanc and Register, *Constant Battles: The Myth of the Peaceful, Noble Savage*.
24. Uncredited, "The Good Guys Wear War Paint."
25. Ibid.
26. Kempton, "Little Big Man Clings to Life," p. 22.
27. Ibid., p. 23.

28. Zimmerman, "How the West Was Lost," p. 61.
29. Champlin, "Tragedy of Indian in *Man*," p. C4.
30. Cohen, "*Little Big Man* Sure to Do Well at the Box Office," p. 1.
31. No fewer than three mainstream reviews described Old Lodge Skins' sense of humor as "Jewish" or "Yiddish." In a film that could easily be understood as Hollywood's first attempt to genuinely privilege Native Americans, critics—and filmmakers, if the critics are right—were privileging an idea of being Jewish.
32. Crist, "Joltin' Joe Never Had It So Good," p. 30. Crist ignores the fact that Hoffman is playing an adolescent for at least thirty minutes of this film.
33. Kanfer, "The Red and the White," p. 49.
34. Blevins, "Penn's *Little Big Man*—Admirable," p. 19.
35. Kael, "Little Big Man,", pp. 92–7. She went on: "The new racial interpretations of history that have come up in the last few movie years have become an insult to the audience's intelligence. ... This is offensively simple. ... It's Stanley Krämerism, and one expects something different from Penn. Custer—'the Devil'—is like the Germans or the Japanese in Second World War movies, but in this movie, as in others now, we in the audience are also supposed to be the Devil. This reversal is no more honest than putting us with the angels, and we experience the discomforts of guilt, confusion, and disbelief."
36. Toward the end of *Little Big Man*, Crabb finally confronts Custer, saying that "It was time to look the Devil in the eye and send him to Hell."
37. Altman, commentary track on 2004 DVD re-release of *M*A*S*H* (originally released 1970).
38. Uncredited, "The Good Guys Wear War Paint."
39. Ibid.
40. Oppenheimer, "Dustin Hoffman: From Odd Jobs to Superstar," p. 50.
41. Ibid., p. 50.
42. Westerbeck, "Stars vs. Actors: The Importance of Being Oscar," p. 8.
43. Uncredited, "Biography: Dustin Hoffman," pp. 1–4.
44. Prince, commentary track on 2003 DVD release of *Straw Dogs* (originally released 1971).
45. Ibid.
46. Wood, *Hollywood from Vietnam to Reagan*, p. 29.
47. Iain Johnstone, "Making *Straw Dogs*."
48. Haber, "Dustin Hoffman—He's Not Really Part of Any Scene," p. 21.
49. Kermode, "Wild Bunch in Cornwall," pp. 4–5.
50. Wolf, "Straw Dogs," p. 44.
51. Sedgwick, *Between Men: English Literature and Male Homosocial Desire*, p. 214.
52. Farber, "Straw Dogs," p. 7.
53. Schickel, "Don't Play It Again, Sam," p. 44.
54. Cook, "The Sex and Violence are Justified in Peckinpah's Tense 'Straw Dogs,'" p. 25.
55. Uncredited, "Straw Dogs," p. 4.
56. Prince, commentary track on *Straw Dogs*.
57. Schickel, "Don't Play It Again, Sam," p. 44.
58. Kael, "The Current Cinema," December 13, 1971, pp. 82–5.

59. Ibid. Kael's tone as she explains the film is more than a review; it's like a report from the cinematic front lines, conveyed with the urgency and perspicacity of a journalist. *New Yorker* readers aren't just hearing about the latest picture; they're getting an update as crucial as any from, say, Vietnam or the Moon. She wasn't alone. *Straw Dogs* was perceived as an important film, reviewed with an urgency and sociological perspective that one does not find in reviews for, say, *Get Carter* (1971). *Straw Dogs* was generally considered a statement, a message, a mirror held up to society. Critics decided that it had something to say, and decided to say something in turn. As many noted, this was Sam Peckinpah's first non-western, his first film made outside the American West, his first contemporary film, and his first film to feature a woman in a major role. This was also Peckinpah's second feature after *The Wild Bunch*, a film that had been reviled, celebrated, and mostly perceived as both the most violent mainstream film ever made and a dark, cynical commentary on man's violent nature. For filmgoers, *The Wild Bunch* had already assumed the stature of a benchmark, and coming into *Straw Dogs*, it was time to see where the envelope could next be pushed.
60. Peckinpah, handwritten letter included as DVD extra on 2003 DVD release of *Straw Dogs* (originally released 1971).
61. Melnick, interview included as DVD extra on 2003 DVD release of *Straw Dogs*.
62. Kermode, "Wild Bunch in Cornwall," p. 5.
63. Weaver, "I Have the Blood of Kings in My Veins, Is My Point of View," pp. 17–18.
64. Davidson, "Do You Have To Go Through Everything Before You Know It's Not Good For You?: An Interview with Dustin Hoffman."

3 Jack Nicholson: The Realistic Romantic

1. Gamson, *Claims to Fame: Celebrity in Contemporary America*, p. 54.
2. Bingham, *Acting Male: Masculinities in the Films of James Stewart, Jack Nicholson, and Clint Eastwood*, p. 12.
3. Ibid., p. 108.
4. But its reception as near-scriptural revelation said something about the zeitgeist as well as about the unexplored nature of a persona like Nicholson's.
5. Talking about this speech, Fonda later called Nicholson "our mouthpiece," because audience members could relate more to a drunk than to a pothead. Peter Fonda, commentary track on 1999 DVD re-release of *Easy Rider* (originally released 1969).
6. Hoberman, *The Dream Life*, p. 192.
7. Canby, "'Easy Rider': A Statement on Film," p. 38.
8. Kauffmann, "Easy Rider," p. 49.
9. Brackman, "Films," September 1969, p. 52.
10. Sarris, "Films," pp. 11–12.
11. McGilligan, *Jack's Life: A Biography of Jack Nicholson*, p. 207.
12. Ibid., p. 205 (quote is from *Newsweek*, December 7, 1970).
13. Uncredited, "*Playboy* Interview: Elliott Gould," p. 64.
14. Clein, "JN Jack Nicholson," p. 14.

15. Rossell, "Riders' Silent Sage," p. 19.
16. Ibid., p. 20.
17. Thomas, "Nicholson Leaves Obscurity in Dust," pp. C1–3.
18. Haskell, "Gould vs. Redford vs. Nicholson: The Absurdist as Box-Office Draw," p. 57
19. Mahoney, John. "'Easy Rider' Facing High Profits, Critical Honors." *The Hollywood Reporter*, June 26, 1969, p. 3.
20. Carnicke, "Screen Performance and Directors' Visions," p. 47.
21. Weaver, "I Have the Blood of Kings in My Veins, Is My Point of View," p. 17.
22. Skolsky, "Tintype: Nicholson Clicks," p. 22.
23. Wedman, "Jack Nicholson has His Film Work Cut Out for Him," pp. 9–10. The piece went on: "He will be 'out of it all by the time I'm 40.' If he's serious, this means he has about seven years to go before retiring to a more leisurely life of writing and music. It's doubtful, though, that he will either want to quit or be able to quit. Meanwhile, Nicholson, Wechsler and Rafelson represent the new breed of Hollywood's creative film-makers." Nicholson is here listed as a film-*maker*.
24. Clein, "JN Jack Nicholson," p. 14.
25. Blume, "Best-Actor Nominee Nicholson Knows How to Play the Game," p. C2.
26. Rossell, "Riders' Silent Sage," pp. 19–20.
27. Schjeldahl, "This is the 'Pieces' that Jack Built," p. 33.
28. Rosenbaum, "Acting: The Creative Mind of Jack Nicholson," p. 13.
29. Bingham, *Acting Male*, pp. 111–13.
30. Ibid., p. 115.
31. Rosenbaum, "Acting: The Creative Mind of Jack Nicholson," p. 12.
32. McGilligan, *Jack's Life*, p. 215.
33. Bingham, *Acting Male*, p. 114.
34. Ibid., p. 114.
35. Kauffmann, "On Films," September 26, 1970, p. 60.
36. Brackman, "Films," November 1970, p. 77.
37. Alpert, "The Homeless Hero," p. 8.
38. Schickel, "Five Easy Pieces," p. 39.
39. Schjeldahl, "This is the 'Pieces' that Jack Built," p. 33.
40. Uncredited, "Five Easy Pieces," September 9, 1970, p. 5.
41. Zimmerman, "The New Movies," p. 27.
42. Haskell, "Gould vs. Redford vs. Nicholson," p. 48.
43. Ross, "Jack Nicholson is, Without Doubt, Hollywood's Hottest New Male Star, but Who is He Really? HIPPIE? HARD-HAT? HERO?," p. 84.
44. Alpert, "The Homeless Hero," pp. 40–1.
45. Bobby has a place, a job, a car, and he can afford enough gas to drive 1000 miles up the coast.
46. Reed, "Odd Man In—Jack Nicholson," p. 25.
47. Ross, "HIPPIE? HARD-HAT? HERO?," pp. 84–6.
48. Uncredited, "Coming Up," p. 6.
49. Audience semioticians rejoice at the asserted impossibility of common signs.
50. Ross, "HIPPIE? HARD-HAT? HERO?," p. 84.
51. Uncredited, "Carnal Knowledge," p. 66.

52. Zwerin, "The Cannes Film Festival," no page number. Hampton was an activist and Black Panther Party official who had indeed been killed by corrupt Cook County officers.
53. Blume, "Best-Actor Nominee Nicholson Knows How to Play the Game," p. C3.
54. Blevins, "Jack Nicholson: A Realistic Romantic," p. 18.
55. Haskell, "Gould vs. Redford vs. Nicholson," p. 57.
56. Uncredited, "Jack Nicholson," *Playboy* interview, p. 86.
57. Uncredited, "Spiritual Disease," p. 58.
58. From a transcript of the program *Sound on Film*.
59. Blevins, "Jack Nicholson: A Realistic Romantic," p. 19.
60. Uncredited, "Jack Nicholson," *Playboy* interview, p. 84.
61. Ibid., p. 87.
62. Kael, "The Current Cinema," July 3, 1971, pp. 97–8.
63. Blevins, "Jack Nicholson: A Realistic Romantic," p. 19.

4   Elliott Gould: The Urban Don Quixote

1. Flatley, "What Ever Happened to Elliott Gould? Plenty!," p. 8.
2. King, "Articulating Stardom," pp. 163–4.
3. Gamson, *Claims to Fame: Celebrity in Contemporary America*, p. 54.
4. McDonald, *The Star System: Hollywood's Production of Popular Identities*, p. 11.
5. Scott, "Gould Blossoms as Actor," p. 22.
6. Ibid., p. 22.
7. Klemesrud, "Now Who's the Greatest Star?," pp. 8–9.
8. Bacon, "Elliott Gould? Who's That?," p. 24.
9. Tusher, "'Bob & Carol & Ted & Alice' is 'Go-See' Movie of the Year," p. 3.
10. Ibid., p. 3.
11. Byrne, "Gould Sparkles in 'Bob and Carol,'" p. 13.
12. Rick, "The Showmen's Trade Reviews: Bob & Carol & Ted & Alice," p. 4.
13. Pelegrine, "Bob & Carol & Ted & Alice," p. 2.
14. Kael, "The Current Cinema: Waiting for Orgy," p. 82.
15. Haber, "Elliott Gould is a Standout All on His Own," p. 1.
16. Paley, "Steamrollered to Stardom," p. 44.
17. Haber, "Elliott Gould is a Standout All on His Own," p. 1.
18. Klemesrud, "Now Who's the Greatest Star?," p. 8.
19. Elliott Gould, commentary track on 2004 DVD release of *Bob & Carol & Ted & Alice* (originally released 1969).
20. Mazursky, *Show Me the Magic*, p. 162.
21. Uncredited, "Elliott Gould: The Urban Don Quixote," p. 28.
22. Klemesrud, "Now Who's the Greatest Star?," p. 8.
23. Canby, "The New Natalie," p. 35.
24. To contradict my statement here, one would have to find an interview with a current or past A-list star who now decries the perks s/he received ten years ago.
25. Schickel, "A Very Human Comedy," p. 52.
26. Hoberman, *The Dream Life*, p. 115.
27. Robert Altman, commentary track on 2004 DVD re-release of *M*A*S*H* (originally released 1970).

28. Haskell, "Gould vs. Redford vs. Nicholson: The Absurdist as Box-Office Draw," p. 50.
29. J. M. Kenny, *Enlisted: The Story of M*A*S*H*, featurette on 20th Century Fox Pictures' 2000 DVD release of *M*A*S*H* (originally released 1970).
30. Donald Sutherland, commentary track on 2000 DVD release of *M*A*S*H* (originally released 1970).
31. Uncredited, "M.A.S.H.," January 21, 1970, pp. 3–4.
32. Kenny, *Enlisted: The Story of M*A*S*H* featurette.
33. Uncredited, "M*A*S*H: Synopsis," pp. 1–4.
34. Alpert, "SR Goes to the Movies: The Power and the Gory," p. 10.
35. Mahoney, "M*A*S*H," p. 5.
36. Schickel, "War Humor in Perfect Taste: Bad," p. 40.
37. Mahoney, "M*A*S*H," p. 5.
38. Canby, "Blood, Blasphemy, and Laughs," p. 28.
39. Uncredited, "M*A*S*H," January 26, 1970, p. 66.
40. Rick, "The Showmen's Trade Reviews: M*A*S*H," p. 4.
41. Mike Nichols, commentary track on 2001 DVD release of *Catch-22* (originally released 1970).
42. Corliss, "I Admit It, I Didn't Like 'M*A*S*H,'" p. 19.
43. Schickel, "War Humor in Perfect Taste: Bad," p. 40.
44. Mahoney, "M*A*S*H," p. 5.
45. Corliss, "I Admit It, I Didn't Like 'M*A*S*H,'" pp. 5–6.
46. Willis, "Letter to the Editor: 'Misogyny,'" p. 9.
47. Kauffmann, "On Films," January 20, 1970, p. 60.
48. Clein, "MASH," pp. 5–6.
49. Uncredited, "*Playboy* Interview: Elliott Gould," pp. 60–8.
50. Uncredited, "Elliott Gould: The Urban Don Quixote," pp. 26–7.
51. Ibid., pp. 28–9.
52. Daley, "Elliott Gould is Making It Big!," pp. 75–6.
53. Skolsky, "Elliott Gould," p. 33.
54. Daley, "Elliott Gould is Making It Big!," p. 75.
55. Uncredited, "*Playboy* Interview: Elliott Gould," p. 65.
56. Ibid., pp. 62–3.
57. Mayer, "Elliott Gould as 'The Entrepreneur,'" p. 42.
58. Carson, "Heartache and Heartburn of Elliott Gould," p. 15.
59. McDonald, *The Star System*, p. 7.
60. Kalin, *The Films of Ingmar Bergman*, p. 99.
61. Uncredited, "Elliott Gould: The Urban Don Quixote," p. 30.
62. Quoted in Meryman, "I Live at the Edge of a Very Strange Country," p. 96.
63. Schickel, "Stars vs. Celebrities: The Deterioration of the Star System," p. 15.
64. Canby, "Bergman's 'Touch' Tells a Love Story," p. 33.
65. Simon, "The Touch," p. 5.
66. Kauffmann, "The Touch," p. 27.
67. Uncredited, "The Touch," page number missing.
68. Zimmerman, "Bergman's Love Story," p. 49.
69. Byrne, "Anderson, Von Sydow Stunning in 'Touch,'" p. 18.
70. Zimmerman, "Bergman's Love Story," p. 49.
71. Champlin, "'The Touch' a Departure for Ingmar Bergman," p. C1.

72. Schickel, "Stars vs. Celebrities," p. 15.
73. Flatley, "What Ever Happened to Elliott Gould? Plenty!", p. 8.

5 Conclusion

1. No source seems to know if it was Paul Newman's role, or Robert Redford's.
2. Kubrick's financiers abandoned the project—supposedly because of the failure of the contemporary *Waterloo* starring Rod Steiger—but Kubrick used much of the same historical research to make his next film, *Barry Lyndon*. And he did go back to Nicholson to star in his next film after *Barry Lyndon*, *The Shining*.
3. McGilligan, *Jack's Life: A Biography of Jack Nicholson*, pp. 233–4.
4. Flatley, "What Ever Happened to Elliott Gould Plenty!," p. 8.
5. Daley, "Elliott Gould Is Making It Big!," p. 75.

Bibliography

Alberoni, Francesco. "The Powerless 'Elite': Theory and Sociological Research on the Phenomenon of Stars," reprinted in *Stardom and Celebrity*, ed. Sean Redmond and Su Holmes. Los Angeles: Sage Publications, 2007, pp. 65–77.

Allen, Robert C. and Gomery, Douglas. *Film History: Theory and Practice*. New York: Random House, 1985.

Alpert, Hollis. "The Homeless Hero." *The Saturday Review*, September 26, 1970, pp. 40–1.

——. "SR Goes to the Movies: The Power and the Gory." *The Saturday Review*, January 31, 1970, p. 10.

Anderson, Terry H. *The Sixties* (Third Edition). New York: Longman Books, 2006.

Andrews, Nigel. "Straw Dogs." *Monthly Film Bulletin*, December 1971, pp. 5–6.

Armbruster, Frank E. *The Forgotten Americans: A Survey of Values, Beliefs, and Concerns of the Majority*. New Rochelle, NY: The Hudson Institute, 1972.

Arnheim, Rudolf. "In Praise of Character Actors," reprinted in *Movie Acting: The Film Reader*. New York: Routledge, 2004, pp. 205–6.

Bacon, James. "Elliott Gould? Who's That?" *Los Angeles Herald-Examiner*, July 28, 1969, p. 24.

——. "Gould Wins Hairy Chest Group Prize." *Los Angeles Herald-Examiner*, November 18, 1970, p. 10.

Barker, Martin. "Introduction," in *Contemporary Hollywood Stardom*, ed. Thomas Austin and Martin Barker. London: Arnold, 2003, pp. 1–8.

Baron, Cynthia. "Crafting Film Performances: Acting in the Hollywood Studio Era," in *Screen Acting*, ed. Peter Krämer and Alan Lovell. London: Routledge, 1999, pp. 39–48.

Baron, Cynthia and Sharon Marie Carnicke. *Reframing Screen Performance*. Ann Arbor: University of Michigan Press, 2008.

Baron, Cynthia, Diane Carson, and Frank Tomasulo. "Introduction: More than the Method, More than One Method," in *More than a Method*, ed. Cynthia Baron, Diane Carson, and Frank Tomasulo. Detroit: Wayne State University Press, 2004, pp. 1–14.

Barthes, Roland. "Myth Today," reprinted in *Stardom and Celebrity*, ed. Sean Redmond and Su Holmes. Los Angeles: Sage Publications, 2007, pp. 44–8.

——. "'THAT-HAS-BEEN'; The Pose; The Luminous Rays, Color, Amazement; Authentification," reprinted in *Stardom and Celebrity*, ed. Sean Redmond and Su Holmes. Los Angeles: Sage Publications, 2007, pp. 49–52.

Bazin, Andre. *What is Cinema?* Vol. 1. Berkeley: University of California Press, 2004 reissue.

Benedetti, Robert. *The Actor at Work* (Eighth Edition). Boston, MA: Allyn & Bacon, 2001.

Benjamin, Walter. "The Work of Art in the Age of Mechanical Reproduction," excerpted in *Stardom and Celebrity*, ed. Sean Redmond and Su Holmes. Los Angeles: Sage Publications, 2007, pp. 25–33.

Bingham, Dennis. *Acting Male: Masculinities in the Films of James Stewart, Jack Nicholson, and Clint Eastwood*. New Brunswick, NJ: Rutgers University Press, 1994.

Biskind, Peter. *Easy Riders, Raging Bulls: How the Sex-Drugs-and-Rock 'n' Roll Generation Saved Hollywood*. New York: Simon & Schuster, 1998.

——. "*Midnight* Revolution." *Vanity Fair*, March 2005, pp. 310–41.

Blevins, Winfred. "Jack Nicholson: A Realistic Romantic." *Los Angeles Herald-Examiner*, February 14, 1971, p. 23.

——. "Knowledge: Brilliantly Executed." *Los Angeles Herald-Examiner*, July 2, 1971, p. 43.

——. "Penn's *Little Big Man*—Admirable." *Los Angeles Herald-Examiner*, December 22, 1970, p. 19.

Blume, Mary. "Best-Actor Nominee Nicholson Knows How to Play the Game." *Los Angeles Times*, April 4, 1971, pp. 30–1.

——. "Elliott Gould: The American in Ingmar Bergman's Troupe." *International Herald Tribune*, November 12, 1970, p. 7.

Bob & Carol & Ted & Alice (1969), directed by Paul Mazursky. DVD Commentary, 2004 release.

Boyum, Joy Gould. "Dustin Hoffman," reprinted in *The National Society of Film Critics on The Movie Star*, ed. Elisabeth Weis. New York: The Viking Press, 1981, pp. 271–91 (first published in 1973).

Brackman, Jacob. "Films." *Esquire*, September 1969, p. 52.

——. "Films." *Esquire*, November 1970, p. 77.

Brake, Elizabeth. "'To Live Outside the Law, You Must Be Honest': Freedom in Dylan's Lyrics," in *Bob Dylan and Philosophy*, ed. Peter Vernezze and Carl J. Porter. Chicago: Open Court Publishing, 2006, pp. 7. "The Dream of Acceptability," in *Stardom and Celebrity*, ed. Sean Redmond and Su Holmes. Los Angeles: Sage Publications, 2007, p. 186.

Brecht, Bertolt. "Short Description of a New Technique of Acting Which Produces an Alienation Effect," in *Star Texts: Image and Performance in Film and Television*, ed. Jeremy Butler. Detroit: Wayne State University Press, 1991, pp. 65–76.

Burke, Tom. "Rosemary has a New Baby." *The New York Times*, March 16, 1969, p. 17.

Butler, Jeremy. "Introduction," in *Star Texts: Image and Performance in Film and Television*, ed. Jeremy Butler. Detroit: Wayne State University Press, 1991, pp. 3–11.

Butler, Judith. "Bodies that Matter," in *Feminist Theory and the Body: A Reader*, ed. Janet Price and Margrit Shildrick. New York: Taylor & Francis, 1999, pp. 237–52.

——. *Gender Trouble*. New York: Routledge, 1999.

Byrne, Bridget. "Anderson, Von Sydow Stunning in 'Touch'." *Los Angeles Herald-Examiner*, August 20, 1971, p. 18.

——. "Gould Sparkles in 'Bob and Carol.'" *Los Angeles Herald-Examiner*, November 2, 1969, p. 13.

Canby, Vincent. "Bergman's 'Touch' Tells a Love Story." *The New York Times*, July 15, 1971, p. 33.

——. "Blood, Blasphemy, and Laughs." *The New York Times*, February 1, 1970, p. 28.

——. "Character Actors vs. Stars: The Distinction is Fading," reprinted in *The National Society of Film Critics on The Movie Star*, ed. Elisabeth Weis, New York: The Viking Press, 1981, pp. 57–64 (first published in 1976).

——. "'Easy Rider': A Statement on Film." *The New York Times*, July 15, 1969, p. 38.

——. "The New Natalie." *The New York Times*, June 27, 1969, p. 35.

——. "No-No Words are Now Yes-Yes." *The New York Times*, July 18, 1971, p. 15.

Carnicke, Sharon Marie. "Lee Strasberg's Paradox of the Actor," in *Screen Acting*, ed. Peter Krämer and Alan Lovell. London: Routledge, 1999, pp. 72–88.

——. "Screen Performance and Directors' Visions," in *More than a Method*, ed. Cynthia Baron, Diane Carson, and Frank Tomasulo. Detroit: Wayne State University Press, 2004, pp. 43–57.

Carson, Rubin. "Heartache and Heartburn of Elliott Gould." *The Sunday New York Times Magazine*, March 29, 1970, pp. 6–7.

Catch-22 (1970), directed by Mike Nichols. DVD Commentary, 2002 release.

Champlin, Charles. "Carnal Knowledge." *Los Angeles Times*, July 2, 1971, p. C2.

——. "Low-Cost, High-Importance Bike Film." *The Los Angeles Times*, August 10, 1969, p. C1.

——. "'The Touch' a Departure for Ingmar Bergman." *Los Angeles Times*, August 15, 1971, p. C1.

——. "Tragedy of Indian in *Man*." *Los Angeles Times*, December 27, 1970, p. C4.

Chapman, Daniel. "The Graduate Turns Bum." *Look*, September 17, 1968, page number missing. From the Margaret Herrick Library collection, Academy of Motion Picture Arts and Sciences, Los Angeles, CA.

Chubbuck, Ivana. *The Power of the Actor*. London: Penguin Books, 2004.

Clark, Danae. *Negotiating Hollywood: The Cultural Politics of Actors' Labor*. Minneapolis: University of Minnesota Press, 1995.

Claydon, E. Anna. *The Representation of Masculinity in British Cinema of the 1960s*. Lampeter, Ceredigion, Wales: Edwin Mellen Press, 2005.

Clein, Harry. "JN Jack Nicholson." *Entertainment World*, November 7, 1969, p. 14.

——. "MASH." *Entertainment World*, January 30, 1970, pp. 5–6.

——. "The MASH Mystique: How One Film Made Such a Difference in So Many Careers." *Entertainment World*, May 22, 1970, p. 3.

Cohan, Steven. *Masked Men: Masculinity and the Movies in the Fifties*. Bloomington: Indiana University Press, 1997.

Cohen, Larry. "Five Easy Pieces." *Hollywood Reporter*, September 14, 1970, p. 5.

——. "*Little Big Man* Sure to Do Well at the Box Office." *Hollywood Reporter*, December 16, 1970, p. 1.

Cook, Bruce. "The Sex and Violence are Justified in Peckinpah's Tense 'Straw Dogs.'" *National Observer*, January 15, 1972, p. 25.

Cook, David. *A History of Narrative Film* (Fourth Edition). New York: W. W. Norton and Company, 2004.

——. *History of the American Cinema—Lost Illusions: American Cinema in the Age of Watergate and Vietnam, 1970–1979*. New York: Charles Scribner's Sons, 1999.

Corkin, Stanley. *Cowboys as Cold Warriors: The Western and U.S. History*, Philadelphia, PA: Temple University Press, 2004.

Corliss, Richard. "I Admit It, I Didn't Like 'M*A*S*H.'" *The New York Times*, March 22, 1970, p. 19.

Counsell, Colin. *Signs of Performance: An Introduction to Twentieth-Century Theatre.* London: Routledge, 1996.

Crist, Judith. "Joltin' Joe Never Had It So Good." *New York*, December 21, 1970, p. 30.

Daley, Robert. "Elliott Gould is Making It Big!" *Cosmopolitan*, November 1970, pp. 75–6.

Davidson, Muriel. "Do You Have to go through Everything Before You Know It's Not Good for You? An Interview with Dustin Hoffman." *Family Circle*, November 1971, page number missing. From the Margaret Herrick Library collection, Academy of Motion Picture Arts and Sciences, Los Angeles, CA.

Daw, Kurt. *Acting: Thought into Action.* Portsmouth, NH: Heinemann, 2004.

DeCordova, Richard. *Picture Personalities: The Emergence of the Star System in America.* Champagne-Urbana: University of Illinois Press, 2001.

Delgado, Richard and Jean Stefancic. "Imposition." Hein Online: Wm. & Mary L. Rev, 1993. http://scholar.google.com/scholar?hl=en&lr=&q=info:kQ6t HbpcGfcJ:scholar.google.com/&output=viewport&pg=1 [accessed on June 25, 2009].

Dyer, Richard. *Heavenly Bodies* (Second Edition). London: Routledge, 2004.

——. *Stars.* London: British Film Institute, 1979.

——. "White," in *The Matter of Images: Essays on Representations*, London: Routledge, 1993, pp. 148–61.

Easy Rider (1969), directed by Dennis Hopper. DVD Commentary, 1999 re-release.

Ellis, John. "Stars as a Cinematic Phenomenon," excerpted in in *Stardom and Celebrity*, ed. Sean Redmond and Su Holmes. Los Angeles: Sage Publications, 2007, pp. 90–7.

Elsa. "The Showmen's Trade Reviews: Easy Rider." *Motion Picture Exhibitor*, July 9, 1969, p. 4.

Elsaesser, Thomas. "American Auteur Cinema," in *The Last Great American Picture Show: Traditions, Transitions and Triumphs in 1970s Cinema*, ed. Alexander Horwath. Amsterdam: Amsterdam University Press, 2004, pp. 54–78.

Engel, Johann Jacob and Henry Siddons. *Practical Illustrations of Rhetorical Gesture and Action, Adapted to the English Drama.* London: Printed For Richard Phillips, No. 6, Bridge-Street, Blackfriars, 1807.

Farber, Stephen. "Straw Dogs." *Cinema*, February 1972, p. 7.

Flatley, Guy. "Whatever Happened to Elliott Gould? Plenty!" *The New York Times*, March 4, 1973, p. 8.

Gamson, Joshua. *Claims to Fame: Celebrity in Contemporary America.* Berkeley: University of California Press, 1994.

Geraghty, Christine. "Re-examining Stardom: Questions of Texts, Bodies, and Performance," in *Stardom and Celebrity*, ed. Sean Redmond and Su Holmes. Los Angeles: Sage Publications, 2007, pp. 98–109.

Gertner, Richard. "Review: *Midnight Cowboy*." *Motion Picture Daily*, May 14, 1969, p. 9.

Giannetti, Louis and Scott Eyman. *Flashback: A Brief History of Film* (Sixth Edition). Boston, MA: Allyn & Bacon, 2010.

Gitlin, Todd. *The Twilight of Common Dreams: Why America is Wracked by Culture Wars.* New York: Metropolitan Books, 1995.

Glazer, Nathan and Daniel Patrick Moynihan. *Beyond the Melting Pot: The Negroes, Puerto Ricans, Jews, Italians, and Irish of New York City.* Cambridge, MA: MIT Press, 1963.

Gleason, Philip. "American Identity and Americanization." *Concepts of Ethnicity.* Cambridge, MA: Belknap Press of Harvard University Press, 1980, p. 135.

Goldstein, Patrick. "*Midnight Cowboy* and the Very Dark Horse Its Makers Rode In On." *Los Angeles Times*, February 27, 2005, pp. D1–D2.

Gosline, Anna. "Babies Prefer to Gaze Upon Beautiful Faces." *The New Scientist*, December 30, 2004. http://www.newscientist.com/article.ns?id=dn6355 [accessed on April 15, 2008].

Gow, Gordon. "Carnal Knowledge." *Films and Filming*, December 1971, p. 8.

Graves, Ralph. "Dusty and the Duke: A Choice of Heroes." *Life*, July 11, 1969, pp. 8–17.

——. "The Graduate." *Life*, December 14, 1967, p. 64.

Greeley, Andrew. "The Alienation of White Ethnic Groups," in *Why Can't They Be Like Us? America's White Ethnic Groups.* New York: E. P. Dutton & Co., 1971, pp. 153–66.

Gussow, Mel. "Dustin." *McCall's*, September 1968, p. 41.

Haber, Joyce. "Elliott Gould is a Standout All on His Own." *Los Angeles Times Calendar*, June 8, 1969, pp. 1–2.

——. "Dustin Hoffman—He's Not Really Part of Any Scene." *Los Angeles Times Calendar*, June 27, 1971, p. 21.

Hampton, Howard. "Everybody Knows This is Nowhere: The Uneasy Ride of Hollywood and Rock," in *The Last Great American Picture Show: Traditions, Transitions, and Triumphs in 1970s Cinema*, ed. Alexander Horwath. Amsterdam: Amsterdam University Press, 2004, p. 262.

Hansen, Miriam. "Introduction," in *Theory of Film: The Redemption of Physical Reality*, ed. Siegfried Kracauer. Princeton, NJ: Princeton University Press, 1997, pp. vii–xlv.

Harris, Mark. *Pictures at a Revolution: Five Movies and the Birth of the New Hollywood.* New York: Penguin Books, 2008.

Haskell, Molly. "Gould vs. Redford vs. Nicholson: The Absurdist as Box-Office Draw," reprinted in *The National Society of Film Critics on The Movie Star*, ed. Elisabeth Weis. New York: The Viking Press, 1981, pp. 47–62 (first published in 1974).

Hoberman, James. *The Dream Life.* New York: The New Press, 2003.

Horwath, Alexander. "The Exploitation Generation, or: How Marginal Movies Came in from the Cold," in *The Last Great American Picture Show: Traditions, Transitions, and Triumphs in 1970s Cinema*, ed. Alexander Horwath. Amsterdam: Amsterdam University Press, 2004, pp. 56–74.

Hughes, Robert. "Arthur Penn 1922–: Themes and Variants," interview and broadcast TV special for WGBH-PBS, 1971.

Jameson, Richard T. "Dinosaurs in the Age of the Cinemobile," in *The Last Great American Picture Show: Traditions, Transitions, and Triumphs in 1970s Cinema*, ed. Alexander Horwath. Amsterdam: Amsterdam University Press, 2004, pp. 154–71.

Johnston, Claire. *Notes on Women's Cinema.* New York: Society for Education in Film and Television, 1973.

Kael, Pauline. "Bonnie and Clyde." *The New Yorker*, October 15, 1967, pp. 69–75.

——. "The Current Cinema." *The New Yorker*, July 3, 1971, pp. 97–8.

——. "The Current Cinema." *The New Yorker*, December 13, 1971, pp. 82–5.

——. "The Current Cinema: Waiting for Orgy." *The New Yorker*, October 4, 1969, pp. 80–3.

——. *Kiss Kiss Bang Bang*. London: Arena, 1987.

——. "Little Big Man." *The New Yorker*, December 28, 1970, pp. 92–7.

——. "Marlon Brando and James Dean," reprinted in *The National Society of Film Critics on The Movie Star*, ed. Elisabeth Weis. New York: The Viking Press, 1981, pp. 144–60 (first published in 1955).

Kalin, Jesse. *The Films of Ingmar Bergman*. Cambridge: Cambridge University Press, 2003, p. 99.

Kanfer, Stefan. "The Red and the White." *Time*, December 21, 1970, p. 49.

——. "The Shock of Freedom in Films." *Time*, December 8, 1967, pp. 15–24.

Kanfer, Stefan, Jay Cocks, and Carey Winfrey. "The Moonchild and the Fifth Beatle." *Time*, February 7, 1969, pp. 35–45.

Kauffmann, Stanley. "Easy Rider." *The New Republic*, August 2, 1969, p. 49.

——. "Little Big Man." *The New Republic*, December 26, 1970, p. 50.

——. "Midnight Cowboy." *New Republic*, June 7, 1969, p. 46.

——. "On Films." *The New Republic*, January 20, 1970, p. 60.

——. "On Films." *The New Republic*, September 26, 1970, p. 60.

——. "The Touch." *The New Republic*, August 21–28, 1971, p. 27.

Kempton, Sally. "Little Big Man Clings to Life." *Esquire*, July 1970, p. 22.

Kermode, Mark. "Wild Bunch in Cornwall." *The Observer Review*, August 3, 2003, pp. 4–5.

Keyser, Les. *Hollywood in the Seventies*. San Diego, CA: Barnes Publications, 1981.

Kinder, Marsha. *Close-Up: A Critical Perspective on Film*. New York: Harcourt Brace Jovanovich, Inc., 1972.

King, Barry. "Articulating Stardom," in *Star Texts: Image and Performance in Film and Television*, ed. Jeremy Butler. Detroit: Wayne State University Press, 1991, pp. 139–52.

——. "Stardom and Symbolic Degeneracy: Television and the Transformation of the Stars as Public Symbols." *Semiotica*, 92(1–2), pp. 1–48.

——. "Stardom as an Occupation," in *The Hollywood Film Industry*, ed. Paul Kerr. London: Routledge & Kegan Paul, 1986, pp. 155–69.

King, Geoff. *New Hollywood Cinema: An Introduction*. New York: I. B. Taurus Publishers, 2002.

Klemesrud, Judy. "Now Who's the Greatest Star?" *The New York Times*, October 5, 1969, pp. 8–9.

Knobloch, Susan. "Helen Shaver: Resistance through Artistry," in *Screen Acting*, ed. Peter Krämer and Alan Lovell. London: Routledge, 1999, pp. 106–25.

Krämer, Peter. *The New Hollywood: From Bonnie and Clyde to Star Wars*. London: Wallflower, 2005.

Krämer, Peter and Alan Lovell. "Introduction," in *Screen Acting*, ed. Peter Krämer and Alan Lovell. London: Routledge, 1999, pp. 1–21.

Krein, Kevin and Abigail Levin. "Just Like a Woman: Dylan, Authenticity, and the Second Sex," in *Bob Dylan and Philosophy*, ed. Peter Vernezze and Carl J. Porter. Chicago: Open Court Publishing, 2006, pp. 53–65.

Lane, Anthony. "The Current Cinema: Hot Stuff." *The New Yorker*, July 30, 2007.

LeBlanc, Steven A. and Katherine E. Register. *Constant Battles: The Myth of the Peaceful, Noble Savage.* New York: Macmillan, 2003.

Lee, Betty. *Marie Dressler: The Unlikeliest Star.* Louisville: University of Kentucky Press, 1997.

Lenburg, Jeff. *Dustin Hoffman: Hollywood's Antihero.* New York: St. Martin's Press, 1983.

Lewis, Jon. *Hollywood vs. Hard Core.* New York: New York University Press, 2000.

M*A*S*H (1970), directed by Robert Altman. DVD Commentary, 2004 re-release.

Mahoney, John. "'Easy Rider' Facing High Profits, Critical Honors." *The Hollywood Reporter,* June 26, 1969, p. 3.

———. "M*A*S*H." *Hollywood Reporter,* January 20, 1970, p. 5.

Manners, Dorothy. "Elliott Gould: Big Man of 1970." *Los Angeles Herald-Examiner,* January 4, 1970, p. B1.

Martin, Andy. "The Phenomenology of Ugly." *The New York Times Online Opinionator,* August 10, 2010. http://opinionator.blogs.nytimes.com/2010/08/10/the-phenomenology-of-ugly/?scp=1&sq=phenomenonology%20of%20ugly&st=cse [accessed on August 12, 2010].

Mayer, Martin. "Elliott Gould as 'The Entrepreneur.'" *Fortune,* October 1970, p. 42.

Mazursky, Paul. *Show Me the Magic.* New York: Simon & Schuster, 1999, p. 162.

McCann, Graham. *Rebel Males: Clift, Brando, and Dean.* New Brunswick, NJ: Rutgers University Press, 1991.

McDonagh, Maitland. "The Exploitation Generation, or: How Marginal Movies Came in from the Cold," in *The Last Great American Picture Show: Traditions, Transitions, and Triumphs in 1970s Cinema,* ed. Alexander Horwath. Amsterdam: Amsterdam University Press, 2004, pp. 109–28.

McDonald, Paul. *The Star System: Hollywood's Production of Popular Identities.* London: Wallflower Press, 2005.

———. "Why Study Film Acting? Some Opening Reflections," in *More than a Method,* ed. Cynthia Baron, Diane Carson, and Frank Tomasulo. Detroit: Wayne State University Press, 2004, pp. 23–41.

McGilligan, Patrick. *Jack's Life: A Biography of Jack Nicholson.* London: Hutchinson, 1994.

Menand, Louis. "Drive, He Wrote." *The New Yorker,* October 1, 2007, pp. 74–80.

Merriam-Webster's Collegiate Dictionary: Eleventh Edition. Springfield, MA: 2003.

Meryman, Richard. "I Live at the Edge of a Very Strange Country," in *Ingmar Bergman: Interviews,* ed. Raphael Shargel. Jackson: University Press of Mississippi, 2007, pp. 96–111.

Michaelson, Judy. "Dustin Hoffman Savors the Bittersweet Taste of Success." *Pageant,* June 1968, p. 21.

Miller, Edwin. "Dustin Hoffman: Coping with Success." *Seventeen,* May 1971, page number missing. From the Margaret Herrick Library collection, Academy of Motion Picture Arts and Sciences, Los Angeles, CA.

Naremore, James. *Acting in the Cinema.* Berkeley and Los Angeles: University of California Press, 1988.

Neale, Steve. "'The Last Good Time We Ever Had?' Revising the Hollywood Renaissance," in *Contemporary American Cinema,* ed. Linda Ruth Williams and Michael Hammond. London: Open University Press, 2006, pp. 90–108.

Negra, Diane. *The Irish in Us: Irishness, Performativity, and Popular Culture.* Durham, NC: Duke University Press, 2006.

Neibaur, James. *Tough Guy: The American Movie Macho.* London: McFarland & Company, 1989.

Newman, David. "Man of the Year: 25 and Under." *Time*, December 22, 1966, pp. 23–32.

Norman, Marc. *What Happens Next: A History of American Screenwriting.* New York: Harmony Books, 2007.

Novak, Michael. "Pluralism in Human Perspective," in *Concepts of Ethnicity.* Cambridge, MA: Harvard University Press, 1980, pp. 41–59.

——. *Rise of the Unmeltable Ethnics.* New York: Macmillan Books, 1973.

Oppenheimer, Peer J. "Dustin Hoffman: From Odd Jobs to Superstar." *Hollywood Citizen-News*, March 29, 1970, p. 50.

Paley, Maggie. "Steamrollered to Stardom." *Life*, December 12, 1969, pp. 44–5.

Pearson, Roberta. *Eloquent Gestures: The Transformation of Performance Style in the Griffith Biograph Films.* Berkeley: University of California Press, 1992.

Pelegrine, Louis. "Bob & Carol & Ted & Alice." *Film and Television Daily*, July 11, 1969, p. 2.

Pudovkin, Vsevolod I. "Film Acting," in *Star Texts: Image and Performance in Film and Television*, ed. Jeremy Butler. Detroit: Wayne State University Press, 1991, p. 36.

Rainer, Peter. "Dean vs. Pryor: Acting in the Seventies," reprinted in *The National Society of Film Critics on The Movie Star*, ed. Elisabeth Weis. New York: The Viking Press, 1981, pp. 22–31 (first published in 1979).

Redmond, Sean. "The Whiteness of Stars: Looking at Kate Winslet's Unruly White Body," in *Stardom and Celebrity*, ed. Sean Redmond and Su Holmes. Los Angeles: Sage Publications, 2007, pp. 263–74.

Redmond, Sean and Su Holmes. "Section Two: Introduction," in *Stardom and Celebrity*, ed. Sean Redmond and Su Holmes. Los Angeles: Sage Publications, 2007, pp. 61–4.

Reed, Rex. "Odd Man In—Jack Nicholson." *Show*, May 1971, p. 25.

Rein, Irving, Philip Kotler, and Martin Stoller. *High Visibility: The Making and Marketing of Professionals into Celebrities.* Lincolnwood, IL: NTC Business Books, 1997, p. 15.

Rick. "The Showmen's Trade Reviews: Bob & Carol & Ted & Alice." *Motion Picture Exhibitor*, July 2, 1969, p. 4.

——. "The Showmen's Trade Reviews: M*A*S*H." *Motion Picture Exhibitor*, February 4, 1970, p. 4.

Rocheleau, Jordy. "'Far Between Sundown's Finish an' Midnight's Broken Toll': Enlightenment and Postmodernism in Dylan's Social Criticism," in *Bob Dylan and Philosophy*, ed. Peter Vernezze and Carl J. Porter. Chicago: Open Court Publishing, 2006, pp. 66–77.

Rosen, Marjorie. *Popcorn Venus: Women, Movies & the American Dream.* New York: Coward, McCann & Geoghegan, 1973.

Rosenbaum, Ron. "Acting: The Creative Mind of Jack Nicholson." *New York Times Magazine*, July 13, 1986, pp. 12–17.

Ross, Marilyn. "Jack Nicholson is, Without Doubt, Hollywood's Hottest New Male Star, but Who is He Really? HIPPIE? HARD-HAT? HERO?" *Movie Digest*, January 1972, pp. 84–5.

Rossell, Deac. "Riders' Silent Sage." *Philadelphia After Dark*, September 24, 1969, pp. 19–20.

Rutsky, Randolph L. "Being Keanu," in *The End of Cinema as We Know It: American Film in the Nineties*, ed. Jon Lewis. New York: New York University Press, 2001, pp. 181–95.

Sarris, Andrew. "Actors vs. Directors: The Actor as Auteur," reprinted in *The National Society of Film Critics on The Movie Star*, ed. Elisabeth Weis. New York: The Viking Press, 1981, p. 72 (first published in 1977).

———. "Films." *The Village Voice*, May 29, 1969, page number missing. From the Margaret Herrick Library collection, Academy of Motion Picture Arts and Sciences, Los Angeles, CA.

———. "Films." *The Village Voice*, July 14, 1969, pp. 11–12.

Schickel, Richard. "Don't Play It Again, Sam." *Life*, February 14, 1972, p. 14.

———. "Five Easy Pieces." *Life*, September 18, 1970, p. 39.

———. "A Lyric, Tragic Song of the Road." *Life*, July 11, 1969, p. 42.

———. "Stars vs. Celebrities: The Deterioration of the Star System," reprinted in *The National Society of Film Critics on The Movie Star*, ed. Elisabeth Weis. New York: The Viking Press, 1981, pp. 15–26 (first published in 1971).

———. "A Very Human Comedy." *Life*, October 3, 1969, p. 52.

———. "War Humor in Perfect Taste: Bad." *Life*, February 20, 1970, p. 40.

Schjeldahl, Peter. "This is the 'Pieces' that Jack Built." *The New York Times*, September 27, 1970, p. 33.

Schwartz, Hillel. "Torque: The New Kinaesthetic of the Twentieth Century," in *Incorporations*, ed. Jonathan Crary and Sanford Kwinter. New York: Zone, 1992, pp. 101–11.

Scott, Vernon. "Gould Blossoms as Actor." *Los Angeles Herald-Examiner*, November 10, 1969, p. 22.

Sedgwick, Eve Kosofsky. *Between Men: English Literature and Male Homosocial Desire*. New York: Columbia University Press, 1985.

Segal, Ronald. *The Americans: A Conflict of Creed and Reality*. New York: The Viking Press, 1968.

Self, Robert T. "Resisting Reality: Acting by Design in Robert Altman's *Nashville*," in *More than a Method*, ed. Cynthia Baron, Diane Carson, and Frank Tomasulo. Detroit: Wayne State University Press, 2004, pp. 123–41.

Sergi, Gianluca. "Actors and the Sound Gang," in *Screen Acting*, ed. Peter Krämer and Alan Lovell. London: Routledge, 1999, pp. 128–40.

Sherrill, John. "New Troubadours." *The New York Times Magazine*, June 20, 1965, pp. 11–15.

Simon. "The Touch." *Hollywood Reporter*, August 9, 1971, p. 5.

Simon, John. "Rape upon Rape." *The New Leader*, July 7, 1969, page number missing. From the Margaret Herrick Library collection, Academy of Motion Picture Arts and Sciences, Los Angeles, CA.

Sklar, Robert. *City Boys: Cagney, Bogart, Garfield*. Princeton, NJ: Princeton University Press, 1992.

———. *Movie-Made America: A Cultural History of American Movies*. New York: Random House, 1975.

Skolsky, Sidney. "Elliott Gould." *Hollywood Citizen News*, August 28, 1970, p. 33.

———. "Tintype: Nicholson Clicks." *Hollywood Citizen-News*, March 27, 1970, p. 22.

Staiger, Janet. *Interpreting Films: Studies in the Historical Reception of American Cinema*. Princeton, NJ: Princeton University Press, 1992.

Stam, Robert. *Film Theory*. Oxford: Blackwell Publishers, 2000.

Stanislavski, Constantin. *An Actor's Work* (reissue). New York: Routledge, 2008.

——. "When Acting is an Art," in *Star Texts: Image and Performance in Film and Television*, ed. Jeremy Butler. Detroit: Wayne State University Press, 1991, pp. 26–44.

Strasberg, Lee. "A Dream of Passion: The Development of the Method," in *Star Texts: Image and Performance in Film and Television*, ed. Jeremy Butler. Detroit: Wayne State University Press, 1991, pp. 41–56.

Straw Dogs (1971), directed by Sam Peckinpah. Commentary Track, DVD release, 2003.

Swartz, Omar. *The View from On the Road: The Rhetorical Vision of Jack Kerouac*. Carbondale, IL: Southern Illinois University Press, 1999.

Thomas, Kevin. "Nicholson Leaves Obscurity in Dust." *Los Angeles Times*, August 28, 1969, pp. C1–C3.

Thompson, David. "The Decade when Movies Mattered," in *The Last Great American Picture Show: Traditions, Transitions, and Triumphs in 1970s Cinema*, ed. Alexander Horwath. Amsterdam: Amsterdam University Press, 2004, pp. 75–104.

Thompson, Kristin and David Bordwell. *Film History: An Introduction* (Second Edition). Boston, MA: McGraw-Hill, 2003.

Thurber, Jon. "Jeff Corey, 88; Blacklist Led Actor to Teaching." *Los Angeles Times*, August 14, 2002, p. C2.

Tietje, Louis and Steven Cresap. "Is Lookism Unjust? The Ethics of Aesthetics and Public Policy Implications." *Journal of Libertarian Studies*, 19(2), Spring 2005, pp. 31–50.

Tusher, William. "'Bob & Carol & Ted & Alice' is 'Go-See' Movie of the Year." *Hollywood Reporter*, July 2, 1969, p. 2.

Uncredited. "Biography: Dustin Hoffman." *Cinema Center Films*, December 1970, pp. 1–4. From the Margaret Herrick Library collection, Academy of Motion Picture Arts and Sciences, Los Angeles, CA.

——. "Bonnie and Clyde Captivates Public, Starts Significant Trends." *The Hollywood Reporter*, March 16, 1968, p. 2. From the Margaret Herrick Library collection, Academy of Motion Picture Arts and Sciences, Los Angeles, CA.

——. "Carnal Knowledge." *Look*, December 1971, p. 66. From the Margaret Herrick Library collection, Academy of Motion Picture Arts and Sciences, Los Angeles, CA.

——. "Coming Up." *Variety*, September 16, 1970, p. 6.

——. "Easy Rider, Film Review." *Variety*, May 15, 1969, p. 3. From the Margaret Herrick Library collection, Academy of Motion Picture Arts and Sciences, Los Angeles, CA.

——. "Elliott Gould: The Urban Don Quixote." *Time*, September 7, 1970, p. 29. From the Margaret Herrick Library collection, Academy of Motion Picture Arts and Sciences, Los Angeles, CA.

——. "Five Easy Pieces." *Playboy*, November 1970, p. 110. From the Margaret Herrick Library collection, Academy of Motion Picture Arts and Sciences, Los Angeles, CA.

——. "Five Easy Pieces." *Variety*, September 9, 1970, p. 5. From the Margaret Herrick Library collection, Academy of Motion Picture Arts and Sciences, Los Angeles, CA.

——. "The Good Guys Wear War Paint." *Look*, December 1, 1970, page number missing. From the Margaret Herrick Library collection, Academy of Motion Picture Arts and Sciences, Los Angeles, CA.

——. "Jack Nicholson." *Playboy* interview, April 1972, pp. 87–106. From the Margaret Herrick Library collection, Academy of Motion Picture Arts and Sciences, Los Angeles, CA.

——. "M*A*S*H." *Cue*, January 24, 1970, p. 18. From the Margaret Herrick Library collection, Academy of Motion Picture Arts and Sciences, Los Angeles, CA.

——. "M*A*S*H." *Time*, January 26, 1970, p. 66. From the Margaret Herrick Library collection, Academy of Motion Picture Arts and Sciences, Los Angeles, CA.

——. "M.A.S.H." *Variety*, January 21, 1970, pp. 3–4. From the Margaret Herrick Library collection, Academy of Motion Picture Arts and Sciences, Los Angeles, CA.

——. "M*A*S*H: Synopsis." 20th-Century Fox promotional material, 1970, pp. 1–4. From the Margaret Herrick Library collection, Academy of Motion Picture Arts and Sciences, Los Angeles, CA.

——. "Midnight Cowboy." *Glamour*, August 1969, p. 36. From the Margaret Herrick Library collection, Academy of Motion Picture Arts and Sciences, Los Angeles, CA.

——. "New Films." *Cue*, July 19, 1969, p. 9. From the Margaret Herrick Library collection, Academy of Motion Picture Arts and Sciences, Los Angeles, CA.

——. "The 100 Greatest Movie Stars of All Time." *Entertainment Weekly*, New York: Time-Life Books, 1999.

——. "*Playboy* Interview: Elliott Gould." *Playboy*, November 1970, pp. 60–8. From the Margaret Herrick Library collection, Academy of Motion Picture Arts and Sciences, Los Angeles, CA.

——. "Spiritual Disease." *Time*, July 3, 1971, p. 58. From the Margaret Herrick Library collection, Academy of Motion Picture Arts and Sciences, Los Angeles, CA.

——. "Straw Dogs." *Saturday Review*, December 18, 1971, p. 4. From the Margaret Herrick Library collection, Academy of Motion Picture Arts and Sciences, Los Angeles, CA.

——. "Straw Dogs: Terror and Threat." *Los Angeles Herald-Examiner*, December 19, 1971, p. 38. From the Margaret Herrick Library collection, Academy of Motion Picture Arts and Sciences, Los Angeles, CA.

——. "The Touch." *New York*, July 26, 1971, page number missing. From the Margaret Herrick Library collection, Academy of Motion Picture Arts and Sciences, Los Angeles, CA.

——. "The Touch." *Variety*, July 1, 1971, p. 7.

Van Hees, Martin. "The Free Will in Bob Dylan," in *Bob Dylan and Philosophy*, ed. Peter Vernezze and Carl J. Porter. Chicago: Open Court Publishing, 2006, pp. 115–23.

Weaver, Neal. "I Have the Blood of Kings in My Veins, Is My Point of View." *After Dark*, October 1969, pp. 17–18.

Weber, Max. "The Nature of Charismatic Domination," excerpted in *Stardom and Celebrity*, ed. Sean Redmond and Su Holmes. Los Angeles: Sage Publications, 2007, pp. 17–24.

Wedman, Les. "Jack Nicholson has His Film Work Cut Out for Him." *Los Angeles Times*, January 11, 1970, pp. 9–10.

Weis, Elisabeth. "Introduction," in *The National Society of Film Critics on The Movie Star*, ed. Elisabeth Weis. New York: The Viking Press, 1981, pp. 1–9.

Westerbeck, Colin L. "Stars vs. Actors: The Importance of Being Oscar," reprinted in *The National Society of Film Critics on The Movie Star*, ed. Elisabeth Weis. New York: The Viking Press, 1981, pp. 8–9 (first published in 1971).

Williams, Linda Ruth and Michael Hammond, "Introduction," in *Contemporary American Cinema*, ed. Linda Ruth Williams and Michael Hammond. London: Open University Press, 2006, pp. 1–11.

Williams, Raymond. "A Lecture on Realism." *Screen*, 18(1), 1977, pp. 64–75.

Willis, Ellen. "Letter to the Editor: 'Misogyny'." *The New York Times*, February 7, 1971, p. 9.

Wilson, Earl. "How to Fail and Yet Win." *Los Angeles Herald-Examiner*, January 29, 1968, page number missing. From the Margaret Herrick Library collection, Academy of Motion Picture Arts and Sciences, Los Angeles, CA.

Wilson, Jane. "Dustin Hoffman (Superstars: Will *Midnight Cowboy* Spawn Another?)." *West*, July 11, 1969, p. 39.

Wolf, William. "Straw Dogs." *Cue*, January 22, 1972, p. 44.

Wood, Robin. *Hollywood from Vietnam to Reagan*. New York: Columbia University Press, 1986.

Zimmerman, Paul D. "Bergman's Love Story." *Newsweek*, July 26, 1971, p. 49.

——. "How the West was Lost." *Newsweek*, December 21, 1970, p. 61.

——. "The New Movies." *Newsweek*, December 7, 1970, pp. 27–36.

——. "Rites of Manhood." *Newsweek*, December 20, 1971, p. 71.

Zwerin, Mike. "The Cannes Film Festival." *The Village Voice*, May 20, 1971, page number missing. From the Margaret Herrick Library collection, Academy of Motion Picture Arts and Sciences, Los Angeles, CA.

Index

Printed and bound in Great Britain by
CPI Antony Rowe, Chippenham and Eastbourne